PELICAN BOOKS
A368
IN AN AGE OF REVOLUTION
CYRIL GARBETT

IN AN AGE
OF REVOLUTION

*

Cyril Garbett

PENGUIN BOOKS

Penguin Books Ltd, Harmondsworth, Middlesex
U.S.A.: Penguin Books Inc., 3300 Clipper Mill Road, Baltimore 11, Md
CANADA: Penguin Books (Canada) Ltd, 178 Norseman Street,
Toronto 18, Ontario
AUSTRALIA: Penguin Books Pty Ltd, 762 Whitehorse Road,
Mitcham, Victoria
SOUTH AFRICA: Penguin Books (S.A.) Pty Ltd, Gibraltar House,
Regent Road, Sea Point, Cape Town

—

First Published 1952
Published in Penguin Books 1956

Made and printed in Great Britain
by C. Nicholls & Company Ltd

CONTENTS

Contents

Contents

PART THREE
The Answer of the Church

INTRODUCTION

THIS book has been written in the conviction that mankind is now in the midst of one of the greatest crises in history. It is due to three causes: the rejection of Christian faith and morals, an uncompromising attack on Western civilization, and the violent social and economic upheavals both in the West and the East. The gravity of the crisis has been intensified by the invention of atomic and other deadly weapons which, used in war, would destroy a great part of the civilized world. Civilized man stands to-day in dire danger, for he is on the verge of a precipice over which he may plunge into ruin from which there might be no recovery.

The duty of the nation in this crisis is clear. It must have a firm grasp of the ideals and standards held by Western civilization; it must re-arm to protect itself and the freedom of mankind against aggression; and it must, by hard work and improved methods, produce more, if it is to re-arm and at the same time maintain a high standard of physical well-being.

But this by itself is not sufficient: loyalty to Western ideals, effective re-armament, and increased production will not remove the restlessness, disillusionment, and sense of frustration felt by millions. For this is an age of longing as well as of crisis. Expectation and hope are found side by side with fear and disappointment. The cause of the crisis in the world is spiritual as well as material. Many are now vaguely conscious of this, and, while once they were indifferent to religion as irrelevant to life, they are now asking if the Church has not some guidance and help to give to a generation which is perplexed at its failure to find satisfaction, and is now groping for light.

An attempt is made in this book to give the Christian explanation of the world crisis, to show the reason for the failure of substitutes offered for Christianity, and to indicate the answer which the Church gives to man's most fundamental and spiritual needs. The first part of the book therefore gives some account of the revolution of the last seventy years, and of the effect it has had both on faith and morals. The second part describes and criticizes some of the alternatives which have gained man's allegiance and which have served for a time as substitutes for Christianity: humanism, the search for wealth, democracy, the State and Communism have been in their different ways the false gods which claimed the loyalty which should be given to God alone. In the last part the Christian answer to the crisis is outlined with some account of the manner in which the Church is adapting its methods of work to changed conditions, and its application of Christian principles to two of the most urgent of problems – man's daily work and peace. The Church will be judged by millions who are totally uninterested in ecclesiastical affairs by the courage and wisdom with which it speaks on these matters which most closely affect their lives.

Through all the chapters there can be heard repeatedly the same notes – the danger of catastrophe, the sovereignty of divine law, the value and rights of the individual man, the need of world fellowship – and the failure of all cultural, economic, and political systems which are of this world only. Throughout an attempt is made to give expression to the conviction that the world crisis will not be solved by human devices; but through obedience to God and by the help of His power. It is only a living faith in God as revealed in Christ, and the hope of life beyond the present world order, which will restore confidence and remove the paralysing sense of despair and frustration which comes from man's repeated failures to create a new and more perfect society. But this faith in God and in the future life must not be a substitute for the resolve to rebuild the present world-order more in accordance with God's laws of righteousness, truth, and love. The Gospel must be preached and practised as a dynamic and living creed which should transform societies as well as individuals.

There is some ambiguity over my use of the word 'Church'. Sometimes it is intended to refer to the whole Church throughout the world, but more frequently it is used of the Church of England; for this is one of three books, of which two have been already published, the first on 'The Claims of the Church of England', the second on 'Church and State', and this concluding volume is concerned with the attitude of the Church of England towards movements and problems outside its own borders.

I am conscious that in the chapters which follow there is some overlapping and repetition. This is partly due to the nature of the book, for it is impossible to confine rigidly subjects such as the State, Communism, or the Gospel, to the chapters which bear their titles. But some of the repetition is due to the circumstances under which the book has been written – not continuously, but in odd hours snatched from full days of work; and occasionally all writing of it had to be suspended for several weeks.

I have had help from more books than I can mention, as well as

Introduction

from friends with whom I have discussed these problems; especially I want to thank Canon A. E. Baker, who has corrected the page proofs most carefully and made many valuable suggestions and criticisms. Most of the chapters have also been read by, and discussed with, my chaplain, the Reverend J. A. P. Kent. Canon A. S. Reeve, the Vicar of Leeds, helped me by reading and criticizing earlier drafts of four of the chapters. On my secretary, Miss Steele, there has fallen the tedious work of typing and retyping the book from the first page to the last; this she has done with cheerfulness and ability. I am grateful to Mr Leonard Cutts, the head of Hodder & Stoughton's religious department, for advice and help, as well as for providing the index. I need hardly add that I alone am responsible for the statements and views expressed in the book.

CYRIL EBOR

entertainment. The vast majority put these purposes in a different order, with entertainment first.'* In Great Britain the wireless is used for worship as well as for information and recreation. Sunday by Sunday, as well as on weekdays, it has brought the sounds of prayer and praise, and the preacher's message, to millions who rarely attend public worship, and it has kept them familiar with passages from the Bible and with Christian prayer and teaching.

Unhappily the wireless can be used both to deceive and to stir up enmity. Through it the rulers of a State can mislead their citizens by falsifying news, and by a campaign of vilification make them hate and fear their neighbours. It is used by unscrupulous men to promote disaffection in the country they have marked down for destruction, and by repeated threats to weaken its resistance against attack or to incite its citizens to take action against their Government. In the war wireless propaganda was used with complete disregard of truth by both Germans and Russians; and while the broadcast talks of 'Haw-Haw' were regarded as a joke at first, they became a nuisance and a menace to morale in the darker years which followed. To-day the wireless is systematically used by Russia to mislead its own citizens, and either to encourage or to intimidate its satellites, as the case may seem to require.

Electricity and petrol combined have made possible in another direction the application of power which has had far-reaching results on our social habits, on recreation, on commerce, and on personal safety. The use of the internal-combustion engine either on the ground or in the air has caused a revolution in communication. It is difficult for those who have not reached middle age to appreciate the greatness of the change due to the coming of the motor-car. Sixty years ago all traffic was by foot, by cycle, by horseback, or horse-drawn vehicles, or by railway or steamer. When we were children my brothers and I often used to walk on the Hogs Back, a ridge of chalk down on which there runs the main road from Farnham to Guildford. The road was narrow, and in dry seasons very dusty; on each side were wide verges of

*Pp. 20 and 21.

grass used by pedestrians and horsemen; there was little traffic on it; now and again we met, or were passed by, dog-carts or private carriages; fairly frequently we saw wagons laden with corn or roots and drawn by sturdy cart-horses; occasionally there were cyclists, riding either on the old penny farthing, then rapidly going out of use, or on the new cycle with solid tyres. Most of the pedestrians were 'tramps', who, unwashed, unshaven, and poorly clad, with small bundles of possessions on their shoulders, were on their dreary walk from one workhouse to another, and who had the reputation of asking, sometimes with threats, for money 'for a night's lodging', or for 'the price of a pint'; but with these exceptions the road was usually deserted. To-day the change is startling – the narrow road has become a wide highway flanked with telephone and telegraph wires; the traffic on a summer's day is incessant; it is used by every make of car from a Rolls-Royce to the latest absurd 'baby'; private, commercial, and military cars, lorries, and vans follow each other in almost unbroken succession; there are convoys of gaily dressed cyclists of both sexes bending over their machines with concentrated earnestness; and on the grass verges there are young, bare-legged pedestrians full of health and vitality, carrying on their shoulders large packs for their night's camping. Only now and again can a horse-drawn vehicle be seen.

The car is no longer a luxury of the few; all sorts and conditions possess it or the motor bicycle. To be able to drive a car is an almost necessary accomplishment of the young man of to-day, and it is his ambition to possess one. It is used for commerce and business as well as for pleasure. It has brought with it social changes of great importance. The well-to-do have deserted their houses in the centres of the cities, leaving them to deteriorate into slums or to be converted into offices, while they have moved to their new homes some miles away in the country, from which they travel by car to their place of business. By the use of motor coaches and the motor bicycle workmen are able to live in the new housing estates some distance from their factory or mill. Holidays farther afield have been made possible for the masses, and on Saturdays and

Sundays the roads are crowded with those intending to enjoy a short time by the sea or in the country. Immense sums of money have been spent in making new roads or reconstructing the old, which were often little more than tracks intended for pedestrians and horse-drawn traffic. But the popularity of the car has brought with it disadvantages and new perils. It has destroyed the quiet and beauty of many villages and lanes, and every day it brings death and mutilation to many. The roads are far more dangerous than they were in the days of highwaymen. Every month some 20,000 are killed or injured on them. It has been estimated that in sixty years over 200,000 have been killed and 5,000,000 injured on the roads. A considerable proportion of these have been young children, many of whom will go through life permanently maimed. This terrible toll of casualties is a blot on our civilization. It is a reckless and wicked sacrifice on the altar of speed.

The conquest of the air has done even more than the car to reduce distances. It was only in 1909 that the Channel was flown, and the Atlantic ten years later. Paris can now be reached from London in a little over an hour, and the Atlantic crossed in a night. In August 1955 a plane was flown to New York and back in fifteen hours. Australia can be reached in four days. Swift and direct personal communication between statesmen and businessmen living in distant towns has now become possible, and international conferences and meetings are frequent. But though the aeroplane has brought all the world much closer, it has also brought a terrible danger: the ruins of Berlin, Tokyo and many other cities show the havoc which can be wrought by bombardment from the air, and the protection so long given to Great Britain by the sea has been neutralized by the possibility of attack and even of invasion from the air.

For modern technics have not only been used for the purpose of peace and for the comfort and convenience of mankind. If the new sources of power and the new materials discovered had been solely devoted to the benefit of the human race, some of its greatest problems would have been solved. But, most tragically, many of the new scientific discoveries have been used for slaughter and destruction, and the ingenuity which should have been given to the service of man has been spent in the invention and the perfecting of machines for his annihilation. One of the most terrifying features of the last seventy years has been the great progress made in the range and destructiveness of weapons of war. High explosives have become more powerful, flame-throwers more horrible, guns are made to be fired with greater accuracy at targets at a longer distance, huge tanks like primitive monsters crush all obstacles in their way; from the air aeroplanes rain down death, and guided bombs bring destruction to unseen cities; poison gas and death-dealing bacilli are ready for use if fear of retaliation does not deter; even the sea is sown with magnetic mines, and beneath it there lurk submarines ready to destroy any enemy ship, regardless of its nature. The climax of destructiveness seemed to have been reached with the atomic bombs which devastated two cities in Japan, but since then their destructiveness has been greatly increased, and should another war break out the far deadlier hydrogen bomb may within a second of time wipe out of existence great cities. Technics have given man weapons which he may use for race suicide.

It would, however, be untrue and ungrateful to write as if modern science had been devoted chiefly to enable men to kill one another. On the credit side of its achievements there must be placed the remarkable advances made in the prevention and healing of disease. In the little village in which I was a child there were recurrent outbreaks of typhus and diphtheria, and a large annual toll of infant mortality. Medicine and surgery have made amazing progress; with the exception of cancer and tuberculosis, the death-rate from every disease has been greatly reduced; infant mortality has been halved, the danger of death from epidemics of smallpox and diphtheria is rare, and Great Britain is fast becoming a nation in which the elderly or aged will predominate.

Within half a century we have been transformed into a mechanically minded people. Everywhere there is keen interest in mechanics and inventions. Children who have only just gone to school will talk learnedly about cars and planes. Far greater space is given to physics in the latest editions of encyclopaedias than seventy years ago. We think in mechanical terms, and dismiss as unreal anything we cannot fit into the categories of mechanics. Professor Toynbee says that the bent of Western civilization is towards machinery, 'a concentration of interest and effort and ability upon applying the discoveries of Natural Science to material purposes through the ingenious construction of material and social clockwork (material engines such as steamships and motor-cars and sewing machines and wrist watches and fire-arms and bombs; and social engines such as parliamentary constitutions and military mobilization systems)'.* The danger is that the machine instead of becoming an extension of man, may so dehumanize him that he becomes its extension, or even its slave. The greatness of man's discoveries will result in his ruin unless his moral and spiritual faculties increase so that he can use wisely the inventions he has made.

POLITICAL REVOLUTION

Seventy years ago there were two great political parties: the Conservatives and the Liberals. They were fairly equal in the number of voters who supported them, and through the swing of the pendulum had alternate periods in power. Though they denounced each other in Parliament and on the platform, the amount of agreement between them was considerable. Compared with the political controversies on the Continent, their fights seemed like the famous battles between Tweedledum and Tweedledee, 'Let us fight until six and then have dinner', but they were stopped by a 'a monstrous crow, as black as a tar barrel'. The black crow in the shape of the Labour Party has now brought to an end the historic struggles between Conservative and Liberal. Labour has taken the place in Parliament of the old Liberal Party, and has become one of the two great political parties of the State. The Liberals are now represented by a small and dwindling group. The change has

*A. J. Toynbee, *A Study in History*, Vol. III, p. 385.

been dramatic. Fifty-seven years ago I was in the Strangers' Gallery of the House of Commons listening to the proposal of a loyal message of congratulations to the Queen on the birth of an heir to the throne. The leaders of the two parties, amidst general acclamation, commended the message to the approval of the House; it looked as if it would be at once adopted without a dissentient voice, when from a back bench there rose a stocky figure, clad in homespun, who amidst great uproar made a solitary protest against the resolution. Keir Hardie was at that time the only representative of Independent Labour in the House. No one then would have dared to predict that within thirty years there would be a Labour Prime Minister. In the election of December 1910 Labour returned 42 candidates and polled 370,802 votes; in 1922 the vote increased to 4,348,379 and 191 Labour members were elected; in 1945 it returned 396 members, and had a clear majority of 186; though in 1950 the Conservatives regained most of the ground they had lost, and the Labour Government had a clear majority of only five. In 1955 the Conservatives have a majority of sixty.

Two other political changes of great importance have taken place. The franchise has been extended until it includes all adult citizens, with the exception of convicted criminals, the certified insane and the members of the House of Lords. Women are therefore entitled both to vote for and to sit in Parliament. While the power of the House of Commons has increased, that of the Lords has diminished. Frequently it has been threatened with abolition or reform. Its rejection of the Budget led to the Parliament Act of 1911, which removed all financial Bills from the possibility of interference by the House of Lords, and restricted its power of rejecting other Bills to two years. In 1950 this was reduced to one year only. The Upper House still has considerable influence both through the high standard of its debates and the power it retains of discussing suggested legislation and of proposing amendments which the House of Commons sometimes accepts as improvements.

With the advent of Labour to power there has been a great

increase in the responsibilities undertaken by the State. It was for long held that its chief purpose was to secure the safety and good order of the nation, protecting its shores from attacks from without, and its citizens from disturbance within; and to preserve individuals and their property from harm. Now the State has been made responsible for the education, health, and welfare of its citizens from the cradle to the grave. It has its pre-natal clinics for expectant mothers, and welfare centres for the young; it provides for the education, feeding, medical and dental inspection of the children of school age; by grants and scholarships it has made a highway from the senior and grammar schools to the universities; it provides community centres for the recreation of adolescents; it has an all-inclusive medical service; it gives security from want to the unemployed and aged; it regulates, directs, controls, and sometimes owns, great national industries. To carry out these functions taxation has been increased to an extent which would have horrified an older generation; in 1912 the standard rate of income tax was 1*s*. 2*d*.; to-day it is 8*s*. 6*d*. in the pound and in the highest range of incomes tax and surtax together may amount to 19*s*. 6*d*. in the pound. In rather over forty years the National Debt has risen from £766,000,000 to £26,582,602,000. In addition, there have been great increases in local rates and indirect taxes of various kinds. The growth of the power of the State, its appropriation of privately earned income for public purpose, its control of business and commerce, and its interference with personal freedom, are some of the most striking changes in the last seventy years.

SOCIAL AND ECONOMIC CHANGES

Many social changes were due to the political causes just mentioned; but the two great wars hastened the social and economic upheaval. Financially the United Kingdom lost heavily through the strain of military expenditure. It was necessary to sell most of its overseas investments to meet the cost of the war and to help its weaker allies. High taxation and death duties have reduced to relative poverty many who once were rich. In the last quarter of the nineteenth century railway carriages marked 'first', 'second', and 'third' were symbolical of the division of the nation into three economic classes: the upper, the middle, and the lower. Heavy taxation at one end, the raising of wages at the other, and a national system of compulsory education have done much to blur, if not entirely remove, these distinctions. There are still a few rich men who live on their capital, but incomes have been so reduced by taxation and changes in the value of money that there are now very few who would be described as wealthy; on the other hand, extreme poverty and hunger have been abolished. There is no clear-cut line between the classes; in this country they have never corresponded to the orders in pre-Revolutionary France, which were separated by impassable gulfs; in Great Britain for many years some of those holding high posts in the Church, the Services, in Parliament, and in business have risen from the working classes. The levelling up and the levelling down in the economic position of the classes are shown by the following figures: in 1939 there were 4,500,000 with incomes between £150 and £200, and in 1951 there were 10,250,000 with incomes between £250 and £500. This is in striking contrast to the figures at the other end; in 1939 there were 7,000 with incomes (after the deduction of tax) of £6,000 or over; in 1951–2 the number had fallen to 36.

One of the social changes which has followed this has been the passing away of the country houses. For many centuries these had been a distinctive feature in rural England; they ranged from the famous historic houses of the nobility to the manors and halls of the country gentry. Often the houses were of great beauty and dignity, filled with valuable pictures and furniture, and their carefully kept parks and gardens added to the loveliness of the country. They were well staffed both within the house and in the grounds; hospitality was on a generous scale: in the summer there was a round of tennis and croquet parties, and in the winter dinners and dances. Readers of Jane Austen and Anthony Trollope know how important was the part taken in the social life of their time by these houses. Death duties, taxation and the increased cost of living are rapidly reducing their number. Many have been sold or leased as hotels, convalescent homes, hostels for the aged, and for other purposes. Some stand dilapidated and deserted, their drives concealed by weeds and overhung by the boughs of trees. In some the owner still lives in a few rooms, he and his wife doing the domestic work once performed by a small army of servants; if he possesses an historic house he may secure some help towards the heavy cost of its maintenance by charging a fee of admission to sightseers and by selling the surplus produce of the gardens; often the owner and his family have moved into the house originally built for the agent or the head gardener. The absence of domestic staff has cut entertaining down to the minimum. When the present owners die it is very unlikely that their sons will attempt to live in these large houses. The loss to the countryside will be great, for though there have been bad and selfish landlords in life as well as in fiction, most of the country gentry have shown a genuine sense of responsibility for the welfare both of their tenants and of the poor who lived in their neighbour-hood.

The clergy are among those who have suffered severely through the combined effect of reduced incomes and large houses. For long the rectories and vicarages had been attractive features of the villages and centres of Christian kindliness and charity. The houses and gardens were usually well kept; the parson who neglected his lawns and flower-beds was looked upon with suspicion by his neighbours. Now the clergy find it impossible to pay the wages required by indoor or outdoor servants, even if they could obtain them; the vicarage garden has gone to ruin, and most of the rooms of the house are closed, and in the winter the incumbent and his family live and feed in the kitchen, the only room in which there is a fire. Through the union of parishes, many of the vicarages have been sold, and many more will have either to be sold or modernized as soon as building conditions make it possible.

The levelling up has been as remarkable as the levelling down. Every class of manual worker and most professional men have had an increase in their wages or emoluments relative to the rise in the cost of living. At the end of the last century the majority of the weekly wage earners were badly underpaid, and in the first quarter of the present century there were many whose earnings kept them only just above the line of destitution. In 1936 Sir John Boyd Orr pointed out the contrast in the amount of protective food consumed by the different classes: 'In the poorest group the average consumption of milk, including tinned milk, is equivalent to 1·8 pints per head per week; in the wealthiest group 5·5 pints. The poorest group consume 1·5 eggs per head per week; the wealthiest 4·5.' As late as 1937 Mr Seebohm Rowntree stated: 'The basic fact is that to-day millions of working-class people in this country are inadequately provided with the necessaries of life, simply and solely because the fathers of families are not in receipt of incomes large enough to provide the necessities of physical fitness for themselves and those dependent upon them.'* Higher wages, equal rationing for all, meals for children at school have changed the position. A striking and satisfactory example of the rise in wages is to be seen in the payment of agricultural labourers; their hours of work were longer than those of most engaged in the factory or mine, and their wages were smaller. Seventy years ago the agricultural labourer had a dull and hard life. His wages were between 15s. and 20s. a week, with a cottage often insanitary and in bad repair. His hours of work were long and in all weathers. Most of the workers on the land were unable to read or write. For many of them the public-house was their chief recreation, though there were few hard drinkers. In 1938–9 their average minimum weekly wage was 34s., in 1955 it was £6. In the same period the General Industrial Wage showed a rise for men over twenty-one to 197s. per week. Against this there must be set the alarming rise in the cost of living and the scarcity of goods once plentiful. This has taken away many of the gains which should have come from increased wages.

*The Human Needs of Labour, p. 9.

But when allowance has been made for this the working classes have opportunities and advantages which they never possessed before; they are better dressed, better read, and are able to take holidays and enjoy recreation to a degree not possible in the past. On this side the social revolution has been all to the good, for it has removed long-tolerated evils.

THE EMANCIPATION OF WOMAN

As a very small boy I remember listening to some of my elders talking while I was supposed to be playing with some toys. They were speaking in the hushed tones of mystery, which at once arouses the interest of any child. I heard the phrases 'shocking', 'very wrong', 'dangerous', and the hope was expressed that 'no one who knew her would have seen her', and that neither the servants nor villagers would ever hear of this scandal. Gradually I put things together: a girl of eighteen, the daughter of a neighbouring vicar, had missed her connexion at a London station, and instead of staying for two or three hours in the ladies' waiting-room, had gone for an evening walk in the neighbourhood of the station, 'by herself, my dear, just think of it!' This trifling incident illustrates the gulf which separates the woman of seventy years ago from the emancipated woman of to-day. Woman was then surrounded by every kind of convention to protect her from harm, real or imaginary. In the upper and middle classes she must be beautiful, well dressed, pleasantly spoken, gentle, submissive, accepting without question or opposition the opinions of the menfolk who were her relatives. It was assumed that if unmarried she would help her happier sisters and older relations with their families, and if she married she would be the passive and loving partner, rendering obedience in all things to her husband. Her place was in the home, where she was an ornament, a graceful hostess, the devoted mother of many children, or a household drudge, according to the decree or the social position of her husband. No tribute can be too great to the wonderful wives and mothers of the 'unemancipated' age. Their goodness and unselfishness were above all praise. But there were women who were neither content helping with the children of others nor had any wish for a husband and family of their own. Most professions were, however, closed to them, and they had been brought up to believe that the place of a woman is in her home. Against this there were sometimes indignant outbursts. Florence Nightingale when thirty-two, in a private note headed 'Butchered to make a Roman Holiday', wrote a furious indictment of family life. 'Women don't consider themselves as human beings at all. There is absolutely no God, no country, no duty to them at all, except family . . . I have known a good deal of convents. And of course everyone has talked of the petty grinding tyrannies supposed to be exercised there. But I know nothing like the petty grinding tyranny of a good English family. And the only alleviation is that the tyrannized submits with a heart full of affection.'*

A more famous protest against the generally accepted view of women was made in 1847 by Charlotte Brontë. *Jane Eyre* was the first novel which had as its heroine a plain woman without beauty, who claimed to live her own life and was not ashamed to show that she loved a man who was not her husband. Jane's outburst to Rochester was something new and disconcerting, and especially so when later it was learnt that the novel had been written by a woman: 'Do you think I am an automaton? A machine without feelings? And can bear to have my morsel of bread snatched from my life, and my drop of living water dashed from my cup? Do you think because I am poor, obscure, plain, and little, I am soulless and heartless? You think wrong. I have as much soul as you, and full as much heart! And if God had gifted me with some beauty and much wealth I should have made it as hard for you to leave me, as it is now for me to leave you. I am not talking to you through the medium of custom, conventionalism, or even of mortal flesh; it is my spirit that addresses your spirit; just as if both had passed through the grave and stood at God's feet, equal as we are.'

*Cecil Woodham Smith, *Florence Nightingale,* p. 93.

Florence Nightingale and Charlotte Brontë wrote of conditions of a hundred years ago, but it was not until this century that women obtained in this country either political or social emancipation. In 1918 the Representation of the People Act gave them the first measure of enfranchisement, and in 1928 they were given the same electoral rights as men. In 1919 the Sex Disqualification (Removal) Act opened to them the legal and other professions, as well as the higher grades of the Civil Service and the magistrature. These measures were due to the vigorous campaign for enfranchisement conducted by women in the years previous to the first war; to the progress made in higher education for women during the last half of the nineteenth century; and to the help given by them to industry during the first war. In the Second World War, in the peak period of employment, there were 7,265,000 women in paid employment. Women now meet men on equal terms in social, political, and industrial life, though they have not yet secured equal pay for the same work. They can lead their own lives, earn their own livelihood, make their own friends, follow their own pursuits without causing surprise or provoking criticism. It is a great social and political revolution. It has not been confined to Great Britain; it has been a world-wide movement throughout the British Commonwealth, and in countries as different as Turkey, Russia, China, and Japan. 'For the first time the particular gifts of mind and heart of one half of the human race, so long of value within the family, are in every civilized community being brought to bear on the wider problems of social life. Women now share with men a measure of civic power and responsibility never before enjoyed in history.'*

REVOLUTION IN EDUCATION

In the spring of 1946 I paid a short visit to Addis Ababa, a fascinating city in which Western civilization jostles with primitive Africanism. One morning was spent with the Ethiopian Director of Education in visiting some newly built

*Chambers's Encyclopaedia, Vol. XIV, p. 645.

schools. They were large and spacious, surrounded with good playing-fields. They were crowded with students of all ages. The keenness of the people for education was remarkable in a country which not long ago was isolated from modern thought and methods, and which had only recently been freed from foreign invasion. There were long waiting lists of children whose parents wished them to be admitted to the schools; but not only children were candidates, there were also many young men who were ready to be taught side by side with children, and who often had to start in the same class with those much younger than themselves. The classes were very large, and the staff of teachers quite inadequate in numbers; but the Emperor was doing all in his power to bring education to his people. This is characteristic of what has been happening almost everywhere in the last fifty years. In country after country the necessity of education has been recognized. The Communists in Russia and China have seen how it can serve their ends. In India, Pakistan, and Turkey, schools have become a national necessity. All over Africa, colleges and universities have come into being. The world is educationally minded as it has never been before. Everywhere it is now accepted as a truism that education can no longer be regarded as a privilege of the few, but as a right of ordinary men and women.

In our own country the development of education in the last seventy years has been remarkable. In the eighties every village had its school, held in a small building divided by a partition into senior and junior departments. In the towns the schools were more pretentious, usually rather dreary-looking buildings of three floors, respectively for infants, young children, and those who were in the closing years of their education. The furnishing of these schools was very primitive according to modern standards: uncomfortable benches and fixed desks for the children; a chair, a desk, a bell, a blackboard, and chalk for the teacher; an ugly stove; two or three maps, and possibly some pictures on the walls; for the infants coloured beads on wire strings to teach them to count; and one or two cupboards. The playgrounds were usually small, and cloakroom and lavatory accommodation was inadequate. All schools were divided into the denominational, the so-called Voluntary schools, and the Board schools, which were maintained by the rates. In the former there was definite denominational worship and teaching, and in the latter undenominational teaching approved by Non-conformists, but disliked by most Anglicans and all Roman Catholics. For the children who had gained scholarships, or whose parents could afford the fees, there were grammar and secondary schools, but most of them finished their education at thirteen, and speedily forgot what they had been taught. High above the elementary and secondary schools were the great public schools, the preserve of the few.

In 1902, 1918, and 1944 a series of educational reforms were carried, by which a comprehensive scheme of national education has been established, though not yet fully implemented. The lowest rung consists of nursery schools to which children between two and five years may be sent. Above this there is compulsory education for children from five to fifteen: those from five to eleven plus receiving primary education, and then moving on to one of three types of secondary schools – the modern, which offers a course of education both practical and general; the technical; and the grammar school, which provides a more academic course. It is intended that when circumstances make it possible there shall be county colleges for those who have gone through the secondary schools. The old overcrowded and unattractive buildings are being replaced by pleasant and spacious schools with plenty of windows and good sanitary and washing accommodation. The larger schools have their gymnasiums and their shower-baths; most of them have good playgrounds and recreation-fields. In the elementary schools there is free milk, and midday meals are provided at a small charge. Regular medical inspections are made by school doctors, and teeth and eyes come under supervision. Great strides have been made in improving the health of the children, who now suffer less from malnutrition than at any previous time in the history of the nation.

To the universities there are no longer a few narrow ladders which can be climbed only by those with special gifts; but there are broad highways leading to them from the secondary schools. While in the past the majority of undergraduates were supported by their parents, now possibly as many as 80 per cent of them receive grants from the local authorities. The intellectual qualification for admission has been raised steeply, and most of the students are of scholarship standard. The nation is determined that neither the social nor the economic position of the parents shall prevent their children from receiving a good education, and so the educational barrier between classes is fast vanishing.

This great development in education has not yet produced all the results once confidently anticipated. The lack of discipline and even of elementary cleanliness among so many of the children evacuated during the earlier part of the war evoked severe criticism of the national system of education; but taking the country as a whole the children of to-day have wider interests, better health, and better manners than those of seventy years ago. When the school-leaving age has been raised to sixteen and large classes are reduced to a more manageable size, then the fruits of education should be seen more clearly. But while education in Great Britain is giving both culture and information, it is somewhat doubtful if it is making the children of to-day more intelligent and more capable of forming their own opinions than the children of yesterday. As its administration becomes over-centralized at Whitehall, and independent schools are gradually absorbed into a unified system, the bureaucrat's ideal of the mass mind comes nearer realization. A French statesman, looking at his watch, is reported to have said to a friend, 'I can tell you exactly what is being taught at this moment in every school throughout the length and breadth of France.' The dual system is rapidly vanishing, and with it a safeguard against uniformity. To the Christian no education can be satisfactory unless it is religious both in its basis and in spirit: half an hour's Bible-teaching dissociated from worship is of little value, for religion will be looked upon by the children as a mere lesson to be discarded with all other lessons as soon as they leave school; but the nation is beginning to see that no education is complete unless its children are taught their heritage as children of God, and their duty towards Him as well as towards their neighbours.

RECREATION

Recreation has such an important place in the lives of many that some reference should be made to the remarkable developments in its extent and character.

In my boyhood there was not much organized recreation for the great masses of the people. For the public-school boy there were the playing fields for football and cricket, and usually a river for rowing. On the village greens cricket was played in the summer months, and in the winter in the elementary school there would be some private theatricals or concert or a penny reading, and occasionally a magic-lantern show. In the large towns building had spread with little attempt to reserve open spaces for games, and the minority who wished to play football had usually to walk, and later to cycle or drive, to fields rented on the outskirts of the town. The Music Hall was popular, and boxing drew crowds. On Derby day and in the case of other famous racing fixtures multitudes poured out from the towns to the race-course. Voluntary societies, especially the Churches, opened clubs for the younger people, to keep them off the streets; but most of the working class had to find their recreation in the public-house or in the streets or in some hobby. To-day the opportunities for recreation have greatly increased. The public libraries and popular editions of books have brought good reading within the reach of the many. The bicycle and the motor-car have opened the seaside and the country to the industrial workers. Holidays with pay and cheap excursions have made change and rest possible for all. But the most popular of recreations are football, the cinema, the wireless, and greyhound racing.

First there is Association Football. Its development to its present position started in the last quarter of the nineteenth century. It was until about 1890 a game played by amateurs for their own amusement. Onwards from then clubs began to develop on business lines for the entertainment of the general public; they hired players as their champions, and huge crowds collected to watch them play. The interest and excitement of the game are no longer confined to the twenty-two men who play in any given match; they are the chosen representatives of cities which follow their fortunes with passionate interest and enthusiasm. The chances and the play of the teams are eagerly discussed and debated: their victories are exulted over as bringing honour to their town, their defeats are deplored as civic calamities. Seventy to eighty millions a year attend football matches in Great Britain; every week during the season nearly a million watch professional football; while about half a million play fairly regularly. Huge sums are paid for the transfer of players from one club to another; the highest figure has been £30,000, though the average earnings of the individual player is not more than £8 a week. Professional football has become a major form of entertainment of local and national importance. 'It gives employment to some thousands of people directly and through ancillary industries: it has, in addition to the daily and Sunday Press, a literature of its own. Its matches not uncommonly draw crowds equal to one-third or more of the population of the town in which they are played, and this must attract the attention of the public authorities responsible for transport and crowd control: even more, the attention of any Government concerned with the problems of industrial absenteeism. Then there are the Pools, developed in isolation from the game and contributing nothing towards it. They are based on the results of League club matches, and from the season 1948–9 it is estimated that their turnover was £60,000,000 and that they employed some 20,000 people.'*

Another popular new form of entertainment is the cinema. The annual cinema attendances are 1,400 million. A wartime social survey in the summer of 1943 showed that 70 per cent of the adult civilian population occasionally went to the cinema, as many as 70 per cent of young wage-earners once a week or

*Planning: The Football Industry, I., Vol. XVII, p. 158. Other figures quoted above come from this interesting broadsheet.

more often, and some six million children between the ages of five and fifteen from time to time. The cinema now is a major form of recreation; on the whole its influence has been good; it has given great happiness to large numbers of young and old, who otherwise would have been at a loss as to how to spend their spare time, and it has opened up to them new worlds of interest. Through it they have become acquainted with lands they are never likely to visit, and with the customs of days long past. Directly and indirectly its influence is great; it helps to form the ideals and morals, as well as the manners, dress, and conversation, of its regular *habitués*. Some of its ideals are false, life is made to appear far more glamorous and sensational than it is in reality, and too often insipid beauty is shown as successful. But usually virtue is automatically rewarded, and self-sacrifice, kindliness, and heroism are held up to admiration.

Reference has already been made in this chapter to the function of the wireless in giving both instruction and recreation. It is difficult to over-state the difference it has made to the lives of many whose homes are in remote villages, far from any communal recreations, and to those who, owing to their work or health, are unable to go to places of amusement. Through its various programmes the B.B.C. offers entertainment to its listeners who differ greatly in culture and temperament. He is indeed hard to please who can find recreation neither in the Home, the Light, nor the Third Programme! Though complaints are made from time to time of vulgarity, the general result of the B.B.C. has been to raise the standard of entertainment, and to enable the ordinary listener to appreciate good literature and music in a way he never did before. But the wireless and gramophone together have reduced the number of those who could sing or play some musical instrument; the indifferent amateur is judged by a higher standard than in the past, for good music can now be had by simply turning a knob, instead of inviting some indifferent performer 'to oblige' on the piano or by a song.

Television, one of the latest inventions, is becoming immensely popular. A forest of masts now breaks the skyline of every town and village. In the spring of 1955 the actual number of television licences was just over four and a half million. Audience research showed that on an average evening more people were viewing than were listening to all three sound programmes combined.

Another popular form of recreation is attendance at grey-hound racing. The first impression of the arena is attractive, the blaze of lights and the crowds filling all the seats. The races themselves are uninteresting, a few dogs chasing a tin hare, but thirty-two million annually attend them. Out of two hours, barely five to ten minutes are usually devoted to the actual racing. There would be no interest in it if it were not for the betting. Many of the audience pay little attention to the racing, but have their eyes fixed on a board which gives the numbers of the winners, and on the bookmaker with whom they have placed their bets. But dog-racing will continue to flourish as long as the hours of leisure increase and so few sensible recreations are provided to occupy them.

The weakness of most popular forms of recreation is that everything is done for the spectator. He pays his money, and no further effort is required of him except to applaud or to criticize. He is not encouraged to make recreation for himself; it is provided for him by professionals. This is unavoidable in many cases, but more playing-fields for the young are an urgent necessity; something has already been done towards meeting this need, but there are still large numbers of men and lads anxious to play cricket or football who have no chance of doing so. Education for the right use of leisure is needed if we are not to breed a race of spectators. Lack of imagination and of initiative, as well as of opportunity, prevent many from making a better use of their spare time.

The Commission on Betting, Lotteries and Gaming (1949–51) finds that the 'spread of gambling is one of the symptoms of an age in which people have more leisure and cannot or do not know how to make good use of it. The remedy lies not in restrictive legislation but in education and the provision of facilities for more healthy recreation'. Gambling in some form or another has always been a national habit, though it has never before become so popular and general as during the last few years. This has been partly due to the nervous strain of two wars and the periods of tension and uncertainty which have followed them, though possibly still more to the existence of great organizations which make the promotion of gambling their business. But whatever the causes may be, there is no doubt about the popularity of gambling as an amusement. The Government Social Survey suggests that at least four out of every five adults have taken part at some time in their lives in some form of gambling; it found that during the 1949–50 season the total number of persons who took part in football-pool betting was about fourteen million. The number who bet on horse-race courses each year is about two and a half million; while the number betting fairly regularly on horse-racing off the course 'appears to be about four million, though probably as many as one in two of the adult population have a bet on such races as the Derby and the Grand National.' The Commission from whose report the above figures have been taken finds 'that personal expenditure on all forms of gambling during the three years 1948, 1949, and 1950 has been rather less than £70 million annually,' and that 'the figure of personal expenditure cannot be higher than 1 per cent of total personal expenditure, and that the proportion of the national resources absorbed by gambling is nearer ½ than 1 per cent.'

In recreation, as in everything else, there has been a revolution. Men of over fifty years of age grew up in a world in which there were no cars, no aeroplanes, no wireless, no cinemas, few League matches, no Pools, and no greyhound races!

THE DECLINE OF GREAT BRITAIN

So far I have been writing only of the changes which have taken place within Great Britain, but her position in the world has changed to an extent which would have seemed incredible to those who lived at the time of Queen Victoria's first Jubilee. The supremacy of Great Britain as a world Power was taken for granted by all true Britons, to the amusement or annoyance of their foreign friends or enemies. In Europe there were four great Powers – France, though weak after her defeat by Germany and restless under her humiliation, was generally regarded as a threat to the peace of Europe in her desire for revenge. Germany was looked upon as a friendly, peaceful State, with a well-fed, contented, musical people, united to Great Britain through the kinship of their rulers – William II and his telegram to Kruger were still in the future. Austria-Hungary was viewed with some hesitation, as there was doubt as to whether the different nationalities of which her Empire was composed would hold together for long. In the background was Russia, threatening and mysterious, always casting covetous eyes on Constantinople and on India; any movements she made either in the Balkans or towards the North-West Frontier of India or Afghanistan were viewed with suspicion. Not much reliance was placed on Turkey, the sick man of Europe; her collapse was frequently prophesied, but it was Great Britain's interest to keep her alive as an obstacle to Russian attempts to reach the Mediterranean. Across the Atlantic the United States took little or no interest in the affairs of Europe, though inclined at the time of a presidential election to engage in some irritating twisting of the Lion's tail. Amidst these various States, Great Britain had recognized supremacy, keeping the peace of the world with her fleets in all the oceans, with an Empire larger than any the world had ever known, drawing wealth from overseas investments and commerce, and her Government stable and settled, in contrast with the commotions on the Continent. The extent of the Empire was still increasing, and every patriotic citizen was certain that nothing would ever destroy it. Queen Victoria's Jubilees in 1887 and 1897 were made occasions for great outbursts of imperialism. From all parts of the world the Empire sent its representatives to the London celebrations, and they were welcomed with delirious enthusiasm by the crowds. Looking back to the eighties I find it hard to exaggerate the complete and absolute confidence we had in the greatness and security of the British Empire; we believed it had been chosen by God to bring justice and good order to all the earth, and that for centuries to come it would stand firm as a rock against all storms.

To-day the contrast is strange compared with the optimistic picture we had in those days, now long past. The world has been ravaged by two great wars, and is now threatened by a third. The empires of Germany, Austria-Hungary and Russia have fallen. Germany is divided into two republics, each over-shadowed by occupying Powers. Austria-Hungary has broken into the fragments which once made up its empire, and the small republic of Austria exists precariously while the victor States dispute over its future; Hungary and Czechoslovakia are the subservient satellites of Russia; France, exhausted by defeat and distracted by internal divisions, is uncertain of herself and her future. Out of the whirlpool of world confusion two huge and powerful States have emerged in bitter rivalry – Russia and the United States. The tyranny of the Tsars has gone and has been replaced by the more ruthless tyranny of Communist rulers, who now with huge armed forces and in-cessant propaganda threaten the peace of the world. The United States no longer remains in isolation; her wealth and power have increased enormously; she occupies among the nations the place which once belonged to Great Britain; she is actively and beneficently concerned with the affairs both of Europe and the Far East, and has taken the position of leader of the free world against the aggressiveness of Russia. Without the moral and material support given by America, most of Europe would by now have come under Communist rule.

The fall of Great Britain from her ancient supremacy has been tragic. In the struggle for freedom she was forced to spend her overseas investments and she has lost much of her trade. Her people are both tired and impoverished: tired through their strenuous efforts in the two wars, impoverished by astronomical expenditure in winning them, and by heavy taxation. Her fleet is small compared with what it was in the past, and is overshadowed by the huge fleet built up by the United States. Her Empire is vanishing, India and Burma are independent. She has been driven out of Palestine by the terrorism and intrigues of the Jews. She has had to withdraw the forces which so long occupied Egypt to the Suez Canal area. In her possessions in West Africa there are riots and demands for independence. The pound, through devaluation, has lost the proud position it so long held, and New York has now replaced London as the money centre of the world. At home the cost of living has gone up by leaps and bounds, and it will be impossible to maintain the standard of living to which we have become accustomed. At heavy self-sacrifice and cost, the United Kingdom is now re-arming in self-defence. General de Gaulle's cruel jibe is true, there are now only two and a half great Powers, and with the utmost difficulty we are now preserving our place as the half. Rarely if ever before has an Empire, not after defeat, but after victory, fallen from its high position with such dramatic suddenness. It has come to pass so rapidly that most of us still fail to realize the grim reality; we console ourselves with memories of past greatness, and with flattering hopes of recovery of which there seems to be no immediate prospect.

It is impossible to hold any reasonable hope that Great Britain will ever recover the place she once held in the international world. Her future greatness may be found elsewhere. She may be able to show the world a nation in which Socialism and freedom are combined, in which reverence for the past is reconciled with a new manner of life; and if her Welfare State is successful, she will show a community neither authoritarian nor Communist; she may take the lead in culture and knowledge, in a high standard of education, in scientific research and in the excellency of the goods she exports. She may give the world the example of a nation in which social justice and freedom flourish. But the glory of Empire has gone from her, and the days of prosperity and wealth have vanished beyond recall.

LOSS OF CONFIDENCE

We have not only lost confidence in the future of our nation, but – what is much more serious – we have no longer confidence in man himself. Of all the changes which have taken

44

place in my lifetime this is one of the greatest. It is almost impossible to describe the strength of the confidence which until the passing of the first decade of the twentieth century the average educated Englishman had in himself, his nation, and in the human race. Education, science, medicine, and material prosperity held out to every individual the prospect of ever-increasing security and happiness. The nation with its mighty Empire would retain unchallenged its mastery. The whole world would share in the welfare of the more advanced nations, and as the blessings of civilization spread to the lower races they would rise above their ignorance. Our feet were set on what we assumed was solid ground; we were sure of ourselves and our future. 'God's in His heaven, all's right with the world' was not a sentiment confined to Robert Browning. It is true the more thoughtful did not share this state of mind without considerable qualification; they recognized regretfully that security was not enjoyed by most of their fellow countrymen, but was largely the privilege of the upper and middle classes. There were millions who did not possess any security, who were never far removed from destitution and want, and who were haunted by the fear of unemployment, which would plunge them and their families into long weeks, or even months, of hunger and distress. But confidence and security were taken for granted by the more prosperous and articulate classes of the community. Recently doubt has banished confidence. For the first time for over a thousand years a deliberate and sustained attack is made on Western civilization by a rival civilization which is armed with immense military resources. Communism is an aggressive and militant religion determined to overthrow and destroy all other religions and political systems. It is a religion of atheism which is propagated with relentless enthusiasm and fiery determination. It is not content to allow any rivals to exist, but is resolved to crush out all opposition. While it threatens the world there can be neither peace nor security, at the best only an uncertain truce which may at any time be broken.

With the danger of another war there goes another danger. If the war comes it will be total, it will be a fight for survival, and if a State finds its existence endangered it will employ without scruple every weapon that the ingenuity of man has invented for destruction. If a State engaged in war possesses nuclear weapons it will use them to destroy its enemy. In a war prolonged over several months most of the cities of the world would be reduced to ruin, vast tracts of country would be so devastated that life would become impossible, and terrified survivors would look for hiding places in forests and mountains. If the hydrogen bomb should be used it is not beyond possibility that the world itself might be destroyed. If life is spared by nuclear weapons, it will be swept away by the deadly bacilli and gases released by one or both of the combatants. It is sheer wishful thinking to imagine that because these weapons are so lethal no one will dare to use them. Fear, hate, and ambition are capable of any crime, however hideous and monstrous. Man has made amazing discoveries before he is capable of using them rightly, and now that he understands the appalling destructiveness of the weapons he has invented he is frightened, as he has not been since his primitive ancestors trembled before the unknown and malignant demons with which their imagination peopled the earth and sky.

The reality and terrible nature of the danger should spur man into activity to avoid it. There is the possibility that emphasis on the imminence of catastrophe may lead to fatalism and recklessness. The 'couldn't care less' mentality will be encouraged to say 'Let us eat, drink and be merry, for tomorrow we die'. The more stoical will be tempted to await the doom they cannot avoid in a spirit of grim and determined resignation. In the early Church there were some who neglected their daily duties in expectancy of the imminent end of the world, and who were sternly rebuked for this by the Apostle. The Christian Church spent its early years in a period of crisis. This is not the first time it has experienced an age of crisis: it has therefore guidance and help to give to mankind in its perplexity and anxiety. But the Church has its own special problems due to the revolution of our time. Both its faith and its morals are under fire.

NOTE

I have not stressed sufficiently the revolution either in habits of reading or of taking holidays away from home in the last seventy years. Reading is the result of national education, of increased leisure, and of the publication of first-class books at a low price: the 'Everyman' and the 'World's Classics' series have brought the great writers of the past within reach of all, while 'The Home University Library' and 'The Teach Yourself Series' are admirable in the help they give for self-education. Mr Seebohm Rowntree and Mr G. R. Lavers in *English Life and Leisure* say that in the Penguins and in the public libraries we have supplies of books of which we should 'feel proud, certain that they have no equal anywhere in the world'.*

The holiday habit during this period has increased amazingly. In 1937 it has been estimated that fifteen million people in Great Britain took a week or more's holiday away from home; in 1954 the number was twenty-five million. This is partly due to the standard practice of a week's paid holiday for all employees earning less than £250; partly it has been due to increased wages, and partly to the activities of the various tourist agencies.

*P. 314.

2

Religion in the Twilight

THE revolutionary changes which have taken place during the
last seventy years have profoundly affected religious faith and
life. This is true not only of the Church of England, but of
other Christian Churches, and also of non-Christian religions.
During the war I met in Cairo the Rector of the great Moslem
University of El Ahzar, who told me that there had been a
striking decline in the number of regular worshippers in the
mosques; he attributed this to the disturbance caused by the
war, and was anxious to know if the Christian Churches had
the same experience. A few years later a distinguished archbishop of a Roman Catholic country spoke to me of his
anxiety over the falling away from Christianity of many who
were living in the industrial areas of his province; here again
he ascribed this to the war and to the German occupation of
his diocese. The United States has not felt the impact of the
war to the same extent as Great Britain or Europe, but in the
State of Utah, the stronghold of Mormonism, one of the
leaders of the Church of Latter Day Saints told me that it was
difficult for the younger members of their community to
adapt themselves on demobilization to the stricter rules of
membership. These are only three examples of the widespread
religious unsettlement which has been caused by the war;
they might be multiplied to almost any extent – for everywhere, to a greater or less degree, religious creeds and customs,
whether Christian or non-Christian, have suffered from the
disintegrating effects of two world wars. It would, however,
be a mistake to think that the falling away from religion is
due solely, or even mainly, to the wars. They hastened
and brought to a head tendencies which had already been
undermining religious faith. If there had been no wars
the Churches would have suffered both from open hostility
and from the far-reaching changes in the intellectual atmosphere.

detailed ... years later Disraeli, speaking at Oxford,
there is a city Goths – Is man an ape or an angel? My
of its inhabitants, is on a ... the angels.' Darwin's theory also
been used to show design in botan... from design as expounded by
cry against Darwin's theories was great; the a... argue to a creator from
among religious people was widespread and ext... which had
though some of his arguments were subsequently disproved,
his main thesis is now accepted by most educated people,
namely that through adaptation and readaptation to environment in the struggle for survival existing forms of life, including human beings, have been evolved. There are few thoughtful Christians who now feel any difficulty over the theory of
evolution. Those who accept evolution are convinced that
God's creative action is as real if spread over millions of years
as over one day, and that man's greatness is to be found not in
what he was, but in what he is becoming in accordance with
God's Will. Moreover, the theory of evolution enables God
to be seen not as an absentee Creator, but as the present and
living God who still continues His creative work, ever fash-
ioning through the long ages something new from that which
is old.

While Darwin disturbed faith by teaching the lowly origin
of man, the geologist and archaeologist upset traditional conceptions about the length of time he had been living on the
earth. Some of the older Bibles boldly printed the date of
man's creation as B.C. 4004; but fossils dug up by geologists
prove that there were plants, fishes, birds, and animals on the
earth millions of years before that time; while excavations by
archaeologists show that it was about six thousand years ago
that civilizations were beginning to appear, and this pre-
supposes a much longer previous existence of human beings.
The existence of man on the earth may go back to nearly a

Life of Charles Darwin (1892 edition), p. 238.

million years ago and that of ...ch the world will con-
eight hundred million ye...yed either by collision with
formed there have been ... man's own inventions, there will
have disappeared or ... two and a half million civilizations to rise
their opinion as ...
tinue to exist ... oments like these seem to make human beings
some star ... into meaningless insignificance, while their civiliza-
be time ... appear as mere flashes of light against a background of
and ...
dns appear as mere flashes of light against a background of
impenetrable darkness.

This impression of man's unimportance was deepened by
the latest discoveries of astronomers. It is impossible any
longer to think of the solar system as the centre of the universe. There are two million known clusters of stars, each of
which contains thousands of millions of stars either formed or
in process of creation. Our sun and its planets are a tiny
system within the galaxy of stars to which we belong, and
which can be partly seen in the Milky Way. 'At a moderate
computation, the total number of stars in the universe must
be something like the total number of specks of dust in
London. Think of the sun as something less than a single speck
of dust in a vast city, of the earth as less than a millionth part
of such a speck of dust.' But notwithstanding the millions and
millions of stars, the spaces between them are vast. 'The universe consists in the main not of stars but of desolate empti-
ness – inconceivably vast stretches of desert space in which
the presence of a star is a rare and exceptional event.'† These
statements make us echo Pascal's cry, 'The eternal silence of
these infinite spaces terrifies me.' Size can intimidate the mind.
The vastness of the universe may conceal its Creator. But if
God can create this stupendous universe, He is also capable of
knowing and caring for every individual in it. While man
seems to dwindle into utter insignificance at each discovery,
yet it is he who has made the discovery. Every discovery

*A. J. Toynbee, *Civilization on Trial*, p. 23.
†Sir James Jeans, *The Universe Around Us*, pp. 86, 87.

should be regarded both as a further revelation of the Majesty of God and of the greatness of the human mind. Reflexion may reassure us, but the first reaction to the size of the universe as shown by the latest telescopes is the apparent inconceivability of God caring for the minute specks of animated dust living on a slightly larger speck amidst the millions and millions of stars wandering in the vastness of space. 'Here we are in this wholly fantastic universe with scarcely a clue as to whether our existence has any real significance,'* writes a modern astronomer; but against this the Christian repeats another saying of Pascal, 'Man is but a reed, the weakest thing in nature; but a thinking reed . . . But though the universe should crush him, man would still be nobler than his destroyer, because he knows that he is dying . . . the universe knows naught of him.'

It is right that the discoveries of the astronomer should fill man with a sense both of awe and fear. The vastness of the universe should have a purgative effect, painfully cleansing him of false ideas of human importance. Astronomy does not make faith easier, it makes it harder and sterner. It should make 'us ashamed of our petty interpretation of the world, ashamed of thinking that the universe was made solely for our benefit; ashamed of thinking that our little scheme of purely human values is valid for the whole; ashamed of our arrogant assumption that we are "the roof and crown of things", so that all the non-human world, including the other living inhabitants of our planet, has a merely instrumental value "made for our use" as some have said.'†

From another side, too, science has brought doubt and perplexity. The study of comparative religion has shown not only the varieties of religion as practised by different races, but also their remarkable similarities. To a limited extent this has always been recognized, and some of the early Christian apologists attempted to account for the resemblances between Christianity and pagan religions by saying either that they were borrowed from Christianity or that they came from the

*F. Hoyle, *The Nature of the Universe*, p. 115.
†W. R. Inge, *God and the Astronomers*, p. 15.

devil in an attempt to mislead and confuse the Christian. It is often held there is no absolute difference between religions, that all are relatively both false and true, for they are conditioned by the climate, the geographical features, and the different civilizations in which they have had their origin; it is thus really a matter of no importance as to which religion a man holds: one religion is as good as another, provided he lives up to its teaching. This attitude encourages indifference to the claims of any specific religion. No one would, however, say this of art in all the ages: there are similarities between the painting of different epochs, but the differences are still greater. The crude drawings of animals on the walls of a cave inhabited by primitive man may be viewed with interest, but only an unbalanced eccentric would claim that they had the same value as the paintings of El Greco or of Leonardo da Vinci. The Christian can appreciate the truth which is found in most religions, for he believes it comes from the One Spirit who teaches truth to all men, but he claims that the Christian religion is as superior to the religion of the animist as Leonardo's 'Last Supper' is to the rough scrawls of a barbaric huntsman on the wall of the cave.

One of the latest sciences recognizes the strength of the religious instinct and then attempts to explain it. Psychology can be used as a dangerous weapon against religion. Over twenty years ago J. B. S. Haldane wrote, 'The psychologists are hauling up their guns into position with a view to an assault.'* The almost universal belief in the existence of a God or gods towards whom man's relationship is of vital importance calls for explanation. Modern psychology is ready with an answer. It explains that the deities which human beings worship have no existence outside themselves; they are the projection of minds demanding security, and satisfy men who otherwise would feel helpless in the midst of natural forces they are unable to control. The origin of the belief in gods is to be found in the shelter which the infant had before birth in his mother's womb; the need for protection is carried into the world; the child finds reassurance in the protective strength

*J. B. S. Haldane, *The Inequality of Man*, p. 133.

of his father, and this is transferred to an imaginary, all-powerful being who has the qualities of fatherhood. Some psychologists find the source of religion not in the individual but in the racial group which projects its aspirations and ideals into an image it has created. Psychology can explain how religious faith has developed, but it fails to explain a historical religion like Christianity, whose faith and devotion are concentrated on One who had lived at a definite time in the history of the world among men who heard His words, saw His deeds and were transformed by the power of His Person. Here is no mental projection, but a Man who was seen and heard by His contemporaries.

Modern psychology does not only claim to explain the nature of religion, but also of sin and remorse. Where our forefathers regarded sin as disobedience to God, and penitence as necessary for forgiveness, the psychologist finds its root in the recesses of the subconscious, and claims to remove it by psycho-analysis. The psychologist takes the place of the priest; complexes and obsessions are resolved, instead of sin repented and forgiven; sublimation of an instinct is substituted for amendment of life. Sin can often be overcome by the patient – for penitents no longer would exist – by his own thinking: assisted by the psycho-analyst, the 'straightener' of *Erewhon*, he can smooth out knots in his life. One of the characters in Mr T. S. Eliot's *Cocktail Party* expresses a very common view of sin:

> Well, my bringing up was pretty conventional –
> I had always been taught to disbelieve in sin.
> Oh, I don't mean that it was ever mentioned!
> But anything wrong, from our point of view,
> Was either bad form or was psychological.
> And bad form always led to disaster
> Because the people one knew disapproved of it.

The psycho-analyst can often give valuable help in restoring a divided personality and in removing irrational phobias; but the tendency of much psychological teaching is to blunt the difference between right and wrong: sins of lust, perversion and temper are excused by a man on the ground that they are 'part of his make-up', and are treated not as sins for which forgiveness is needed, but as inherited twists which can be straightened out. Readers of *Erewhon* will remember that in that country 'if a man forges a cheque, or sets his house on fire, or robs with violence from the person, or does any other such things as are criminal in our own country, he is either taken to a hospital and most carefully tended at the public expense, or if he is in good circumstances, he lets it be known to all his friends that he is suffering from a severe fit of immorality, just as we do when we are ill, and they come and visit him with great solicitude . . . for bad conduct, though considered no less deplorable than illness with ourselves . . . is nevertheless held to be the result of pre-natal or post-natal misfortune.' Psychology is often taught and understood as if it gave a satisfactory natural explanation of religion and a valid reason for not 'worrying' about sin.

THE BIBLE

There were many who looked upon the Bible as an impregnable citadel against assaults on the Christian faith. For centuries it had been reverenced as verbally inspired, and all within its covers accepted as literally true. But at the end of the last century a great change began to be made in the traditional views of the Bible. The so-called Lower Criticism had examined the received text, and compared and corrected it with ancient manuscripts. Later the High Criticism inquired into the authorship, the composition and dates of the different books, and weighed their value as historical documents. This study of the Bible was undertaken mainly by Christian scholars, their only purpose being the search for truth, and thus to understand better the book they valued above all others. The Bible could not be exempt from the literary and historical criticism already applied to all other ancient literature. The results of this investigation were alarming to those who had been taught to look upon every page of the Bible as guaranteed from all error. It was found that many of the books were written by authors different from those whose names they bore; that some of them were composite documents, the work of various hands; that the dates of their writing were frequently later than those generally accepted; and that the authors shared many of the opinions and errors of their time. It soon became plain that there were statements in some of the books which could not be accepted as historically correct, and that the earlier writers approved of customs and deeds condemned in later and more civilized ages. As these results were gradually made known, there were vehement protests from many Christians, and a shout of triumph from the secularists, who believed that the Bible had been proved to be untrue.

At first, indeed, it looked as if the extremer criticisms would sweep all before them, but reflexion and further research led to the abandonment of many radical theories and often to a return to positions not far removed from those which had been traditionally held. It was seen that while all the books of the Bible were not equally inspired, nor of the same level of importance, together they gave a unique account of progressive revelation showing how in various ways and manners God had gradually revealed His Nature and purpose. It is now accepted that most of the books of the New Testament had been written well within the first century. 'If fair play is given to them, it must be recognized that the New Testament books stand in a very strong position, the strength of which has been increased by recent discoveries and investigation. Short of the discovery of first-century manuscripts, their traditional first-century dates are confirmed by as strong evidence as it is reasonable to expect.'* The Christian believes that notwithstanding the new views on the books of the Bible, it is the inspired Word of God; and though it does not give authoritative information about science, geology, history, or astronomy, which must be looked for elsewhere, it speaks to man as no other book does about God and His purpose. Its inspiration is experienced by all those who with reverence and patience turn to it for spiritual help and use it as a lantern which gives light to their feet on the way to eternal life.

*Sir Frederick Kenyon, *The Bible and Modern Scholarship*, p. 51.

Much of the perplexity caused by the new views on the Bible as they reached the man in the street, or even the man in the pew, was due to past failure to give intelligent teaching. The fear the clergy felt of disturbing the faithful by plain statements led many of their congregations to be caught unawares by Biblical criticism, and in violent reaction from the traditional views they rejected the Bible as the Word of God. They discovered that the description of the creation in Genesis is not a scientific account of the origin of life, that the world was not covered with a flood, that a great fish did not swallow Jonah, and therefore hastily concluded that most of the Bible is unworthy of belief. My own experience in this respect was fortunate: when I was a small boy my father taught me that many of the stories of the Bible should not be taken literally, that some of the events described with approval in the Old Testament should be condemned by the Christian as cruel and wicked – Jael's killing of Sisera he described as a treacherous murder – and that while all good books, especially poetry, were inspired, the Bible stood supreme above all others in its truth and wisdom, and in the knowledge it gave of God. This teaching saved me from the heart-searching experienced by so many when later in life they learnt that some of the assured results of Biblical criticism could not be reconciled with views of inspiration which they had been taught.

THE WARS AND RELIGION

The discoveries of science and Biblical criticism spread gradually and slowly down from the educated to the great mass of ordinary people; their results on religious faith and practice became evident only after many years, but the impact of the two great wars on religion was immediate, and affected millions who had only the vaguest idea, if any, of the bearing of science on faith. In three directions the years of war had a disintegrating effect on religion.

First, they were physically destructive. In England and on the Continent they destroyed thousands of churches and other buildings which in some cases had been used for centuries for worship. I shall never forget going into Southampton on a Sunday morning at the end of 1940 after a severe raid. Five of the Anglican churches had been destroyed, some were blackened shells, others were still burning. In previous raids churches had been destroyed or damaged, and in the weeks which followed more were rendered unusable. Nonconformists and Roman Catholics suffered in the same way. In the larger neighbouring city of Portsmouth, many of the churches were destroyed, and more of them damaged. In the dioceses of London and Southwark the toll of destruction far exceeded anything experienced in the Provinces. Large numbers of churches were scheduled as complete ruins and abandoned; in others an aisle or chapel or even the vestry was hastily adapted for the use of the small congregation which remained; sometimes a hall or school was used for worship; or some neighbouring church which had escaped serious damage was used by parishes which had no buildings left in which services could be held. Conditions were far worse on the Continent; whole cities with their churches were reduced to heaps of ruins. In addition to the destruction of churches both in Great Britain and on the Continent, ecclesiastical property of all kinds – parsonage houses, halls, institutions, and schools – shared in the general ruin. Nor was this all: in many cases the buildings which had escaped destruction were requisitioned for military or civil purposes. Flourishing Sunday Schools and Bible Classes were expelled for years from their premises, and their work suspended.

Over and above the actual destruction of buildings, Church work suffered from the dislocation and confusion caused by war. Thousands of the younger clergy left their parishes to serve as chaplains; the best of the younger men abandoned their colleges and training to enlist in one of the services; during the war the supply of ordinands dried up almost completely, and the bishops ordained only a small handful either of men past the age for military service or incapacitated through ill health or injury. Single-handed the older clergy had to minister to parishes in which there should have been a staff of assistant curates. Many of the organizations, and most of the pastoral visitation, customary in well-worked parishes, had to be brought to an end. Only very gradually will the vacancies among the clergy be filled as the men now at the universities or theological colleges are ordained; and as fast as the younger men come forward many of the older men who in ordinary circumstances would have resigned some years ago drop out of the ranks.

Equally serious was the dislocation caused among the congregations and lay helpers. At the time of the 1914–18 war I was Vicar of Portsea, a great naval and dockyard parish of over 40,000 people. On the first Saturday afternoon in August the order was issued by bugles blown in the streets for men to join their ships immediately; on the Sunday half the choir of my church, many of the bellringers, the caretakers of our buildings, large numbers of Sunday School teachers and a considerable proportion of the men usually in the congregation had vanished. Before the war was over ten of my staff of sixteen curates were serving as chaplains. Notwithstanding the black-out we were allowed to hold evening services, on the condition that they did not exceed an hour, and that all lights could be extinguished at a moment's notice; in the reading-desk and pulpit I had candles to light if an emergency arose. There were no air raids – only once, and then possibly by mistake, a zeppelin came over Portsmouth – and throughout most of the war we had an evening congregation of nearly two thousand. But my successor found in the last war everything far more difficult: his staff was reduced to a minimum, the black-out was complete, thousands of children were evacuated to safety, the church itself was damaged and one of the mission churches destroyed in air raids, and numerous streets in the parish were wiped out. When the war came to an end much of the work had to be restarted from the beginning. This was the experience of thousands of parishes; even those which were spared actual bombing were affected by the black-out, which necessitated afternoon instead of evening services, and the movements of population: often the child population of a parish in a danger area vanished, while parishes in areas regarded as safe had sudden invasions of children and their mothers. It is not even now always realized how great was the movement of population in the early months of the war. Not 'until the fifth year of war did the Health Department know that whereas they had evacuated nearly 1,500,000 mothers and children, about 2,000,000 had evacuated themselves.'* In addition, large numbers of men and women left their homes for service either in the armed forces or in the munition factories. Established habits of regular church-going were broken, and they were not always resumed when the men and women returned to their homes. Sheer exhaustion also must be taken into account; those who had been accustomed to the help of servants, found themselves without domestic staff and compelled to do all the household work; their difficulties were frequently increased by the necessity of sharing their house with those whose homes had been destroyed. Church work voluntarily undertaken in the past had to be abandoned, and church attendance became irregular.

There was a third and deeper way in which the war affected religious faith. Generations of peace disturbed only by minor wars felt the two wars as a great spiritual and psychological shock. 'Why does God allow the war?' was the cry of many who had never previously questioned their faith. The years after the first war were a time of bitter disillusionment. We deluded ourselves with the hope that it had been the war to end war, that it had purged the world of much that was evil, and that out of the suffering there would emerge an international order of justice and peace. As the years passed the sense of depression and frustration deepened, and when another war with all its horror broke out, with its fearful atrocities and cruelties, and the devils of lust and brutality seemed to have been unloosed, the doubts as to whether there is a God who reigns became deeper. Many who had never heard of the intellectual arguments for or against Christianity found themselves asking how could a God of love permit the appalling horrors and the flagrant injustices of which they heard day after day. When I was walking through the still-burning streets of Southampton after a severe raid a man

*R. M. Titmuss, *Problems of Social Policy*, p. 102.

called out to me, 'What does One above think of all this?'
Some who in the past had accepted Christianity without hesitation now rejected it because their experiences of war had convinced them it was not true. It is only the superficial optimist who imagines that from war there will come a religious revival; history shows that war leads either to crass superstition or to widespread falling away from faith and worship.

THE FALLING AWAY FROM RELIGION

Modern science, Biblical criticism, and the war thus have had almost everywhere a disturbing effect on the work of the Christian Church. In the United States this has probably been less than anywhere else, and it is claimed that while a large percentage of the nation has no connexion with organized religion, yet Church attendance is larger than at any previous time. This is exceptional, for both on the Continent and in Great Britain there is abundant evidence to prove that religion has lost the hold it once had on the peoples of the Old World.

There is more open and aggressive atheism than at any other period of human history. In a later chapter this will be discussed more fully, but now it is sufficient to say that the dominant form of Communism, which is Marxian in its philosophy, is bitterly opposed to Christianity as a dangerous enemy and mischievous superstition. At the hands of twentieth-century atheism Christianity has suffered from persecutions far more severe than anything it had to endure from the paganism of the Roman Empire. In Russia, in Germany, in France, and in many of the Central European and Balkan nations Christianity is treated either with hatred or with contempt. Apart from organized atheism there are probably more individual atheists than in the past. Many who once would have called themselves agnostics, refusing either to deny or to believe in God, but asserting that nothing could be known about Him even if He did exist, would now describe themselves as atheists. Some do so with deep sorrow – they respect and even reverence the faith of the Christian and wish they could share it, but intellectual honesty seems to compel them to hold that there is no evidence which would justify belief in the existence of God, still less to believe He is love, and that they would only be deceiving themselves if they found comfort in the hope of a life after death. But there is another type of atheist who looks on Christianity as the great lie, and on the Church as the instrument of tyranny, falsehood, and superstition. He is filled with hatred of it and its faith; with crusading zeal, he will do all in his power to destroy, or at least to discredit it. This fanatical atheism is rare in Great Britain, but from time to time it shows itself in some venomous attack on institutional religion, in the gloating over any scandal committed by Christians, in misrepresenting, vilifying, and pouring contempt on its faith and worship.

Far more general is the attitude of almost complete indifference to religion and ignorance of its nature. Except for occasions such as baptisms, marriages, and funerals, the ordinary man has little contact with the Church or its ministers. The Chaplains to the Forces during the two wars often expressed amazement at the indifference and ignorance of the men under their care; but the parish priest who knew the people was not surprised. For years he had been alive to the fact of indifference and to the widespread opinion that religion was good for children, sometimes for women, but it had nothing to do with the average man. To most its prohibitions were known, 'Thou shalt not', but of its positive teaching they had no knowledge. In an inquiry it was found that three out of five of those questioned did not know the names of the four Gospels; out of a club of thirty boys only one knew what had happened on Good Friday; the majority of a larger group of men had the vaguest ideas as to who was Jesus Christ, 'a good man' was the usual answer; but when or where He lived, or even if He had lived at all, still less what He taught, few of them could say with confidence. Men who take an intelligent interest in political and social problems, take it for granted that religion has nothing to do with them; it has no help to give, no guidance to offer. There is not much hostility, there is often friendliness to individual ministers of religion, and in rural districts there is considerable respect and affection for the ancient parish church, and large sums of money are contributed by those who rarely enter its doors, as well as by the regular worshippers, to keep it from falling into ruin; but religion as an effective power which concerns the whole of life is remote from the thoughts of ordinary men and women. What was learnt at school, both on Sundays and on weekdays, on the Christian religion has gone almost completely out of their minds, and if they still have some recollection of the teaching they once received, it is rarely regarded as having any practical bearing on life. The majority of men and women neither say their prayers, except in some terrifying emergency, nor read their Bibles, unless to look for help in a crossword puzzle, or enter a church from one end of the year to the other, except for baptisms, marriages, or funerals. A Mass-Observation Inquiry in a London Borough showed that only one out of every twelve people questioned had attended any place of worship in the previous six months; and the same Inquiry showed that 'nearly half the women, and nearly two-thirds of the men, incline to think that there is no after-life or are undecided about it.'* Elsewhere in the same Inquiry it is stated: 'Many people look upon religion as something quite harmless and purely personal – an innocuous hobby, like collecting stamps. One of the results of this attitude is that these same people often feel that religion is exceeding its legitimate grounds if it "interferes" with more practical matters. Religion to them is all right in its place, but it shouldn't get involved in everyday affairs outside the private life of believers.'†

The results of unbelief, ignorance, and indifference on the life and work of the Church are very grave. Churches once full now have small congregations, though here and there they are as large as ever; Sunday Schools have greatly diminished in their membership, though this is partly due to the decline in the birthrate; and many of the organizations for young people have come to an end. On Sunday a huge stream of cars, coaches, and cycles flows from the towns to the country or the sea, and no thought is given by the

*Puzzled People, pp. 18 and 28.   †Op. cit., p. 84.

holiday-maker to worship. The Sunday opening of cinemas, the radio, concerts, excursions, and games have all in different degrees discouraged church attendance. The influence which the Church once had on the nation has diminished; religion is now the active concern of a minority of its people; its claim for the whole of life is no longer made with any confidence, and only very rarely treated as serious.

NO REASON FOR PESSIMISM

Later on some account will be given of the way in which the Church is meeting this position, but lest the foregoing seems unduly pessimistic, it should be remembered that this is not the first time the Church has had to pass through a period of indifference and opposition. As long ago as the fifth century a pope complained that the people of Rome were neglecting their religious duties for the games and other amusements. Since then at frequent intervals the religious have deplored, and the irreligious have rejoiced over, the decline of faith. There have been periods of dryness and neglect followed by spiritual revival. Professor Latourette, the historian of the expansion of Christianity, sums up the position as follows: 'Since in the past Christianity has demonstrated its ability to survive the passing of the order which it has helped to shape and of which it has seemed to be an inseparable part, it is to be expected that this again will be the record and that after what may be a decline Christianity will revive and with increased power go on to mould, more than before, the human race. Even if it should lose in some areas where it once has been strong – perhaps in some sections where it has been strongest – this will be no new phenomenon. That has happened before. Past experience gives ground for the expectation that elsewhere, perhaps in some quite unexpected region, Christianity can achieve a fresh extension, and in which and from which it can continue its growth.'*

The Christian must avoid both undue optimism and pessimism. His optimism must not lead him to ignore the gravity

*The Unquenchable Light, p. 128.

and difficulty of the present crisis. To prophesy smooth things with the promise of an immediate revival or of 'the world for Christ in our time' may call forth some temporary enthusiasm which will soon be replaced by disappointment in face of hard and unyielding facts. There must be no shouting on the part of the Christian to keep his courage up. On the other hand, he must avoid the despondency of pessimism. There are already some signs of a return to religion. The generation which is most indifferent is now chiefly composed of middle-aged people, while the rising generation is showing more interest in religion than was formerly the case. Mr Charles Morgan in one of his essays tells of a young girl who recently said to her father, 'You spent your time, when you were young, in breaking down the walls. We are going to build them up again.' Mr Morgan is not quite clear as to the nature of the walls which the girl had in mind – though the first wall he assumes would be the wall of European peace – she and her contemporaries have not the faith of an earlier generation in blueprints; but he goes on to say that unless they 'expect to have communal shelters built for them, they are reasonably determined to build walls for themselves – of custom, of responsibility, of decorum probably, of principle perhaps, even of privilege.'* But these walls will soon collapse unless they are built on a sure and solid foundation, and for this the Christian points to One who is the Rock.

Liberties of the Mind, pp. 116 and 122.

3

Moral Chaos

THE loss of faith has been followed by moral chaos. The agnostics of Victorian days were confident that the Christian ethic, which they reverenced, would remain unshaken even if the faith with which it had always been associated should be abandoned. Occasionally warning voices were heard insisting that Christian morals were the result of Christian doctrine, and that they would inevitably wither and perish if separated from the root from which they derived their life. Little attention was, however, paid to these warnings, and it was confidently assumed that the Christian ethic would continue to be accepted as the ideal standard of conduct even if Christian dogma should be discredited by natural science and modern criticism.

NATURAL LAW

The moral standards of Western civilization had their origin in theistic and Christian faith. Before the coming of Christ, pagan philosophers, especially the Stoics, had taught that there was a law of nature which was binding on all men at all times and in all places. Medieval philosophers and theologians took over and strengthened this teaching. Natural law 'is the eternal law of God, imprinted in our conscience by Him naturally, so that all men know or may know what is essentially right or wrong by the light of their own conscience. This is the sense in which St Paul says the Gentiles, who have not the Law (*sc.* of Moses), do by nature the things of the law (the natural law of God). This natural law is promulgated by God in making human nature. No power can abrogate it or dispense from it.'* This law speaks of justice, truth, honesty, self control. It is the law which should be recognized and obeyed by the heathen as much as by the Christian. It is the

*Adrian Fortescue on 'Law (Christian)'. *Encyclopaedia of Religion and Ethics*, Vol. VII, p. 832.

foundation on which international law is built. Christians believe its authority is derived not from human speculations, nor from enlightened self-interest, but from the conviction that above all nations and individuals there is the Sovereignty of God, who demands obedience to the laws by which He governs the world He has made.

THE CHRISTIAN ETHIC

When Christ came He did not abolish the natural law, nor did He supplement it by an elaborate code of laws made binding upon His disciples. If He had done this He would have given His Church for all time a rigid system which would have left no room for progress and change. Some of the laws intended to govern conduct in a small province of the Roman Empire in the first century would have proved inapplicable in the changed conditions of the modern world. He assumed the natural law and gave a wider interpretation to the Jewish law; but in addition He set before His disciples a new and far higher ideal of the *summum bonum* – the Christian was to love God with all his heart, with all his soul, with all his mind, and with all his strength, and his neighbour as himself. By His teaching and, above all, by His life and deeds, He showed how this ideal should be realized in ordinary life. Love to God was revealed in such complete surrender of self that it led to the cross on Calvary; love to man was made plain in acts and words of mercy and kindness to all sorts and conditions of men; and hatred for an enemy was to be replaced by forgiveness. He taught His disciples that pride, anger, self-sufficiency, and contempt were to be renounced by those who would be members of the Kingdom of God; instead they should show themselves the true children of God by their meekness, humility, and forbearance. Perfect chastity was to govern the relationships between man and woman, and the married were to be faithful to each other until parted by death. Christ's ethical demands on His disciples were far more searching than those made by heathen moralists; for He was concerned not only with external conduct, but with the secret motives behind it. Later St Paul described the chief Christian virtues as fruits of the spirit and enumerated them as 'love, joy, peace, long-suffering, gentleness, goodness, faith, meekness, temperance', while the opposite qualities, the works of the flesh, are 'adultery, fornication, uncleanness, lasciviousness, idolatry, witchcraft, hatred, variance, emulations, wrath, strife, seditions, heresies, envyings, murders, drunkenness, revellings, and such like'. Christian discipline and self-denial were not intended for the sake of causing pain or discomfort, but as necessary training which would harden the spiritual athlete to resist the temptations of the flesh, and would encourage the growth of the fruits of the spirit.

The Christian therefore was never given a comprehensive ethical code; instead he has the example and teaching of Christ, which he must endeavour to apply to his own personal life and to the conditions of the age in which he lives. He must learn to enter into and to understand the Mind of Christ. To enable the whole fellowship of believers to do this, Christ promised that He would send His Holy Spirit to guide it into the way of all truth. The Church therefore has taught that instead of a set of unchanging moral laws which must be literally obeyed, it has been given the Spirit of Jesus to enable it in successive centuries to apply His teaching to new circumstances, and to bring out of the treasure-house with which it has been entrusted things both new and old.

It would be absurd to claim that the moral teaching of Christ has been accepted throughout the world; the millions of Hindu, Moslem, and heathen owe Him no allegiance, though some of the greatest of non-Christian teachers, of whom Gandhi is the most striking, have been profoundly influenced by Him. It is not possible to claim that even Western civilization has faithfully followed His teaching; though until recently it accepted the Christian ethic as the highest and most authoritative standard of life ever set before the human race. Even when nations and individuals acted in direct contradiction to the Christian way of life, nevertheless they judged themselves by it, and often attempted to persuade themselves and others that their actions were not in reality flagrantly opposed to the Christian standard. Individuals who had been brought up in an environment impregnated by centuries of Christian teaching were conscious of a sense of wrong-doing if they deliberately broke the Ten Commandments or ignored the Christian standard of right and wrong, and they feared a final day of judgement when they would have to give account for their words and deeds.

THE REJECTION OF THE CHRISTIAN ETHIC

The great difference between our age and the past is that while the Christian teaching on right and wrong used to be accepted as the ideal to be realized, now often it is either treated with contempt as impractical, or attacked as false and mischievous.

This falling away from the Christian ideal is due to a number of different causes. The most influential of these has been the decline of belief in the supernatural. The authority of the law of nature depended ultimately upon belief in a Righteous and Living God, the Sovereign of the Universe, and the Supreme Law-giver. When God was banished to a remote corner of His creation, or treated as an unnecessary hypothesis, the natural law lost its authority and became merely a collection of man-made laws or customs which experience had shown to be of some value in regulating both the relationship between nations and the conduct of individuals. The natural law had therefore no binding force beyond that which States and individuals cared to give it. The Christian way of life had depended upon the acceptance of Christ as the Lord to whom God had given all authority and power and who would come at the last day to judge mankind. When this faith went, Christian morality lost its binding character and was treated as a series of beautiful, though largely impractical precepts laid down by a somewhat unorthodox Jewish Teacher of the first century. With the weakening of the belief in a future life and of judgement to come, an incentive to the good life was destroyed and a deterrent to bad conduct removed. The hope of reward and the fear of punishment are not the highest motives for right conduct; but Our Lord spoke frequently of the reward of heaven and the punishment of hell. There can be no doubt that millions have been encouraged to persevere in doing good through the hope of future bliss, and many more have abstained from evil out of fear of the eternal consequences which might follow from their wickedness. With the loss of faith both in the divine authority of Christ and in a judgement to come, Christian morality is looked upon as one system of life among many; those who reject it often pay a somewhat patronizing tribute of respect to it for the contribution it made to civilization at an earlier stage of man's development; but they assume it is now out of date, and therefore while a wise man will select from it that which he approves, he may discard any of its precepts which he finds inconvenient to observe.

Secondly, great difficulty has been felt in the application of teaching given to a rural community in the first century to the very different world of to-day; it has been enlarged beyond any possible conception; space and time have been annihilated by modern means of travel and communication. On my first visit to Palestine, when it was still under Turkish rule, it took two long and exhausting days to travel in a primitive carriage without springs from Jerusalem to Nazareth; on my last visit it took just over an hour to do the same journey by car and plane. In September, 1949, a traveller who had been round the world in eight days announced on the wireless that he had knocked the nought off Jules Verne's imaginary eighty days. It is now possible to dine in London and breakfast in New York. The word 'neighbour' therefore can no longer be confined to a group of people living in the same town or village. There are industrial, social, and economic problems which could never have entered the minds of the men of ancient Palestine. The absolute nature of great works of art or of poetry is not denied merely because their origin was often in small cities, but there is hesitation in accepting as binding moral conduct which received its noblest expression in a small Eastern country. To many it seems impossible to transfer to the planned society of industrial Europe and America duties laid upon individuals whose interests and obligations were limited to their family or tribe. 'Christian values were originally expressed in terms of a neighbourhood community in an agrarian world. They are virtues of a primary group. That is to say, they are virtues which directly apply to conditions where personal contacts prevail. In primary groups the commandment "Love your neighbour" is not paradoxical, whereas it is least not immediately evident how one should follow the commandment in Great Society, where you do not even know the members personally, let alone love them, which is a personal attitude *par excellence*.'* This has not been kept sufficiently in mind by Christian moralists who have concentrated on the development of virtue in the individual, without due attention to the enlarged social environment in which he lives. The failure to show that Christian moral teaching is as applicable to the modern world as it was to the small communities in which it was first given has encouraged many to reject Christian morality as irrelevant to their time.

There are some who look upon the Christian ethic not merely as impractical and irrelevant, but as false and dangerous. Love and sacrifice are scorned as weak and enervating; patience and humility are branded as 'slave virtues' unworthy of free men; self-control is condemned as an obstacle to the complete realization of the self. The most unrestrained of these attacks was made by the German Nietzsche, who hated Christianity as the foe which for centuries had sought to master the 'blond beast'. Two quotations will show the bitterness and thoroughgoing nature of his attack on Christian morality: 'In the early years of the Middle Ages, during which the Church was most distinctly and above all a menagerie, the most beautiful examples of the "blond beast" were hunted down in all directions – the noble Germans, for instance, were "improved". But what did the "improved" German who had been lured to the monastery look like after the process? He looked like a caricature of man, like an abortion; he had become a "sinner", he was caged up, he had been imprisoned behind a host of appalling notions. He now lay there, sick, wretched, malevolent even towards himself; full of hate for

*Karl Mannheim, *Diagnosis of our Time,* p. 150.

the instincts of life, full of suspicion in regard to all that is still strong and happy. In short a "Christian". In physiological terms in a fight with an animal, the only way of making it weak may be to make it sick. The Church understood this: it ruined man, it made him weak, but it laid claims to having "improved" him.'* Nietzsche scorns pity. 'Christianity is called the religion of pity. Pity is opposed to the tonic passions which enhance the energy of the feeling of life; its action is depressing. A man loses power when he pities ... On the whole pity thwarts the law of development which is the law of selection. It preserves that which is ripe for death, it fights in favour of the disinherited and the condemned of life; thanks to the multitude of abortions of all kinds which it maintains in life, it lends life itself a sombre and questionable aspect ... Nothing is more unhealthy in the midst of an unhealthy modernity than Christian pity.'† In more restrained language many others have made the same attack on Christian virtues; they are despised as slave virtues, and condemned as undermining man's vigour and ruthlessness. Since the rise and fall of Nazism less has been heard of the noble qualities of the 'blond beast'; for under Hitler's regime he was given complete freedom, and all who valued civilization were appalled at the results.

The intellectual criticism of Christian morality was reinforced by the experience of two wars and the intervening period of darkening clouds. The two wars and the years that followed them did more to discredit and shake in the popular mind traditional morality than all the attacks of the intelligentsia. The wars came with shattering impact upon a world which had been accustomed to generations of peace and had accepted the most optimistic predictions of the spread of brotherhood between the nations and of a new order of justice and peace. In the midst of war deeds were done and passions unleashed which had always been condemned by Christianity. Christianity taught the sacredness of human life, but in war men were killed and mutilated in battle on a gigantic

*The Twilight of the Idols, p. 45. Translated by A. M. Ludovic.
†Op. cit., pp. 131, 133.

scale. Christianity taught consideration for the weak and helpless; in war night after night fire rained from the skies, destroying men, women, and children, without discrimination between the soldier and the civilian. Christianity taught meekness, gentleness, and pity, but in war for the sake of survival these virtues had to be set aside. Christianity taught goodwill and peace between men; in war hatred was fanned to white heat. Christianity taught the value of truth; but in war lying propaganda was used to terrify and to confuse the enemy. It is true that war also brought out the nobler side of human nature, and its darkness was relieved by splendid self-sacrifice and endurance, and by the homely qualities of kindliness and friendliness. Though war is almost the worst of all evils, injustice and cowardly refusal to protect the weak threatened with slavery and oppression are the greater sins. But if war can sometimes be justified as the lesser of two evils, history shows that it always has a demoralizing effect on both public and personal morality. The enforced familiarity with brutality and slaughter blunts the sensitiveness which makes civilized men shrink from violence. In the occupied countries the most law-abiding citizens felt it a patriotic duty to deceive and mislead the invader; treachery and dishonesty often became the duty of those who loved their country. War accustomed many to condone actions which in peace time they would have condemned; but when peace came it was found difficult to give up habits which had been encouraged in the years of strife.

Loss of faith, the difficulty of applying the Christian ethic to modern conditions, the continued attacks upon it by bitter opponents of Christianity, and the two wars, have broken down many of the moral defences of past centuries. This, however, is by no means universal. There are still millions in all parts of Christendom who out of definite conviction attempt to follow the teaching of Christ, and there are millions who, though they do not call themselves Christians, yet accept and reverence the Christian moral standard as the highest which man has ever known. It is, however, an open question whether Christian conduct will long survive the rejection of the faith from which it comes. There are many who have no

74

definite moral ideals, who want to do what is right, but who are uncertain as to what is right. The old signposts have gone and new and wider roads open in various directions. On all sides puzzled men and women hear the clamour of self-appointed guides who really are as baffled and ignorant as themselves. 'Whirl is king, having driven out Zeus.' Life seems to have no clear purpose. But the more thoughtful are not content with drifting through life without chart or compass; they want light and guidance. Stephen Spender expressed the thoughts of many when he wrote: 'Yet in the end I wanted to know the answer of good and evil; what was unbearable was to think that there is no moral awakening, that we creep from moment to moment deceiving ourselves, sometimes guilty and remorseful, sometimes happy, but never knowing the answer, never seeing things as a whole.'*

SUBSTITUTES FOR THE CHRISTIAN ETHIC

The rejection of faith and morals leaves a void which must be filled. Most men need some standard of conduct which will help them to judge themselves and others, and some purpose in life to which their conduct should conform. In our century the ordinary man looks for guidance not to the theologian or philosopher, but to the popular writer, the novelist, and the dramatist. The three writers who have had the widest popular influence in Great Britain in the last half-century are G. B. Shaw, D. H. Lawrence, and H. G. Wells. They are in agreement in their rejection of traditional Christian morality, but they are confused and uncertain when they attempt to find a substitute for it. Bernard Shaw, the greatest of the three, in prefaces almost as brilliant as the plays which they introduce, proclaims the gospel of Life Force. In *Man and Superman* Don Juan declares, 'I tell you that as long as I can conceive something better than myself I cannot be easy unless I am striving to bring it into existence or clearing the way for it. That is the law of my life. That is the wakening within me of Life's incessant aspiration to higher organization, wider,

World Within World, p. 210.

deeper, intenser self-consciousness and clearer self-understanding. It was the supremacy of this purpose that reduced love for me to the mere pleasure of a moment, art for me to the mere schooling of my faculties, religion for me to a mere excuse for laziness, since it had set up a God who looked at the world and saw that it was good, against the instinct in me that looked through my eyes at the world and saw that it could be improved.' Twenty years later, in *Back to Methuselah*, Shaw returns to the same theme; in the closing speech Lilith, the source of all life, declares of human beings, 'Best of all, they are still not satisfied: the impulse I gave them in that day when I sundered myself in twain and launched Man and Woman on the earth still urges them: after passing a million goals they press on to the goal of redemption from the flesh, to the vortex free from all matter, to the whirlpool in pure intelligence that, when the world began, was a whirlpool in pure force.' The final results of the Life Force as seen in the 'Ancients' are not very attractive! But for the full operation of this Force self-control is essential, 'the self-controlled man survives all such changes or circumstances, because he adapts himself to them, and eats neither as much as he can hold nor as little as he can scrape along on, but as much as is good for him. What *is* self-control? It is nothing but a highly developed vital sense, dominating and regulating the mere appetites.'* It is doubtful if by self-control Shaw meant the deliberate action of the will, or whether it is only the description of some mysterious vital sense. In this doctrine of Life Force there is nothing which will help the plain man to know the purpose of life and the conduct which subserves its true end.

Mr D. H. Lawrence, whose popularity will puzzle future generations, if indeed his writings are still read by them, despises the intellect which Shaw extols. His belief is that complete life is found in the gratification of the sexual side of man. In language which is almost hysterical, he writes of the dark sensual underworld which lies beyond the boundaries of man's conscious mind, and from which surge up impulses and wants which must be gratified if true life is to be experienced.

Back to Methuselah, p. 411.

In one of his letters he states this baldly: 'My great religion is a belief in the blood, the flesh, as being wiser than the intellect. We can go wrong in our minds. But what our blood feels and believes and says is always true. The intellect is only a bit and a bridle. What do I care about knowledge? All I want is to answer to my blood, direct, without quibbling intervention of mind, or moral, or what not. I conceive a man's body as a kind of flame, like a candle flame, forever upright and yet flowing: and the intellect is just the light that is shed on to the things around ... The real way of living is to answer to one's wants. Not "I want to light up with my intelligence as many things as possible," but "For the living of my full flame – I want that liberty, I want that woman, I want that pound of peaches, I want to go to sleep, I want to go to the pub and have a good time, I want to look a beastly swell to-day, I want to kiss that girl, I want to insult that man." Instead of that, all these wants, which are there whether-or-not, are utterly ignored, and we talk about some sort of ideas.'* Combine this philosophy of the gratification of wants with physical power and we have the picture of the 'blond beast'. If everyone aimed at the fulfilment of his wants as they rise from the dark, mysterious depths, the result would be a world of chaos. The claims of others, the discipline of self-control, must be swept aside if man's real and complete life is identical with his satisfaction of sexual hunger. It is only fair to add that Mr Aldous Huxley in his Introduction to the Letters remarks 'that Lawrence's doctrine is constantly invoked by people, of whom Lawrence would passionately have disapproved, in defence of a behaviour which he would have found deplorable or even revolting.'† It is difficult, however, to give any other interpretation to this doctrine except as the assertion that the true end of life and the most direct road to knowledge of things as they are can be found only through the complete gratification of sex.

H. G. Wells as a writer is on a lower plane than either Shaw or Lawrence. He has neither the brilliancy of the one nor the mysticism of the other, but his influence on his contemporaries

*The Letters of D. H. Lawrence, pp. 94, 95.   †Op. cit., p. xiii.

was probably greater. His writing is simple and direct; but apart from his earlier books, in which he gave his imagination full play and in which many think he is at his best, he lacks humour or depth of insight. He is incapable of describing a gentleman, or a Christian. Kipps is perhaps the most real of his many characters. Wells despises the homely virtues; the freedom he demands is usually little more than freedom from traditional sexual morality. His final conception of Utopia is the cold world of sham classical buildings and priggish intellectuals described in *The Shape of Things to Come*. Progress, he taught, was certain through the spread of science and education; together they would triumphantly destroy old conventions and build a new order in which all men would be happy, intelligent, and free. But the years between the wars, and the outbreak of the second war, shattered this easy optimism, and the last books he wrote contained a cry of bitter disillusionment and disappointment. 'Our universe is not merely bankrupt; there remains no dividend at all; it has not simply liquidated, it is going clean out of existence, leaving not a wrack behind.'* Before his death he had learnt that neither science nor education could by themselves create the new order of which he had at one time been the confident prophet.

When absolute values vanished, an attempt was made to find some substitute for them by a pragmatical system of relative values. If men could no longer say, 'This is right or wrong at all times and places,' they could at least say, 'This action is right or wrong at this special time in the group in which I live and work.' So we find a local and group morality substituted for the morality which is above place or time. A man will often fully recognize his duty towards his family and make great sacrifices for their welfare, but feels he is under no obligation to extend forbearance, consideration, or even courtesy to those who belong to families other than his own. He will be honest and straightforward in dealings with those who are his fellow-workers in the factory or mine, but he has another code

*'Mind at the End of its Tether', quoted by N. Nicholson in *H. G. Wells*, p. 95.

of conduct towards his employers or towards those who belong to a different social class. Loyalty to his own family or his mates is shown in self-sacrifice and generosity; but those outside these groups are treated as neutral or even hostile, and, without any sense of wrongdoing, he may behave towards them in a manner which would fill him with shame if he acted similarly towards his own mates. An interesting example of group morality is given by Colonel Peniakoff (Popski) in his book *Private Army*. 'We got on very nicely without religion. We preserved the decencies through the violence and licence of war: raped no women, tortured no one, looted in moderation and only from those who could well afford to lose, drank decorously (by soldierly standards) and refrained from bullying, went wenching only with the best, and, when we could, we looked after the girls we got into trouble. As a matter of course we helped a companion in trouble, took our duties to heart, looked after our men, loved our enemies (in the persons of the prisoners we took), and laid down our lives without making a fuss. Our behaviour was modelled on that Victorian ideal of a gentleman, which has, in the course of time, drifted down from the clan which first formed it (but has long since discarded it) to the bulk of the people for whom it is now the naturally accepted standard of conduct. There occurred many misdemeanours – mostly of a technical nature – for which I had to take sanction, but the men themselves always saw to it there should be no stealing, no lying, no quarrelling, no bullying, no disloyalty, no cowardice, no shirking of responsibility, nor any of those monstrous ill-defined crimes which come under the heading of "letting down the boys".'*

The loyalty which at one time would have been called forth in defence of the Christian moral standard is now transferred to causes limited in their claims and their scope. If there can be found more rarely than in the past complete devotion to the cause of Christ, remarkable devotion is shown in lesser and more provincial loyalties. One man is a patriot, loving his native land and ready to live and die to save it from ruin.

*Pp. 412-413.

Another will give his time and energy for the promotion of some political cause or social reform which has gained his allegiance. The position of the Labour Party to-day is the result of the zeal, hard work, and sacrifice of tens of thousands of working men who devoted themselves to the realization of its programme with the same enthusiasm as Christians have shown in spreading the Kingdom of Christ. It is not true to say that with the decline of the Christian faith all standards of morality have disappeared. There is plenty of idealism, and there are numerous standards of morality, some of which demand exacting self-control and sacrifice from those who have accepted them; but both their ideals and standards are local and relative, compared with the unlimited demands made by the natural law or by the standards of morality accepted and taught by Christianity. A number of different codes lead to division and confusion, the group ideals frequently conflict and result in strife; Communists and democrats have ideals for the preservation of which they are ready to make great sacrifices, but the greater the zeal they show in the promotion of their respective ideals, the more certainly will tension result, and as this increases the greater will be the danger of war. The capitalist employer has his ideal of good and efficient business; to realize it he will work from early in the morning to late at night, he will aim at an ever higher degree of efficiency, and he will look for ever-increasing returns; but his employees also have their ideals, of a higher standard of life, of better conditions of work, of a fairer distribution of profits; they are ready to make great sacrifices to attain these ideals, they will make regular contributions to their union, and if need be they will spend weeks in voluntary unemployment in defence of what they are convinced is a just standard of life; but the more strongly the employer and the employed hold their respective ideals, the more likely is a clash between them.

There is no longer any single absolute moral standard which modern society accepts as universally authoritative and by which actions can be tested as right or wrong. Christianity teaches that there are values given by nature and revelation which are binding upon all men at all times; and there are deeds which a man with an instructed conscience will at once either recognize as good or condemn as wicked. But in the modern world there are ideals and codes of conduct which society has created for its own welfare and safety, and which are accepted or rejected as each thinks expedient unless obedience is commanded by the State of which he is a citizen. An absolute moral authority is repudiated, and it is thought tyrannical to command certain conduct and intolerant to forbid all compromise with what is opposed to it. Men choose or make their standard of conduct as they go along, changing it whenever expediency seems to require its abandonment or modification. This loss of an absolute standard and the consequent widespread chaos and confusion have led to insecurity in the international world, the recrudescence of cruelty, a threat to home life, and a widespread departure from personal honesty.

CHANGED VALUES

(a) *International.* In the world of nations the rejection of traditional standards has been disastrous. In medieval Christendom the nations recognized that they were under a sovereignty mightier than that of any single State. There were frequent wars, often conducted with great barbarity, but they were wars within the same family, and the combatants accepted that there were certain rules of conduct which they should observe. The Holy Roman Empire, notwithstanding its shadowy nature, membership of one Church under the spiritual sovereignty of the Pope, and a Canon Law which transcended frontiers, afforded some check to the development of the excessive nationalism which looked upon the advancement of national interests as the supreme good. Long after the break-up of the visible Church, nations still recognized that they were all under the natural law, and this led to development of international law. Both the League of Nations and the United Nations Organization attempted to set up a sovereignty greater than that of national sovereignty. Both in the Middle Ages and in the centuries which followed, the law of nations has frequently been broken by those who paid lip service to it, but the existence of such a law was not questioned. Even the aggressor attempted to show that the action he had taken was of an exceptional nature and was forced upon him by the threats and intrigue of his enemy. Nations suffering from tyranny appealed to the common conscience of mankind. There were certain acts, such as the massacre of minorities, which no nation until recently would deliberately authorize or defend, for they would be condemned by the rest of the world.

To-day, however, even the theory of international justice has been abandoned by States which once were regarded as civilized. In the first war Germany tore up treaties as mere 'scraps of paper'; in the last war she broke at her convenience the treaties she had made with and the assurances she had given to Poland, Czechoslovakia, Holland, Belgium, and Russia; and since the war Russia has gained complete control of States in Central and Eastern Europe whose freedom she had promised to preserve. Fear and suspicion now bedevil international relationships; no nation can rely for very long on the most solemn treaties made with a possible enemy. Treaties are made with the reservation that they can be broken when it is found inconvenient to observe them. Wholesale lying propaganda is used to soften the morale of neighbours marked down for destruction, and is the most powerful weapon of the cold war. Nations negotiate with each other in an atmosphere of cynicism, their statesmen inwardly convinced that few treaties are of much value unless they are the result of self-interest or of fear. Lip homage is sometimes paid to international justice, but the division of the world into two great camps with diametrically opposed ideals makes it impossible to appeal any longer with confidence to standards of conduct recognized by all nations.

(*b*) *The Revival of Cruelty.* One of the most ominous signs of the times has been the revival of cruelty. A feature of Western Civilization had been the progressive abolition of cruelty as a means of punishment or judicial investigation. It had been used in the Middle Ages to intensify punishment when, for certain crimes, it was felt that death by itself was too lenient, and also as a means of extorting information from an unwilling witness, or confession from the accused. As late as the eighteenth century great crowds used to collect to watch the last agonies of the criminal condemned to be hanged; to be amused by the spectacle of a public flogging; and later on, when human beings were no longer tortured, by the baiting of bulls and bears. To witness an act of cruelty was the pastime of thousands who themselves lived under brutal conditions. Gradually public opinion learned to condemn cruelty and to revolt against its public exhibition. It was seen to be useless as a deterrent; long ago Montaigne had declared, 'All that exceeds a simple death appears to me absolute cruelty; neither can our justice expect that he whom the fear of being beheaded or hanged will not restrain should be any more awed by the imagination of burning pincers or the wheel.' It was found unreliable as a means of extracting truth from a recalcitrant witness or criminal. The growth of humanitarianism in all classes led to public opinion condemning cruelty. Dr Inge, writing between the wars of 'Christian Ethics and Modern Problems', said that the abolition of cruelty was one of the signs of civilization: 'It would be unnecessary to enumerate all the cruelties which have been abolished within the last two hundred years. The moral advance has been prodigious, and there is no other field in which we may feel so confident that the change of heart has been spontaneous, genuine, and permanent. Cruelty now excites a degree of moral indignation which is not felt towards any other class of offence ... This has been the most important change in ethical sentiment during the modern period. We are amazed at the callousness which tolerated public strangling for criminals, an extremely painful mode of death which sometimes tortured the victim for five minutes or longer; savage flogging in the army and navy and even in schools; the chaining and beating of lunatics, and many other atrocities which it would be easy to mention.'* Since those words were written, less than

*P. 274.

twenty years ago, we have seen a return to deliberate and horrible cruelty on a gigantic scale. In the war the Nazis committed barbarities from which primitive savages would have shrunk; by the gas-chambers, by mass shootings, and by slow starvation they massacred millions of helpless men, women, and children; they exercised fiendish ingenuity in torturing prisoners from whom they wished to extort information or upon whom they gratified their sadistic lusts. Belsen, Buchenwald, and other concentration camps will long be remembered as examples of the depths of bestiality to which human beings can descend. Since the defeat of Germany cruelty has flourished elsewhere. From behind the iron curtain there come horrible stories of torture systematically inflicted. We read now with little emotion stories of cruelty which at one time would have made Europe and America blaze with indignant protest.

(c) *The New Morality*. In Great Britain there has been something like a revolution in the attitude of public opinion towards questions of sex. This has been by no means all evil. It has brought some striking changes for the better. One of the most important of these is the emancipation of women. With the freedom of women, the double moral standard has gone; it is no longer said that conduct permissible to a man is unpardonable in a woman. The critics of the double standard always assumed that its abolition would condemn in the man conduct which had in the past been condemned in the woman; but for a time at any rate it seems that this hope has been reversed in practice, and immorality which was regarded as permissible to a man is now claimed as permissible equally to the woman.

Another gain has been the removal of an unhealthy secrecy over sex. For long it was tabooed or treated chiefly as a subject for lavatory jokes. Though of interest to all, it was shrouded in secrecy and discussed with shame. The results were unhealthy furtiveness and quite appalling ignorance about some of the so-called 'facts of life'. It was felt sufficient to tell the growing boy that he must neither do nor say anything which he would be ashamed of doing or saying before his mother.

Information was acquired through prurient books secretly obtained, or through the whispered confidences of contemporaries almost as ignorant as himself. This secrecy was partly due to the Church's knowledge of the vehemence and danger of uncontrolled sex, and its anxiety to raise against it strong barriers of self-control. But however foolish were some of the statements made by individual Churchmen, the Church has never been so stupid as to condemn sex; instead it has sought both to hallow the sexual impulses and to see that they are rightly used. The official attitude of the Anglican Communion was clearly expressed at the Lambeth Conference of 1930, when it was formally declared that 'the functions of sex as a God-given factor in human life are essentially noble and creative,' and 'emphasizes the truth that the sexual instinct is a holy thing implanted by God in human nature. It acknowledges that intercourse between husband and wife as the consummation of marriage has a value of its own within that sacrament, and that thereby married love is enhanced and its character strengthened.' Archbishop Temple, commenting on these resolutions, wrote: 'The first demand of the bishops is that we should grow out of the tendency to suppose that whatever concerns sex is of itself unclean or nasty . . . and the first necessity for a truly Christian philosophy of sex is to pass from the phase where sex is a matter of shame to that where it becomes an object of reverence.'* The modern freedom to discuss sex is often abused, and sometimes becomes an almost intolerable nuisance. Some novelists are obsessed with the problems of sex, and forget there are other interests in life; and there are plays which are a reversion to the type common in the Restoration age, though usually without their brilliancy. The perpetual discussion of sex now tends to become as boring as the endless repetition of the crude indecencies of schoolboys would be to a fairly intelligent adult. But notwithstanding these disadvantages, it is all to the good that sex can now be discussed with both intelligence and frankness.

The departure in matters of sexual conduct from traditional Christian morality has been very great. Christianity taught

*W. Temple, *Thoughts on Some Problems of the Day,* p. 42.

that all sexual intercourse outside marriage was sin; that marriage was the lifelong union of husband and wife until parted by death; and that the primary purpose of marriage was the procreation of children. These three principles were widely accepted as the ideal, though often in actual practice they were neglected. How widely the ideal was departed from even when it was not openly challenged was to be seen in the existence of prostitution, in the leniency with which a man was judged who kept a mistress provided she was kept in decent seclusion, and by the large number of illegitimate births among the poor. Now the Christian ideals of sex are not only disregarded in practice, but criticized and rejected as mischievous and dangerous. A recent writer in somewhat exaggerated terms sums up the position: 'Actions which do not give mental or physical pain no longer cause horror. A woman co-habiting without marriage is no longer "living in sin", but has become "an unmarried dependant living as a wife". Divorce has increased gigantically, and save in official circles, the fact of having committed adultery carries no stigma.'*

Continence before marriage is denounced as an impractical demand which leads to dangerous psychological and physical results. It is argued that it deprives men and women of pleasure which otherwise they might have enjoyed, and the necessary self-control may lead to strange perversions and nervous breakdowns. The demand for freedom in sexual intercourse has been assisted by the spread of the knowledge of methods of birth control, which reduce the possibility of the birth of unwanted children resulting from intercourse. The new moralists claim that sexual freedom can now be enjoyed without the risk of the woman being subject to the inconvenience of an unwanted child, and of the man to the danger of paying for its maintenance. It is argued that anything that stands in the way of pleasure is harmful, and therefore full rein should be given to the sexual impulses, provided that harm is not inflicted on others. In the United States sexual licence has gone much further in college life than in Great Britain. Before the war promiscuity between the students

*F. Sherwood Taylor, *A Century of Science*, p. 261.

became so common and harmful that Judge Lindsay, who had great experience in juvenile courts, advocated in much-discussed books 'companionate marriage' as a remedy. Young people were to be allowed to live together openly without censure or blame, provided that they had no children, and on the condition that if one or both became tired of this experimental union a divorce could at once be obtained without any claim for an allowance from the man. These proposals aroused much discussion in the United States, and as a result their author had to resign his judgeship. He received, however, some support on this side of the Atlantic: Mr Bertrand (now Lord) Russell went even farther than Judge Lindsay: 'I think that all sex relations which do not involve children should be regarded as a purely private affair, and that if a man and a woman choose to live together without having children, that should be no one's business but their own. I should not hold it desirable that either a man or a woman should enter upon the serious business of a marriage intended to lead to children without having previous sexual experience.'* There is no doubt that there is widespread laxity in sex. What was done in secret is now proclaimed openly. It is a matter of common knowledge that large numbers of men and women have sexual intercourse without any thought of marriage with their casual partners. This is the result of the greater freedom (good in itself) between young people of both sexes, of the nervous strain of the war, of life under conditions which make abstinence extremely difficult, and of the erotic atmosphere created by an unending stream of emotional novels and films. Only definite moral conviction based upon religious faith will give the necessary self-control.

Lack of control before marriage is not easily replaced by self-control after marriage. Immorality before marriage paves the way for adultery in marriage, though there are many who after sowing their wild oats make good husbands and wives. The Christian teaching on divorce is now widely ignored. Between the Reformation and 1857 there were in all only about three hundred cases of divorce in this country, and these

*Marriage and Morals, p. 132.

could be obtained only by costly Acts of Parliament. In 1857 an Act made it possible for a man to divorce his wife on the ground of adultery, while she could divorce him for adultery and cruelty; this resulted in about three hundred divorces being granted a year. In 1937 divorce was made more easy both in procedure and by an increase of causes for which it could be claimed, and the decrees granted rose at once from 4,547 in 1935 to ten thousand in 1938. Since the last war the increase has been alarming; the peak figure was fifty-two thousand in 1947, irrespective of 25,400 separation orders granted for judicial separation. Since then there has been a decline, though the numbers are still far bigger than those of pre-war years. These huge figures must not be ascribed solely to the new legislation, which was intended to deal with the misery of unhappy married life due to adultery, insanity, cruelty, and desertion. These unhappy marriages were not caused by the Act; they would have existed even if there had been no such legislation. But the increased facilities for divorce have had some serious results on the stability of marriage. Marriage is entered upon with increasing lightheartedness after a short emotional acquaintance, with the knowledge that if a mistake has been made there is now a way out; it need no longer be a union for life; it is in a sense an experiment which both hope may be successful, but if it fails, the results need not be disastrous. While in the past husband and wife often at some period went through a difficult time of disappointment and disillusionment, they knew they had to make the best of it, for they had pledged themselves to each other 'until death us do part', and even if they wished to break their promise there was no way in which they could easily do so; often after some years of tension there came to them a new and different happiness in marriage, the old emotional affection was replaced by steady companionship and mutual help. To-day when disappointment replaces the first emotional love and each detects the faults of the other, or some more attractive person appears, no time is given for the heart to heal; the divorce court is looked upon as the natural remedy, and the husband gives his wife evidence of his unfaithfulness in an hotel. To many marriage has become an emotional experience, and divorce the means by which another experiment can be made. Pleasure is tacitly accepted as the chief end of marriage, and when that fails, marriage itself is written off as a failure. There are occasions when divorce is justified: sympathy and not censure should be given to those whose married life has been wrecked by deliberate and persistent unfaithfulness, by calculated cruelty, or incurable insanity. But divorce, once intended for exceptional cases, has become the normal way of escaping from the obligation of vows solemnly taken. It is destroying the security of the home, which is built on the life-long union of husband and wife; in so doing it destroys both the discipline which is needed for the growth of love and character of the partners, and the stability needed for the development of good and stable emotions in the children.

Christians condemn this sexual laxity as contrary to the law of Christ. There are, however, many who refuse to recognize His authority. To them another argument may appeal: by fornication people use persons as mere instruments for their pleasure, and this is no less true when the two concerned mutually agree. The use of persons as means instead of ends leads to an attitude of contempt towards them; this is the Nazi mentality of regarding all men as possible slaves, and it rots the mutual respect which is the cement of the social fabric. Between husband and wife living in harmony sexual union is a spring of joy and beauty; the promiscuous are indulging in a sad and sordid imitation of true love, and wonder gloomily at their disillusion.

There is another contrast between the teaching of the Christian Church and the new morality. The marriage service makes it plain that the primary purpose of marriage is the pro-creation of children, to be 'brought up in the fear and nurture of the Lord and to the praise of His Holy Name'. For many years past there has been a striking decline in the birth-rate. From 1700 to 1900 the increase of population in Great Britain had been abnormal: it had grown from seven million to forty-nine million. If the increase had continued at this rate, by the year 2000 Great Britain would have had a population of a hundred and thirty million. But in 1910 there commenced a decline in the number of births, while in each of the ten years between 1871 and 1911 the birth-rate had been about four million, in the ten years between 1931 and 1941 it was little more than one million. The mid-Victorian family of five to six children had fallen to two. The Royal Commission on Population which reported in 1949 dispelled some of the more gloomy prognostications of the effect of the decline by the end of the century, and stated that the proportion of the population under fifteen years, which is now 21·4 per cent, would not fall below 19 per cent in this century. The decline has, however, already seriously affected the age balance, and soon the nation will include an unduly large proportion of 'old people' – that is, those who are over sixty-five. If it continues, the nation will be unable to defend itself against attack, or to send emigrants overseas, and its position as a Great Power will disappear. The Commission confirms what for long has been generally known, that the decrease in the birth-rate is the result of deliberate decision on the part of parents who are now familiar with the methods by which they can limit the size of their families. Most parents are anxious to give their children the best possible opportunities for a good start in life, and they know that the more children they have the greater difficulty they experience in providing for them. The commissioners repeatedly urge that the larger the family the more the parents are handicapped in a struggle with poverty. The Joneses with one child are able to afford a higher standard of living than the Smiths, who on the same income have three children to feed, clothe, and educate.

The Report of this influential Commission concentrates almost entirely on the economic, social, and political results of the decline in the birth-rate. There is, however, another side which the Christian must not forget: while he recognizes that in married life there should be self-control and foresight, and that it is wrong for parents to have a larger family than they can afford to bring up with a reasonable standard of comfort, he also knows there are many men and women who find real happiness in parenthood, and joy in the sacrifices they make for their children. A family of four or five is a wonderful school of character, in which daily give and take teach the art of co-operation and afford early training in the quality of un-selfishness. Where there are children there is less likelihood of disagreement between the parents reaching such an extent that it leads to divorce. It is significant that both in this country and in the United States a large proportion of those who go through the divorce courts have no children. The Lambeth Conference carefully avoided an absolute condemna-tion of the use of artificial methods of birth control, but it is their misuse which in so many cases has deprived the husband and wife of the happiness of a family, robbed the one child of his natural playmates, and has brought the nation into danger through the declining birth-rate.

INCREASE IN CRIME

The moral chaos of our time can be seen also in the increase of crime. The facts shown by the criminal statistics issued by the Home Office should give rise to great anxiety. The command 'Thou shalt not steal' is broken as frequently as the command 'Thou shalt not commit adultery'. The most serious feature of these statistics is that they show a large number of these offences have been committed by children and young people. But the cases of dishonesty known to the police and resulting in conviction are small compared with the large amount of pilfering from the sheds and the docks, from the railways, from the factories and from the shop. In 1948 the University of Liverpool Department of Social Science issued a report on 'The increase in crimes of theft'. In its summary it stated that 'crimes of theft have increased very rapidly during the decade 1938–47. It estimates that the increase in thefts from railways has been 315 per cent and 'the value of property stolen within the country has increased from about £2,500,000 to an order of magnitude of £13,000,000 during the same period'.

The causes for this increase in crime, especially in dis-honesty, are many: among them are the scarcity and high prices of goods which at one time were easily obtainable and inexpensive; the lack of discipline among young people due to the wartime interference with home life;* the scrounging habits of war carried over into the years of peace; and the inadequate number of police. But behind them is the change in public opinion about honesty and truthfulness; they are no longer regarded as qualities which must be respected at all times and towards all. Dishonesty is looked upon much more leniently than in the past, and lying is a legitimate means of escape from detection and punishment. The delinquent feels little or no shame about his conduct, and excuses himself by pleading that he is only doing what others would do to him. The only commandment he respects is 'Thou shalt not be found out'. Among juveniles a successful theft is a matter for pride and boasting; they have neither the imagination nor the sympathy to see the suffering or inconvenience they have caused to those from whom they have stolen. It means nothing to them if they are told they are committing by their theft an offence against society, and they have not been taught that whether or not their offence is detected by man, it is known to God and is disobedience to Him. While the increase in crime among both adults and juveniles is due to a number of different causes, with the loss of faith in God and of responsibility to Him a strong motive for honesty and truthfulness has been removed.

The moral chaos of our time is the natural result of the rejection of God. For the first time in history man claims to make the laws which govern his conduct without reference to anything higher than that which he has created. 'For the first time in his history man has assumed the undisputed captaincy of his soul. Until our own day he has always acknowledged a master, whether it was God, or the gods, or the Law or the Way. Always there has been a Rule which he accepted, a rule which was beyond amendment and beyond dispute. To-day there is none. He knows no master. He has freed himself at

*'To be torn up from the roots of home life and to be sent away from the family circle, in most instances for the first time in the child's life, was a painful event. This was no social experiment: it was a surgical rent only to be contemplated as a last resort.' R. M. Titmuss, *Problems of Social Policy*, p. 109.

last. He has thrown off his chains. He has cast aside his outworn superstitions. And in so doing he has surrendered himself to a tyrant more arbitrary and more capricious than any he has ever known. That tyrant is his own will. We have been overtaken at last by the nemesis of humanism.'*

*R. Law, *Return from Utopia*, p. 28.

PART TWO

SUBSTITUTES FOR CHRISTIANITY

4

Humanism

THE preceding two chapters were devoted to an account of the falling away in recent years from Christian faith and morals. But man cannot live by bread alone, and though he may reject Christianity he will still need some religion to inspire and guide him. The nineteenth and twentieth centuries have been prolific in substitutes for Christianity; though some of these have been influenced by Christian thought and conduct, and in their ideals have often come close to Christianity. But there are other substitutes which reject and attack Christianity and any religion which has a supernatural creed. The chapters which follow will discuss the most influential of these substitutes: humanism, democracy, Mammon, totalitarianism and Communism, and their relationship to Christianity. Though they are often separated from one another by unbridgeable gulfs, they are all secularist in outlook, and assume that man in his own power can create a new and more perfect society.

HUMANISM

Modern humanism had its origin in the fifteenth and sixteenth centuries, the period of the Renaissance and Reformation. At first the term 'humanist' was applied to those who valued the ancient culture of the Greek and Latin classics. A humanist in this sense was not necessarily a philosopher, but one who studied the literature of the classical age, worked at its texts and sought for its sculpture. But very soon the phrase took a wider meaning, and humanism came to mean belief in man and confidence in his powers. In the earlier Christian renaissance of the twelfth and thirteenth centuries there had been a great revival in the conception of man as a spiritual being; painting, architecture, and poetry reached unexampled heights as an expression of his spiritual nature and of his worship of God. The paintings of Giotto and Fra Angelico were the fruit of an age of faith; Dante's *Divina Commedia* was a profound exposition in poetry of man's responsibility to his Creator, and of the eternal consequences of right and wrong; the cathedrals within and without were both an offering of man to God and witnesses in stone to His majesty, beauty, and love. In this period, however, man's spiritual nature was exalted at the cost of his humanity. In his realization of the holiness of God, man despised himself and the world in which he lived. The vision of the splendour of God was so dazzling that it hid the gifts which God Himself had bestowed upon His children. Man forgot that he had been given freedom so that he might serve and worship God by the exercise and development of his talents. As the Middle Ages passed away there came a new renaissance which was more interested in man and nature than in God and the unseen world. It has been held that its chief characteristic was the discovery of man, but a Russian writer says more truly, 'The Renaissance once more discovered the natural man, the old Adam of the pre-Christian world, for whom Christianity had substituted the new Adam or the spiritual man. Christianity had declared war on the natural man and on the baser elements in the name of a spiritual forging of the human personality and for the sake of man's Redemption. Medieval Christianity had bound the natural man hand and foot; it was engaged in forging human forces, and it divorced man from both the nature within him and that of the environing world. In the Middle Ages nature was a closed book . . . The Renaissance represented the discovery of both nature and antiquity.'*

*N. Berdyaev, *The Meaning of History*, pp. 131, 132.

In the early days of the Renaissance there was little denial of God and the supernatural. 'It is still, if you like, the age of the Son of Man; but one in which men pass from the cult of the God-Man, of the Word made flesh, to that of Humanity alone.'* There was, however, tension, often severe and unresolved, between the honour now given to man and the worship of God. Occasionally there were violent protests against the new art and literature; the most dramatic of these was the burning of books during the brief period when Savonarola's influence was supreme in Florence, and at his order inscriptions were placed on all the public buildings of the city declaring that Jesus was its King. But usually the men of the Renaissance kept their art and their religion in separate compartments, exercising with complete freedom their art, but at the same time accepting the Christian faith. A striking example of this was seen in the Papacy; a succession of Popes associated themselves with the latest scholarship and culture; they patronized the leading artists and sculptors, spent great sums of money in acquiring ancient manuscripts, and enriched their palaces with splendid paintings and sculptures; at the same time they were punctilious in the observance of religious rites and in excommunicating those found guilty of heresy. 'Under Leo X scholarship had become one of the surest avenues of preferment in the Church . . . Scholars were in the high places of the Vatican. They gave the tone to the Court and Roman society. It was a world pervaded by a sense of beauty in literature, in plastic art, in architecture, in painting.'†

Benvenuto Cellini, Michel de Montaigne, and Sir Thomas More can be taken as typical examples of men of the Renaissance. Cellini is better remembered for his memoirs than for his sculptures, though his Perseus is one of the important minor statues of this period. He describes with complete frankness his quarrels, his jealousies, his hatreds, and his murders. In the squalor of his dungeon in the Castle of Sant' Angelo, Cellini commenced reading the Bible with the utmost delight; meditated on the power of God; spent the days of his

---

*J. Maritain, *True Humanism*, p. 8.
†*Cambridge Modern History*, Vol. 1, p. 565.

imprisonment in singing psalms and hymns; and was cheered by supernatural visions. He is a remarkable example of a man who combined apparently genuine religious devotion with a complete lack of morality.

Michel de Montaigne, born in 1533, some thirty years later than Cellini, was a very different man. He had none of Cellini's recklessness. His essays, from which his autobiography could be composed, show a man of the world, highly cultured, greatly intrigued by every kind of discovery and speculation; quiet, tolerant, and friendly. There are no other essays which give the reader so naturally the impression of a well-informed man talking to him by his fireside on all manner of subjects. There is hardly an essay of his from which enjoyment cannot be obtained. He is an amiable, cynical materialist, interested in all human beings, especially in himself; by his charm and versatility he continues to win the interest and friendship of many in the twentieth century. He is suspicious equally of asceticism or of excess. In all things he aims at walking on the road of moderation. 'The Via Media was the one road he would travel on, and he insisted on good inns by the way, with a proper provision of crayfish and clean linen.'* His outlook is pagan, and yet he would claim to be a good Catholic. He could write: 'We see every day that when human nature swerveth, however slightly, from the main road, and wandereth from the beaten track traced out by the Church, in an instant it misseth its turnings and loseth its way, it groweth confused and entangleth itself, drifting hither and thither, airless, unbridled, in the vast sea of tossing waves, the sea of opinion. As soon as it departeth from the great high road, it goeth on, dwindling and scattering itself on many different paths.'

Sir Thomas More is a noble example of a Christian humanist who combined devotion to the best learning of his time with unswerving loyalty to his religion. He was born twenty-two years before Cellini, and reached manhood at a time when the riches of England filled foreign visitors with amazement. England, though inferior to the Continent in painting and poetry, had splendid architecture, craftsmanship, and scholarship.

*Edith Sichel, *Michel de Montaigne*, p. 181.

Scholars like Erasmus came as visitors and would gladly have settled here. Sir Thomas More was one of a circle of English humanists who had been influenced by the Continental Renaissance. But they did not separate faith and morals. They were anxious to apply the new knowledge to practical life and to the society of their time. More, in his *Utopia,* gave a description of a new order from which abuses were banished and in which all lived in ideal fellowship. But he was first and foremost a devout Christian, ready to die rather than to disobey the dictates of conscience.

The early days of humanism were thus marked by the recovery of a past culture and delight in a new sense of freedom. Humanism in Italy has its origin in the recognition of the ancient greatness of Rome and Greece: 'The barriers so long imposed on the exercise of the reason were broken down, not all at once, but by degrees. It was discovered that there had been a time when men had used all their faculties of mind and imagination without fear or reproof: not restricted to certain paths or bound by formulas, but freely seeking for knowledge in every field of speculation, and for beauty in all the realms of fancy. Those men had bequeathed to posterity a literature different in quality and range from anything that had been written for a thousand years. They had left, too, works of architecture such that even the mutilated remains had been regarded by legend as the work of supernatural beings whom heathen poets had constrained by spells. The pagan view was now once more proclaimed that man was made not only to toil and suffer, but to enjoy.'* The newly recovered freedom led on the one hand to the Christian Renaissance in the Reformation and Counter-reformation, and on the other to a humanism which became divorced from the Christian religion and its moral standard.

As man increased his mastery over the natural world he became bolder in speculation. In the 'enlightenment' a new philosophy rejected the medieval philosophies which were built on, or justified by, an appeal to religious dogmas. God seemed to be unnecessary to the new world of science and

Cambridge Modern History, Vol. 1, p.532

discovery. It is said that Napoleon on a clear night at sea pointed to the stars and asked a scientist who was present how he could account for them without belief in God the creator, and received the reply, 'I have no need of God as an hypothesis.' Some indeed of the deistic philosophers were anxious to make it plain that they did not deny the existence of God, however remote He might be from the world He had created. Voltaire claimed to be on 'bowing terms' with God. His attitude was that of many eighteenth-century philosophers; their tendency was to crowd God out or to relegate Him to a distant background, while man, instead of God, became both the centre and the crown of the universe. The humanist no longer felt it necessary even to render lip service to God and still less to concern himself with His hypothetical existence. While disliking the iconoclasm of the atheist as stupid and vulgar, he gloried in the beauty and power of the world in which he lived, and above all in the amazing gifts and inventivenesses of man, who from the lowliest origins had reached the proud position of the Lord of all creation; instead of raising hymns of praise to God, the humanist addressed them to man, bowing down in adoration of himself: 'Glory to Man in the highest! for man is the master of things.'

MODERN HUMANISM

Modern humanism has three characteristics: first of all it appreciates all that is noblest and most lovely in the works of man and nature. It inherits the Renaissance love of the great Greek and Latin classics, and one of the most honoured of contemporary humanists, Gilbert Murray, has made Euripides and Aristophanes living poetry and drama to our time. Humanism loves beauty in all its different forms, and by the plastic arts and literature attempts to express and interpret it. It seeks knowledge for its own sake and not merely for the benefits which come from its application. Its interests are as wide as humanity itself, and many of its protagonists in their fight against wretchedness and poverty have proved that they are humanitarians as well as humanists. Man is the supreme object of their study and care; there is nothing higher than him, nor is there anything in the world of nature more worthy of their devotion and service. They are thus opposed to the totalitarianism which treats the individual as a mere tool of the State, or to an industrial system which regards him as a mere cog in a gigantic wealth-producing machine, or to the Philistinism which would subordinate beauty to material gain. But the thorough-going humanist finds no room for God and the supernatural; this world is all-sufficient.

Secondly, the humanist has complete faith in the power of science and education to create a new and more perfect order. Science rightly used will bring to all, irrespective of wealth or rank, the amenities and knowledge which not so long ago were confined to the few. The poorest now enjoy in their homes conveniences which once would have been regarded as luxuries only within the reach of the wealthy. Electric light, hot and cold water, good sanitation, a variety of food, much of it from overseas, swift conveyance to and from work or recreation by tram, bus, bicycle, car, or underground; the wireless, the cinema, and television as forms of amusement; shorter hours of labour in well-lighted and ventilated factories and mills; higher wages and regular holidays, have immensely improved the lot of millions. If so much has been done by applied science in a little over a hundred years, there is good reason to hope that it will bring in the next hundred even greater boons. The inventiveness of science seems to be unlimited. Universal education gives to the children knowledge which their parents could never have possessed, and teaches them how best to use the advantages offered by modern civilization. The humanist can rightly point to vast improvements – the buildings in which the children are taught, the longer period over which their education extends, and the care now taken over both their minds and bodies. With an extension of education, with better-trained teachers, with smaller classes, and with the development of infant schools at one end of the scale and of secondary schools at the other, the humanist hopes that the present generation of children may be the intelligent citizens of the future.

This leads to the third characteristic of modern humanism: its belief in progress. The humanist is convinced that the world and all its inhabitants will get better and better as the generations succeed each other, until at last there is formed a perfect community built on an international order of justice and peace. In support of this he appeals to the great material progress which has been made since the dawn of history, and especially during the last century and a half. He contrasts the barbarism of the past with the civilization of to-day, and the static character of a thousand years with the extraordinary advances in knowledge of the last century. He claims that the process of evolution in the natural world is a good reason for believing in the continued advance of the human race. Herbert Spencer used Darwin's theory of evolution as an argument for belief in the continuous progress of mankind, and in various forms the same argument has been used by the exponents of emergent evolution. The humanist therefore is an optimist; he has a gospel of hope, and though he admits that there may often be interruptions and even temporary recessions in human progress, he is certain that presently the onward movement will be resumed. He looks beyond the darkening mist and assumes it will presently give way to a better and brighter future. His faith in man's natural goodness and inventiveness is so great that he is confident that the future holds better things in store than any which have yet been enjoyed by man in his long and painful upward progress.

Of all the alternatives offered to Christianity in the twentieth century, humanism is the most attractive to educated men and women. 'It commonly connotes wide human interests, a rich and genial appreciation of human nature and its manifold works, and the fascinating lights and shadows of character. It means to love people more than theories; to enjoy the rich movement and colour of the ever-moving drama of human life; to be sensitive to all true forms of value; to discriminate the real from the counterfeit.'* It makes, however, no appeal to the great mass of the uneducated; its strength is to be found among the intelligentsia, more especially among those who

*F. R. Barry, *The Relevance of Christianity*, p. 115.

have the leisure to enjoy natural beauty and art. At its best it is seen in a gracious appreciative spirit, thankful for man's past achievements and confident about his future progress. It has no formal creed, it finds room for men of very different religious and political opinions; it asks no questions and imposes no conditions, except that of belief in man as the master of his destiny.

CHRISTIANITY AND HUMANISM

There is much in humanism which Christianity should welcome. It is true that the Christian Church has from time to time feared and rejected what humanism has valued. Christianity has always had a strong vein of Puritanism which has suspected both beauty and learning as detracting from concentration on the things which are spiritual and heavenly. Art has so often been associated with sensuality that the Church has occasionally attempted to bar its admission to its worship and buildings. The sculptures, paintings, and literature of classical days seemed to the Puritan to pander to the lowest side of human nature, and must be cut off as drastically from the Christian life as a man might cut off an offending hand or pluck out an offending eye to save himself from hell fire. Christian devotion has been responsible for the destruction of much that was beautiful. The Reformers in England, and later the Puritans, smashed images and windows, defaced sacred emblems and robbed the churches of gifts which had long enriched them. The influence of Puritanism for many generations separated religion from beauty. Art was allowed to enter a church only if it could be proved to be either useful or edifying, but it was rejected if its only claim was that it was beautiful. The loveliness honoured by the humanist was frowned on by the Puritan; the one exception he made was in favour of music, for the admission of beauty through the ear was considered to have few of the dangers of admission through the eye. There was often an unhappy contrast between the beauty of the singing in a church and its hideous architecture and cumbrous furniture; the richness of the music was challenged by the bareness of the whitewashed walls and by the massive pews which crowded the floor. But if good music was admitted because it was also sacred, poor and insipid music too often crept in when it claimed that it was religious. No wonder that the humanist felt that the Church was opposed to all that he valued most. It was not only towards beauty that he felt the hostility of the Church; far more serious was its attitude to new discoveries: by the Inquisition, and later by denunciation and ostracism, it attempted to stifle them. It is not necessary to go back to the fate of Galileo for examples of obscurantist timidity; there were plenty of occasions in the last century when the discoveries of geologist, biologist, and astronomer were denounced not because they were untrue, but because they might prove unsettling to the faith. Humanism is often non-Christian because the Church in the past rejected its affirmations as well as its negations.

The Christian should welcome and claim all the values of truth and beauty to which the humanist holds fast. No one in recent years has done more to state the relationship between Christianity and humanism than Dr Barry, now Bishop of Southwell. While recognizing fully the errors of humanism, he urges Christians to treat it as an ally rather than a foe. 'Who are the friends of man and who are his enemies? In the ever-narrowing strip of no-man's-land between the high religions and secularism, are the light and scattered patrols of Humanism, attempting gallantly to defend man's cause, yet without supplies or reinforcements and under no organized command. Unless they are re-formed and embodied within the Christian lines they will melt away and be rapidly overwhelmed by the enemy. For it is on the Christian side that they belong. It might seem to betray a strange lack of insight when Christian apologists denounce Humanism, even in its all-too-human forms as an enemy to be attacked. It is a weak ally to be succoured . . . If the Church is to rally the forces of goodwill, if it is to baptize into the faith of Christ whatever may be still vital and creative in the flux of the world situation and build from its elements in dissolution a new form of Christian civilization, then it must at least know where to look for them . . .

The Gospel and Humanism belong together.'* In days when the value of the individual is scorned and denied, the Christian and the humanist should be allies in asserting and defending the dignity of man. The beauty which is admired by the humanist should be seen by the Christian as a revelation of the beauty of God Himself. Every new discovery of truth should be welcomed by the Christian, for all truth, whether from the theologian, the philosopher, or the scientist, has always the same source, God Himself, and is a further unveiling of the perfect truth in Him.

THE FAILURE OF HUMANISM

So far the Christian and the humanist can go together, but the Christian goes much farther. The humanist stops at the barriers of this world, the Christian looks beyond to a world without any limits of space and time. The humanist is concerned with man and with this world only; the Christian looks on man as a child of God called to eternal life. The humanist believes that man is all sufficient and can work out his own destiny; the Christian believes that man is a sinner, unable to do anything by himself, and that he has been redeemed by God, who will guide and uphold him.

Humanism both under-estimates and over-estimates man. It under-estimates his value, for it fails to see that he is a child of God and has a spiritual nature which will not be satisfied even if he is given all the material goods which the world possesses. Thomas Carlyle spoke truly when he asked, 'Will the whole Finance Ministers and Upholsterers and Confectioners of modern Europe undertake, the Joint Stock Company, to make one Shoeblack *happy*? They cannot accomplish it! above an hour or two; for the Shoeblack also has a soul quite other than his stomach.' It is because he is a child of God and of value in His sight that man can claim rights over and beyond any which the State might please to grant or to withhold; it is because he has gifts and talents given to him by God to use in His service that he has the right to freedom, to economic

*F. R. Barry, *Recovery of Man*, p. 17.

security, and the opportunities of a full life. It is on man's dignity, as called to be a child of God and loved by Him, that his rights truly depend. The humanist, by denying or ignoring his spiritual nature and destiny, not only fails to satisfy the deepest side of man's nature, but leaves him defenceless in front of the tyranny of the totalitarian State and the harshness of an industrial system which treat him as a means either to the power of the State or to the acquisitiveness of capitalism.

On the other hand, humanism greatly over-rates man's capacities. Its fundamental conviction is that with education and knowledge man can create a new and perfect order. It has formed a romantic and unrealistic picture of human nature, and imagines that by natural goodness, unselfishness, and wisdom man will so use the inventions of science that he will be able to banish war, poverty, and ignorance. Two great wars should have destroyed these delusions. Man has learned to control nature before he has learned to master himself; and though he has discovered how to bend to his will many of the forces of nature, he does not yet know the secret of living in peace with his fellow men. Never has the world had so many blueprints produced by idealists, and never has there been such a deep sense of frustration and disappointment at the repeated failures to carry them into effect. The humanist has closed his eyes to human nature as it actually is, obstinately refusing to recognize that within man there is something which perpetually corrupts the good and perverts it to evil. Lord Keynes in an interesting Memoir recognized the weakness of the humanism of his younger days. 'We were among the last of the Utopians, or meliorists as they are sometimes called, who believe in a continuing moral progress by virtue of which the human race already consists of reliable, rational, decent people, influenced by truth and objective standards, who can be safely released from the outward restraints of convention and traditional standards and inflexible rules of conduct, and left, from now onwards, to their own sensible devices, pure motives and reliable intuitions of the good ... In short, we repudiated all versions of the doctrine of original sin, of there being insane and unrational springs of wickedness in most men. We were not aware that civilization was a thin and precarious crust erected by the personality and the will of a very few, and only maintained by rules and conventions skilfully put across and guilefully preserved.' Later he writes that towards 1914 'the thinness and superficiality, as well as the falsity of our view of man's heart became, as it now seem to me, more obvious.'* Not all humanists have been so ready to recognize the weakness of their position, though events of recent years should have been sufficient to shatter the optimism of the most self-complacent.

Inventions which might have banished poverty have often been used to enrich the few and to degrade the many. The discoveries recently made in the application of atomic energy, which should be of great benefit to mankind, have been used to make nuclear weapons which may destroy the human race. The League of Nations failed through the failure of the statesmen and the countries they represented to use wisely and courageously its powers; and now the United Nations Organization is threatened by the same dangers. The Professor of Modern History in the University of Cambridge, in his lecture on Christianity and History, stresses again and again the way in which the best schemes fail through the imperfection of human nature. 'It is essential not to have faith in human nature. Such faith is a recent heresy and a very disastrous one.' Or again, 'We know now that there is an inadequacy in human nature which makes the reality so different from the idea – time has brought out new patterns of human wilfulness not anticipated by the political dreamers of a century ago.'† The old doctrine of original sin is coming back in a different form through the rediscovery that there is a tendency in the human race to choose the evil and to reject the good. The most perfect organization will fail unless there are the right men to work it, and of 'the right men' something far more than wisdom is required; the moral qualities of self-sacrifice and unselfishness are of greater importance than intellectual cleverness. The gravity of the position in the world to-day

*J. M. Keynes, *Two Memoirs*, pp. 98, 99, 101.
†Herbert Butterfield, *Christianity and History*, pp. 47, 56.

does not, however, arise so much from the existence of a few wicked individuals who out of selfish ambition manipulate international machinery for their own purposes, as from an atmosphere of cynicism and distrust which makes it easy for them to do so. Christian humanism neither under-rates nor over-estimates man; it believes in his greatness as a being made and loved by God and called by Him to live as His son and to the inheritance of eternal life; on the other hand, it understands man's sinfulness and knows that his pride, lust, greed, and folly will bring on him misery and failure. The Christian humanist has a far deeper and more thorough understanding of the nature of man than that possessed by the secular humanist. The Christian knows that man is of value in the sight of God and made by Him in His image, but that he is also a sinner who has failed to carry out God's purpose in creating him. The secularist humanist looks on man as a being who has emerged from the earth, who in the course of centuries has acquired great skill of brain and hand, but who after a brief period of life will return to the earth from which he came. The Christian humanist believes that life here is only a beginning, and its full fruit will be on the other side of death.

TWO VIEWS OF PROGRESS

The Christian view of progress is in sharp contrast to that of the humanist. The idea of progress is essential to the faith of a humanist; he anticipates continuous progress through the different generations until at last a perfect order has been established. This idea of unbroken progress is comparatively recent. It was unknown to the ancient world, which looked back to a golden age in the distant past. Later both pagan and Christian writers assumed that the century in which they were writing was an advance on the barbarism of the earliest days of history, but they expected no further progress; the wheel had reached its height and would now move downwards. No one will deny that in certain directions there has been remarkable progress in man's understanding and mastery of the world of nature, but it is more doubtful if man himself has made much advance. It is a legitimate question to ask whether if men of the twentieth century were deprived of all the material advantages given to them by science and discovery, they would be wiser, more efficient, and of a higher morality than their distant ancestors who lived in an unscientific environment. Professor A. J. Toynbee holds that in an advancing society progress has been confined to a few gifted individuals, while the great majority remain passive and unchanged: 'Growing civilizations differ from static primitive societies in virtue of the dynamic movement, in their bodies social, of creative individual personalities; and we should add that these creative personalities, at their greatest numerical strength, never amount to more than a small minority in the society which their action pervades and animates. In every growing civilization, even at the time when it is growing the most lustily, the great majority of the participant individuals are in the same stagnant quiescent condition as the members of a primitive society which is in a state of rest. More than that, the great majority of the participants in any civilization in any phase are men of like passions – of identical human nature – with Primitive Mankind.'* As far as peasants are concerned – and the great mass of human beings are living and working on the land – Dr Toynbee is supported by an older scholar, Sir James Frazer, who, with his great knowledge of anthropology, writes, 'The truth seems to be that to this day the peasant remains a pagan and a savage at heart; his civilization is merely a thin veneer which the hard knocks of Life soon abrade, exposing the solid core of paganism and savagery below.'† From time to time with terrible force there break loose primitive human lusts for murder and rapine which degrade outwardly civilized men to a level below that of primitive savages. The wholesale massacres in the recent wars, the failure to discriminate between belligerent and civilian, and still more the calculated extermination or enslavement of minorities in days of peace, should shake the optimist who assumes so easily that human nature has changed fundamentally for the

*A Study of History, Vol. III, p. 242.
†The Golden Bough, Part VII, pp. vii-ix.

better. Montaigne in his essay on 'Caniballes' says that men stigmatize as barbarism customs with which they are not familiar, and they condemn others for customs which are not really worse than those which they themselves practise – we are horrified, for instance, at savages eating their captives after they had killed them, but 'there is more barbarism in eating men alive, than to feed upon them being dead; to mangle by torture and torments a body full of lively sense than to roast and eat him after dead'. We contrast complacently the barbarism of past ages with our civilization, unmindful that it has perpetrated crimes which would have been utterly abhorrent to the moral sense of our distant ancestors. But if it is open to doubt whether we can speak with unqualified praise of past progress, it is still more doubtful if there are grounds to justify confidence in the future of mankind. The rapid material progress made in the West in the last century and a half gives no ground for assuming that this will be continued indefinitely. There are great tracts of the world – in Central Europe and in China – whose inhabitants both materially and spiritually are worse off than they were half a century ago. There are reasons also for dreading that before many years are over man may use some of his latest weapons for race suicide, and that nuclear weapons in a third war may wipe out our Western civilization, leaving a few survivors in the mountains of Abyssinia or Central Asia to make a new start in human history.

But even if the humanist is right in predicting continued progress towards an earthly paradise, it is impossible to contemplate with complete satisfaction either the process or the climax. Each successive generation, on this interpretation, would look back upon its predecessors as mere steppingstones to its own greatness, while in its turn it would become a means to the further advance of those who followed it. Each generation is a rung in the long ladder of ascent. Only a minority will reach the summit, and from the heights will look down with mingled pity and contempt on those who failed. But if the summit should be reached, the need for discipline and effort would be over, and no further progress would be possible; it would then be probable that ease and self-satisfaction would result in enfeeblement of body and mind, and after a short interval a rapid descent would commence.

The Christian Church has a different doctrine of progress. It has a Gospel of hope founded upon an historical fact: the coming, the life, death, resurrection, and ascension of Jesus Christ. It looks back to what it regards as a unique event in the history of the world, but it looks forward to the future, for 'the best is yet to be'. But this best is quite distinct from future material prosperity. Christianity has no Gospel of material progress, and does not share the conviction of the humanist that human beings and communities will get better and better as the centuries pass. Our Lord spoke of wars and rumours of wars, of destruction and ruin in the years to come. The Church recognizes that this world may get worse, that the material progress it has made may be arrested or reversed, that chaos and tribulation may fall on the whole human race, and yet nevertheless it proclaims its Gospel of hope. But the Christian does not look forward to some future, and possibly very distant, date in history when at last the strivings of the past will come to fruition and a higher order of men and women will dwell in a world their predecessors have made perfect; rather he believes that the men and women of each generation will carry over into the world on the other side of death the qualities which with God's help they have developed here; death will not arrest their progress, but it will open to them fields of greater scope. On this view the world is an elementary school in which the first lessons of love, truth, and beauty are learnt; it is the ante-chamber to the vast university of eternity, in which there are many colleges and schools for those who have reached different degrees of faith and holiness. Into it there have passed an unending series of men and women of every century who have responded in some degree to the light which shineth in every man, and especially to Him who is the Light of the World. Their progress will not have been abruptly cut short by death, but it will continue, under far more favourable conditions than in this life, towards that perfection which is found only in Christ. There are those in every generation who have deliberately rejected the light they had, or who have so consciously used for evil the talents entrusted to them that their light has become darkness; for these there seems no hope of progress, and they may remain for ever in the darkness they have chosen. The other-worldly hope is an essential part of the Christian faith, but it does not mean that the Christian should despise the world in which God has placed him; for the Christian should rejoice with the humanist in the goodness, wonder, and beauty which this world reveals; but he has the additional reason for viewing it with gratitude and reverence, for he knows that it is God's creation, and that through it God makes known to men His Majesty, His Wisdom and His Beauty, and imparts thereby a health of soul which is not achieved by 'religion' alone. If it should be that man is swept from the earth and all his works perish by fire, and a deserted world should roll on for millenniums, those who once dwelt on it and sought to do God's Will would not be annihilated, but would still live in other abiding places of God's great Kingdom, still moving onward, with the help of His love and guidance, to ever greater perfection.

5

King Mammon

UNRESTRAINED capitalism and Marxian Communism have been the most dangerous enemies which have challenged Christianity in the last two centuries. Both are atheistic, for though many individual capitalists have been convinced Christians, capitalism as a system ignores God and breaks His laws; Marxian Communism is not content with merely ignoring religion, but hates and repudiates with fanatical zeal belief in God and in the supernatural. Both deny the value of the individual; the capitalist system treats him as a cog in a gigantic profit-making machine, the Communist as an instrument to be used in promoting the power of the State. Both make such absolute demands that God tends to be crowded out either by absorption in money-making or by unconditional loyalty and service in the Communist cause. There is, however, one important difference: unrestricted capitalism has had its day; it is dead or moribund, for though in the United States it still has its protagonists, in the United Kingdom State ownership, planning, and control have replaced the capitalism of the Industrial Revolution; but Communism is still spreading, especially in the Far East, and though it may undergo many changes and modifications from the orthodox teaching of Marx and Lenin, it will for long continue to exist as a powerful and dangerous foe of Western civilization.

Capitalism was known long before the eighteenth century. From time immemorial there have been some who have saved instead of consuming the results of their labour, and have used them to gain further wealth. Mr A. L. Rowse in his book on *The England of Elizabeth* points out that at that time there were striking advances in industrial technique, in the opening up of the natural resources of the nation, in the capture of markets by England which until then had been monopolized by foreign nations; in the building up of the wealth of the nation, and in the accumulation of wealth; and he goes on to say that while under the early Tudors economic life 'proceeded on a simple medieval basis, shortage of capital was its chronic limiting factor. Elizabeth's reign saw an expansion of credit and an extension of credit facilities along with the growth of capital.'* But the capitalism of the Elizabethan age did not mould and change the life of the whole nation. Business and commerce were still influenced by religion, by the State, and by the general moral and social atmosphere. Capitalism was something exceptional in its nature, affecting only a minority of the people, and regarded by both Church and State with dislike and suspicion.

Until the coming of industrialism in the middle of the eighteenth century the economy of the nation was mainly rural. Most of the people lived in the country, London was the only large city, and even there a short walk was all that was necessary to reach the woods and fields. For centuries the people lived in villages, hamlets, and farms, either working for the Lord of the Manor, or on their own independent holding. Privileges and duties were alike the result of ancient custom, safeguarded and enforced by the manorial courts. Industries were conducted in the country, and under the cottage roof the parents and their children made what was required by their fellow villagers; it was only the surplus that was taken to the towns to be sold. Occasionally the industry was sufficiently large to be carried on in a shed adjacent to the cottage with the help of a few hired workmen and apprentices. There was little manufacturing in the towns; they were the markets in which country produce and made goods were brought to be sold; and the ports were the centres of commercial traffic by sea. In town and country alike, both employer and workman, rich and poor, were under the rule of custom or law, though the binding force of custom was much stronger in the village than in the town.

The new capitalism was very different from the old. Its strength lay in the discovery that machines worked by steam could make goods more cheaply, in far greater quantities, and in a much shorter space of time than those produced by the old

*P. 111.

cottage industries. But machinery was expensive, capital was needed to obtain it, and capital had to be paid for by interest. Machinery also needed coal, so existing mines had to be worked more vigorously and new pits opened. Mines and factories both required labour, so they soon became centres of population. Improved methods of communication gave the new industries another advantage over the old: the roads denounced so vehemently by Cobbett were improved; canals were made; then came the railways and the use of steam for ships. At the end of the eighteenth century the supply of labour for the new industries was made more easy through the break-up of the traditional rural economy. The enclosure of the open fields and commons, advantageous as this was to agriculture, took from the peasant the land on which he had depended for his livelihood; he was thus compelled to migrate from the country to the town in the hope of obtaining work in the mill or factory. The older capitalism had left untouched the main structure of English life; the new capitalism revolutionized it, and within a century substituted an urban for a rural society; it destroyed the old manorial customs, it reduced the population of the rural districts and it created the great cities. It changed England from a nation of countrymen to a nation of townsmen.

THE GOOD RESULTS OF PRIVATE CAPITALISM

In the reaction from the excesses and cruelties of the Industrial Revolution, it is now usual to find nothing good to say about the capitalist system during the century and a half when it was at the height of its power. It had, however, some good results. It increased enormously the wealth of Great Britain. Karl Marx, notwithstanding his hatred of private capitalism, recognized and admired its efficiency. New methods of manufacture, the development of the mines, and the improvement in transport brought to the country unprecedented riches. The enclosure of the common fields ended a wasteful method of cultivation, and by the adoption of more scientific methods the land produced larger crops and sustained more cattle than had previously been the case. The wealth of England brought her into the first rank of the Great Powers. The increase of riches was such that she was able to finance great industrial undertakings in her overseas possessions and in foreign lands; and the investments thus made brought, until the two world wars, a large return to the nation. The early capitalists did not usually spend their wealth on themselves, nor did they always invest it in profitable undertakings; often they used it to benefit their birthplaces or the town in which their works were situated. The wealthy self-made capitalist living in simplicity frequently made large contributions for the erection of civic buildings, municipal halls, schools, hospitals, and almshouses. There are few of our cities in the north which are not the richer through the generosity of some of their citizens who had made their money in their midst. Nor were the benefits in the increase of national wealth confined to a few; goods which in the past could have been bought only by the well-to-do were produced so plentifully and sold so cheaply that they were brought within the reach of the multitude. Clothing, shoes, stockings, pottery, and other articles, useful and ornamental, were easily obtained by all except the very poor. Capitalism also developed some of the moral virtues: wealth could be acquired only by hard work, self-discipline, and by the readiness to take risks in the hope of obtaining rich returns. The defenders of capitalism used to dwell upon the good qualities it fostered: frugality, saving, total abstinence and simple living, rising early and working hard throughout the day, were extolled as its moral fruits. Sometimes, indeed, those who praised the moral results of capitalism went absurdly far in claiming that it brought spiritual advantages to the poor, as they were delivered from the temptations of riches! In one unexpected direction capitalism also brought good to the wage-earner. The massing of workmen together in towns and their powerlessness as individuals against the tyranny of their employers compelled them to combine together in self-defence and for effective resistance against intolerable conditions of employment. The hardships of the poor were the cause of the working-class movements which led in time to the transfer of political power from the employing to the employed class.

The defenders of capitalism can thus fairly claim that the system brought to the nation results which have been of much benefit. The higher standard of living, the better conditions of labour and the freedom now enjoyed by all members of the working classes would not have been possible if the capitalist system had not so increased national wealth that the State could acquire the means to assist the poorer members of the community, and that the employers had profits large enough to meet, though reluctantly, the demand of their workers for higher wages and shorter hours. But the cost in human life and suffering was terrible. The capitalist system was based on three principles which were contrary to the teaching of Christianity, and the results of their application were such that it is difficult to understand how they could have been tolerated even for a time in a civilized nation. The years in which the capitalistic system was supreme inflicted upon Christianity injuries from which it is still suffering.

THE BASIS OF CAPITALISM

Capitalism was successful because it had clearly in view the ends which it sought to attain. Its *summum bonum* was wealth. The purpose which every capitalist set before himself was the making of profits, and yet more profits. In the past men had aimed at power, at success, at a sufficient livelihood for themselves and those dependent upon them. Men and women often had given themselves in complete devotion in the service of their Church, their nation, and their fellow men. Capitalism as a system aimed at wealth, and to this everything else had to be subordinated. The employment of children in mines and factories, the long hours of work for both men and women, the wretchedly low wages, the repressive regulations and fines which governed work within the factory and made it a dismal and unhealthy prison, were defended by the plea that better conditions, higher wages, and shorter hours would reduce profits. Money-making was considered as sufficient justification for any hardness in their business life of men who in their own homes were good husbands and fathers. Through the upper and middle classes there ran like a fever in the veins a burning urge to make money and yet more money. Honour, duty, kindliness all had to give way to the worship of Mammon. Money-making became the highest end of man: the rich were the favoured of God, while poverty was looked upon as the natural result of deficiency in moral qualities. The warning of Our Lord against riches was ignored or explained away. The man who had become rich, who 'had made good', who by his hard work, by resourcefulness and relentless drive had become one of the employers and was reputed to have tens of thousands of pounds to his credit in the bank, was given the respect which once had been paid to the saint, the artist, or the warrior.

Secondly, in the pursuit of wealth complete freedom was necessary both for the individual and for the market in which he operated; that money-making must be free from all restraint was one of the postulates of the new morality. In the past economy had been under the Christian ethic. It would have been inconceivable in the Middle Ages for trade, investments, and commerce to have claimed that they were governed by laws of their own, independent of Christian teaching. At the time of the Reformation and for some time afterwards the supremacy of the moral law over economic relations continued to be recognized. 'In its insistence that buying and selling, letting and hiring, lending and borrowing, are to be controlled by a moral law, of which the Church is the guardian, religious opinion after the Reformation did not differ from religion before it.'* The Industrial Revolution swept aside these restraints: religion was treated as a special department of man's private life, and it would only lead to confusion, or possibly disaster, if it interfered with his business. If the owner of a factory or mine went devoutly to church or chapel on Sunday and sought conscientiously to apply to his private life the teaching and exhortations he then heard, he shut them off by an iron curtain from his business on the other six days of the week. Here he claimed complete freedom from all laws

*R. H. Tawney, *Religion and the Rise of Capitalism*, p. 157.

except those which political economy made for itself. 'Thou shalt love thy neighbour as thyself' was superseded by 'Thou shalt buy in the cheapest market and sell in the dearest.' In another and more justifiable way he claimed freedom. In the past, commerce had been hindered by a large number of regulations which nations and cities had set up with the intention of protecting their own interests. Adam Smith's *Wealth of Nations* was the classic attack on these restrictions. Few books on political economy have had a greater influence than this treatise of a Glasgow professor. He regarded freedom of internal trade in England as one of the causes of its prosperity as contrasted with the restrictions on the Continent. His advocacy of universal free trade was welcomed by the new industrialists. They urged that everywhere there should be the open market with complete freedom to buy and sell. But this demand, unfortunately, was not limited to material goods; it included human labour: the workman must have the right to sell his labour as profitably as he could, while the employer had equal right to buy it as cheaply as he could. But the workman's very life depended on selling his labour; if he failed to do so, hunger and starvation followed; if the employer failed to buy it at a low figure, he could wait, until hunger compelled the vendor to reduce to a lower amount the price he demanded for his labour. There was fierce competition between the manufacturers of goods, each trying to undersell their rivals, and success in doing so would largely depend on their ability to obtain cheap labour; but between the hungry workman and the wealthy employer there could be no equality in competition; the scales were always weighted on the side of the employer, and until the workmen learnt to combine in defence of their vital interests, wages were kept low and demands for their increase were easily defeated.

Some moral principle was required to support the rigour of economic competition and the unrestrained search for riches. A convenient and comforting formula was provided by the economist Jeremy Bentham, who taught that if every man sought without hindrance his own interests the welfare of the whole community would be served. He assumed that each individual knows what is best for him; therefore if each can attain it freely, the sum total of the benefits thus secured must result in the welfare of the nation. It was only the eagerness to find some ethical justification for the competition for wealth which concealed the obvious fallacies of this theory. There are many who have never known their true interests, and have sought after ends which give neither themselves nor their contemporaries any happiness. There are also conflicting interests between individuals and groups, when the struggle for supremacy is ended by the defeat and ruin of one of the contestants. The interests of the employer and the employee are often starkly opposed. It is true that in one sense the prosperity of the business in which they are engaged is the concern of all, for if it became bankrupt all would suffer; but it does not follow that all have an equal share in its prosperity; the respective interests of the employer and the employed often conflict, the former aiming at keeping wages as low as possible, the latter urging their increase. Nor do the respective interests of an industry and of the community necessarily coincide; the owners of a business sell as profitably as possible for themselves, though to the community this may mean high prices and inferior goods. Sometimes, too, it is in the interest of an employer, or of a group of employers, and of their employees, to limit production, and thus an artificial scarcity is created for the sake of higher profits, while the community suffers from the shortage and is forced to pay excessive prices.

The driving power behind capitalism was the desire for gain, its methods were complete freedom and unrestricted competition, its ethical system false in theory and disastrous in practice. The principles of unrestricted capitalism were a challenge to the teaching of love, mercy, and justice as given to men by the prophets and by Christ Himself.

THE PRACTICAL ABUSES OF THE CAPITALISTIC SYSTEM

The results of the application of these principles were appalling – the degradation of human beings, the infliction of untold suffering on those least able to defend themselves, and class disunion.

1. In the village and in the cottage industries each individual had his place. For good or for ill he counted for someone among those who lived and worked with him. The agricultural labourer, badly paid and wretchedly housed, yet had some room for initiative and independence in his work; the hired labourer in the cottage industry was part of a family, however hard his employer might be. But the peasant sucked into the vortex of industrial life and submerged in a town far larger than the village which had been his birthplace soon lost his identity. The workman from the small cottage industry found himself in the strange and confusing environment of a great factory. Here, for a wretched wage, in dark and unhealthy surroundings, he had to work from morning to night; in many factories the doors were actually locked to prevent the secret departure of any of the workmen; here his work was decided for him: he had no choice, no room for initiative, no scope for skill; he was under orders which he had to carry out mechanically under pain of dismissal. He was no longer an intelligent individual, he was a cog in a machine; he was no longer a person, but a 'hand' to be used by those who hired him. He was given no education; he was deprived of his rights of combination with his fellows; he was forced to live in a jerry-built house, damp, overcrowded, insanitary, the breeding place of pestilence; he was even grudged amusement, as his employers felt it would interfere with his work. The industry in which he was engaged gave him no opportunity of developing skill; his whole working life might be spent in tending automatically the same type of machine, or repeating hour after hour the same monotonous act required for the completion of the article under production. There was justification for the burning words of the Communist Manifesto of 1848: 'Modern industry has converted the little workshop of the patriarchal master into the great factory of the industrial capitalist. Masses of labourers, crowded into the factories, are organized like soldiers. As privates of the industrial army they are placed under the command of a perfect hierarchy of

officers and sergeants. Not only are they slaves of the bourgeois class, and of the bourgeois State; they are daily and hourly enslaved by the machine, by the overlooker, and above all by the individual bourgeois manufacturer himself. The more openly this despotism proclaims gain to be its end and aim, the more petty, the more hateful and the more embittering it is.' Man, intended to be an end in himself, was degraded by capitalism into an instrument for the creation of wealth of which he would receive only a minute portion. His condition was not that of a slave, for he still had the freedom to leave his employment and to die of starvation, for it would be unlikely that he would be employed elsewhere in the locality in which he had been working.

2. The system inflicted terrible suffering on those who were caught in its grip, especially those who were unable to defend themselves. More labour was required; so fierce was the competition for it that it was a great relief to hardly-pressed employers to discover a new source for it in the children of the workhouses. In all of these there were large numbers of parentless and dependent children; what could be more economical to the nation and more valuable a training for the children than to apprentice them to work in the mills? Here was a plentiful and cheap supply of labour. 'These children were consigned to their employers at the age of seven and upwards, till they were twenty-one. Next door to the mills prentice-houses were built, and in these two buildings their young lives were spent, at best in monotonous toil, at worst in a hell of human cruelty. If their master failed in business their labour ceased and they were cast adrift on the world.'* In one case a bankrupt employer turned the young children whom he could no longer afford to pay to fend for themselves on the sea-shore. The guardians were anxious to get rid of the children and the mill-owners equally anxious to obtain cheap labour which they could use as they thought fit: 'in one case at least a Lancashire mill-owner agreed with a London parish to take one idiot with every twenty sound children supplied.' Once in the hands of the mill-owners they were at their mercy,

*J. L. and Barbara Hammond, *The Town Labourer*, p. 145.

unless a child was resourceful and bold enough to complain to a neighbouring magistrate of ill treatment. In some of the mills the working hours were from 5 a.m. to 8 p.m., and in cases when the pressure of work was great until 9 or 10 p.m. It was not until forty years had passed that Parliament abolished this child slavery.

But soon there was a new source of child labour. With the application of steam to machinery, the factories were built in towns, and no longer necessarily by rivers or streams. The parents who were already working in these factories and mills found their wages too small to provide for themselves and their families, and it therefore became customary to send the children as wage-earners to the mills. They began work officially at the age of six or seven, but there were many even younger. They had to work the same long hours under the same unhealthy conditions as the children who had been apprenticed from the workhouse; the temperature in which they worked from 5 a.m. to 8 p.m. without respite varied from 75 to 85 degrees. Fourteen or fifteen hours a day was the normal time of employment, Saturday included, though sometimes this was considerably extended. The children lost all the joy of youth; they were stunted and deformed, anaemic and consumptive; many were crippled for life by some accident in tending an unprotected machine; many died when very young. 'It was physically impossible to keep such a system working at all except by the driving power of terror ... The punishments for arriving late in the morning had to be made cruel enough to overcome the temptation to tired children to take more than three or four hours in bed. One witness before Sadler's Committee had known a child who had reached home at eleven o'clock one night, get up at two o'clock next morning in panic and limp to the mill gate. In some mills scarcely an hour passed in the day without the sound of beating and cries of pain.'* It was not only the mills in which children were compelled to work. Boys and girls of tender years were employed for long hours in the darkness of the mines. Still younger children, from five to eight years of age, sat for

Op. cit., p. 159.

twelve hours at a time in complete darkness so as to open and shut the ventilating doors in the mines. It is hard to believe that employers actually attempted to defend these conditions of work, asserting that the tasks given to the children were light and within their physical powers, that they taught them at an early age the necessity of work. Whenever legislation was threatened, the employers prophesied that interference with child labour would increase costs and would be injurious to the economy of the nation. For long years therefore the childhood of the nation was offered as a sacrifice to the god Mammon, more relentless than Moloch, who also could only be propitiated by the sacrifice of human lives.

3. Unrestricted capitalism divided England into two nations: into the England of the country and the England of the city. Before the Industrial Revolution most of the nation lived in the country, in villages and hamlets, earning their livelihood by work on the land. There were few large towns; London alone approached the size of the modern town. Though there was a great difference between the upper classes and the poor, yet there was a common interest in the life of the country. Even the townsman was never far from the country, and was familiar with its fields and woods. There were dissimilarities both in speech and in custom between those who lived in the north and in the south, and the natives of many remote villages looked upon all strangers as 'foreigners'. But beneath these differences and prejudices the common heritage in and knowledge of the country made men akin. The barriers of birth, class, and place were not so high as the barrier of wealth was to become, for there was still general recognition that privileges carried with them corresponding duties. The Industrial Revolution separated country from the city. The enclosures both of the common fields and of the commons deprived the villager of his independence, turned him into a wage-earner dependent upon the landowner and farmer, or drove him in desperation to find work in the towns which were springing up round the new industries. As the population of the towns increased, the country was bereft of its best and most vigorous sons. Here, crowded together in

wretched and insanitary houses, and working for long hours in factories, shut off from morning to night from the sight of the blue sky, and separated from the country with its fields and woods, they became a new race, a species of Englishmen not known before, with occupations and interests remote from those of their forefathers who for centuries had lived and worked in the country. Within a generation the migrant from the country had become assimilated into city life; within three generations he looked with dislike upon the country as an aristocratic preserve, associated in his mind with an outworn feudal system, with high prices for corn which forced up the cost of living, and with servile dependence upon the owners of the land. When the years of agricultural depression came, the industrial elector disregarded the appeal of farmers and labourers and refused to allow any remedies which might save agriculture if they meant any rise in the cost of bread. Within a hundred years the capitalist system had changed England from a rural into an industrial nation, and had dug a gulf between the countryman and the towns-man.

Even more serious was the division created by the capitalist system between employer and employed, or, as Karl Marx would say, between the bourgeoisie and the proletariat. Often in the past the relationship between the farmer and his labourers, and between the owner of a cottage industry and his employees, had been far from ideal. But there was a personal relationship; in the farm, master and men worked in the same fields, and had common interest in the crops, the beasts, and the weather, and often sat for their meal at a common table in the farm-house. In the cottage industry all worked under the same roof, and shared the same interests. In the new industrial world as the wealth of the owner increased he began to move away from those who had worked for him; by the second or third generation most of his responsibilities for the factory were transferred to managers and foremen, and the owner no longer knew his workmen either by name or by sight. His house, his children, his food, his leisure, the whole of his social surroundings, were in glaring contrast to the misery of those who worked to provide him with his wealth. The personal relationship in many of the industries disappeared. The workman, as he saw the contrast between his poverty and the comfort of his employer, was filled with burning bitterness. The employer looked on the workers as hands whom he was entitled to use to the fullest extent; he resented their complaints, he felt cheated if they were slack in their work, and would accept no responsibility for their safety, health, or general welfare in the over-heated and ill-ventilated mill or factory. In John Galsworthy's play *Strife* John Anthony, the old employer, the representative of an age-long past, expresses views once prevalent in the first half of the last century: 'It has been said that Capital and Labour have the same interests. Cant! Their interests are as wide asunder as the poles. It has been said that the Board is only part of a machine. Cant! We *are* the machine, its brains and sinews; it is for us to lead and to determine what is to be done, and to do it without fear or favour. Fear of the men! Fear of the shareholders! Fear of our own shadows! Before I am like that I hope to die. There is only one way of treating men, with *the iron* hand. This half and half business, the half and half manners of this generation have brought all this upon us . . . The middle-class sentiment or socialism, or whatever it may be, is rotten. Masters are masters, men are men! Yield one demand and they will make it six.' Roberts, the leader of the strike, is equally vigorous on the other side. The fight in which they are engaged is 'the fight of the country's body and blood against a blood-sucker. The fight of those that spend themselves with every blow they strike and every breath they draw, against a thing that fattens on them, and grows and grows by the law of *merciful* Nature. That thing is capital. A thing that buys the sweat off men's brows, and the torture o' their brains, at its own price.' Long after injustices have been removed, the old bitterness and suspicions still smoulder, the owner class accusing the workman of dishonesty and laziness, the workmen deeply suspicious of 'they', the capitalists and employers, often applauding the call to 'soak the rich' for the benefit of those who are poorer.

King Mammon

THE INDUSTRIAL REVOLUTION AND RELIGION

Triumphant capitalism had a disastrous result on the religious life of the people. There were always some capitalists who were devout and sincere Christians, and who gave munificently in response to religious or philanthropic appeals. There were always some, too, who took a personal interest in their workmen, helping them and their families in sickness. But the Industrial Revolution as a whole had a deplorable effect on religion, from which it has not recovered. In the country the parish church or the plain whitewashed chapel meant much to the villagers; in the Sunday worship they found help and inspiration; the church was sacred to them through many intimate associations; they and their children had been christened at its font, at its altar rails they had been married, and in its God's acre their bodies would be laid to rest beside those of their forefathers; and though the parish clergyman was sometimes remote from his people through living in a large house and his connexion with the squire, he was usually the kindly friend of his parishioners to whom they could turn in sorrow or sickness. But with the migration from the country to the town the villager was lost amidst strangers; the town church and its clergy meant nothing to him. The mother church was soon almost submerged by the great population so suddenly springing up round it; it was too dignified and large to make much appeal to the newcomers, it had none of the homeliness which they had associated with their country church or chapel. Soon, too, it was quite inadequate for the needs of the teeming population. The church and its staff of clergy, able to minister to the spiritual and physical needs of a parish of five thousand, could do little for fifty or one hundred thousand. The new population, desperately poor, terribly overworked, bewildered at the new conditions of life and labour, had neither the initiative nor time to seek for the clergy whom they did not know even by sight. The Church, like the State, was taken unawares by the unprecedented and sudden increase of population which outpaced the organization intended for the spiritual needs of the village or market town, though the census of 1851 showed that two thousand churches had been built in the previous twenty years, compared with the five hundred built in the thirty years between 1801 and 1831. Towns came into existence without churches and without clergy. The children were neither baptized, nor taught the elements of religious faith; driven to work at an early age and often crippled or dead before they reached adolescence, religion meant nothing in their short lives; and those who survived to manhood looked upon the Church and its worship as remote from and irrelevant to their daily lives. It was not until years later, when habits of non-churchgoing had become fixed, that churches were built and clergy provided in sufficient numbers for the poorest districts of the industrial towns. The Church at the critical moment, when its help would have been of the greatest value to the dispossessed from the country, missed the opportunity, and has never completely regained the ground that it then lost. In almost every city there are parishes which have a splendid record of work among the poor and oppressed, but there are many which came into existence half a century or more after the new population, and ever since have been gravely handicapped by this late start. In subsequent years the Church created many new parishes and mission districts with their places of worship and halls, and has staffed them as far as possible with clergy and lay helpers; but this did not take place at the time when the expansion of the towns was at its greatest.

But in a more serious way unrestrained capitalism injured religion in Great Britain. The Church of England made no determined protest against the wrongs perpetrated upon the weak and helpless. It allowed itself to be hypnotized into silence by incantations about economic laws. Most of its leaders felt that there was really nothing which could be done to alleviate the hardships inflicted by fierce competition without creating evils which were still greater. Some Christians who were aware of the sufferings of the poor attempted to quiet their own consciences by the belief that in a future life wrongs would be righted and the joy of heaven would be compensation for the brief sufferings of this world. Wilberforce, the great anti-slavery leader, wrote about the poor 'that having food and raiment they should be therewith content, since their situation in life, with all its evils, is better than they have deserved at the hand of God; and finally that all human distinctions will soon be done away, and the true followers of Christ will all, as children of the same Father, be alike admitted to the possession of the same heavenly inheritance.'* Here and there were individual clergy who protested against the sufferings of the poor, but as a whole the Church was silent. As an established Church it was closely associated with those who governed; its relationship with the landowning classes made it suspicious and fearful of social and political agitation, and its fears had been increased by the excesses of the French Revolution; it was more alive to the dangers of possible disorders than to existing social injustice. The judgement of the Hammonds on the Church of England at the time of the Industrial Revolution is stern but fair: 'Religion was, in fact, part of the civil constitution of society. The English Church accepted that position. It knew its place in the domestic establishment of the State, and it took its colour for good and evil from the world of the ruling class. It had no persecuting spirit, no patience with emotion, no curiosity about doctrine, no prejudice against "this wicked world". Above all, it did not obtrude any view of life, but made men less able or less likely to enjoy it.'† The agitator contrasted the poverty and compassion of the Founder of Christianity with those who claimed to represent Him. The palaces and wealth of the bishops and the large rectories of absentee pluralists were held up to hatred and derision. Even the churches seemed to indicate that religion was for the well-to-do, and not for the poor, with their comfortable pews for the squire and farmers and the bare benches at the back for the labourers. Later on the pew-rent system intensified the evil, and many of the churches became the spiritual homes of

*Wilberforce, *Practical View of the System of Christianity*, p. 314. (Quoted by J. L. and Barbara Hammond in *The Town Labourer*.)

†J. L. and Barbara Hammond, *The Town Labourer*, p. 275.

the prosperous into which the poor dare not enter; and in which even the well-dressed visitor had to stand until the pew-owners were safely seated. Pamphlets and tracts attacked the established Church as the enemy of the people. By contrast the chapels of the Nonconformists offered a warm welcome and gave to the working man opportunities of learning the art of public speech and of administration; to many they became the spiritual home in which they received help and guidance for their daily toil. But Puritanism and Nonconformity were disliked by the average workman on account of the rigid Sabbatarianism which made them object to any kind of recreation and enjoyment outside the chapel on the one day in the week in which there was leisure from the toil of mill and factory. The Hammonds, while paying a high tribute to the chapel for giving the poor man a share in its life and responsibility for its work, which by 'its summons to the emotions, its music and singing, took the place that theatres, picture galleries, operas, occupied in the lives of others,'* go on to say of Methodism: 'If we look into the life and teaching of this new religion, we can see that the whole spirit of its teaching was unfavourable to the Democratic movement and the growth of the Trade Union spirit. The Methodist movement was a call not for citizens but for saints; not for the vigorous, still less for the violent redress of injustice, but for the ecstatic vision: the perfect peace of expectation.'† In a greater degree for the Church, and in a lesser degree for Nonconformity, the Industrial Revolution and the reign of capitalism dug a deep ditch, which has never been bridged, between institutional religion and the working classes. One of the most difficult problems which the Churches have to solve is how to remove the prejudice and suspicion which made the working-class movement look upon them and their Gospel as irrelevant and unsympathetic.

Possibly an even more harmful legacy left by capitalism is the honour and deference which came to be paid to wealth: birth and position had always received respect, but honour due to money alone was something which was new and

Op. cit., p. 273.   †*Op. cit.*, p. 282.

exceptional in English life. A class came into existence whose members demanded respect and service not because of their merits, but because of the money which their fathers or grand-fathers had made. The early capitalists lived simply and worked hard, often living in small houses in the town in which their business was situated, but their descendants built pretentious mansions, and expected to receive the honour which had in the past been given to the old families or to those who had distinguished themselves in the service of Church or State. Once the question asked about a newcomer to a county was: 'What is his family?' presently it became: 'What is he worth?' A man's claims were judged by the wealth he possessed; money became the key which would open every social door. Poverty was looked upon as a sin, or as the stigma of failure. There were many who would agree with Undershaft in *Major Barbara* – poverty 'is the worst of crimes. All the other crimes are virtues beside it; all the other dishonours are charity itself by comparison. Poverty blights whole cities; spreads horrible pestilences; strikes dead the very souls of all who come within sight, sound, or smell of it. What you call crime is nothing: a murder here and a theft there, a blow now and a curse then: what do they matter? they are only the accidents and illnesses of life: there are not fifty genuine professional criminals in London. But there are millions of poor people, abject people, dirty people, ill fed, ill clothed people. They poison us morally and physically: they kill the happiness of society: they force us to do away with our own liberties and to organize unnatural cruelties for fear they should rise against us and drag us down into their abyss. Only fools fear crime: we all fear poverty.'

Money was assumed to be the remedy for all evils. But this is not only the creed of Midas; it is held to-day as fervently by the middle class who must go one better than 'the Joneses' next door: they must have the new car, the latest television set, the new dress, so as to prove their superiority and larger income over those who live near them. The same greed for money infects every class. The difficulty of raising the wages of the lower-paid worker is often due to the knowledge that those who are already better paid will also demand an increase to preserve their relative superiority in money over those who are engaged in work of less importance. The craze for betting and gambling in sweepstakes and pools is not only for the sake of excitement and adventure, but for many it is the one and only chance they have of becoming rich. Speculation in any form is due to the same urge – to obtain money. Money is necessary as a means to what is fully legitimate: reasonable comfort, security, books, music, holidays abroad; but when it is sought as an end in itself, or as a means to unworthy ends – power, ostentation, self-indulgence – then it becomes sin. The urge for wealth in the Industrial Revolution, and the respect given now to riches, are in glaring contrast to the New Testament, where we read of Christ saying, 'Ye cannot serve God and Mammon.' 'Lay not up for yourselves treasures upon the earth: where rust and moth doth corrupt, and where thieves break through and steal: but lay up for yourselves treasures in heaven: where neither moth or rust doth corrupt, and where thieves do not break through and steal.' Standards of value were degraded by the triumph of the capitalistic age, and they have not yet been restored to their rightful position. It is still largely assumed that money can remedy all ills, and that higher incomes and wages of themselves will bring an increase in happiness.

THE COUNTER-REVOLUTION

As far as Great Britain is concerned, unrestrained private capitalism has long disappeared. Where private capitalism still exists – and there are very large numbers of smaller firms still worked by those who own them – it has none of the freedom which was abused so terribly in the Industrial Revolution. The change-over from uncontrolled to controlled or State-owned capitalism is so great that it is itself a revolution. The change is due to several causes. As public opinion became aware of the conditions under which women and children were working in factories and mines, it demanded that Parliament should interfere for their protection. A series of

Factory Acts were passed which gradually controlled the ages, the hours, and the conditions of work of all employed in industry. The first Factory Act, of 1802, limited the hours of apprentice children to twelve a day for six days of the week. In 1819 another Act forbade the employment of children under nine in cotton-mills and limited the hours of children under sixteen to twelve. In 1833 an Act limited the work of children under thirteen to nine hours in any one day, and provided for inspectors to enforce the regulations. In 1842 public opinion was stirred by the report of a commission on conditions of employment in the mines, which showed that in nearly every district children under six were working in them. An Act was passed prohibiting the employment of women and girls under-ground and of boys under ten years of age. A great Church-man, Lord Shaftesbury, took the lead in pressing for better conditions in all mills and factories, and in 1844 an Act was passed securing a day of six and a half hours for children between eight and thirteen, and twelve hours a day for all women. In this Act there was, for the first time in the factory laws, a regulation explicitly affecting adult men by providing for the fencing in of machinery.* In 1847 the Ten Hours Act was passed; though this was confined to limiting work to ten hours for persons under eighteen, it really meant that all workers would share in this reduction. 'It had become clear by this time that it was impossible so to organize the working arrangements of the mill so as to combine a twelve hours day for adults with a ten hours day for persons under eighteen. A ten hour day for persons under eighteen meant that the day for persons over eighteen would also be a ten hour day.'† These Bills were opposed by the majority of the employers, who asserted that their business would be ruined. John Bright was one of the leaders of the opposition. The Ten Hours Bill was strongly supported by many of the clergy of the Church of England: 'The Vicars of Leeds, Bradford, Wakefield, Huddersfield, Dewsbury, and of many smaller towns, acted as Chairmen regularly at meetings for the Ten Hours Bill;

*For the above see E. L. Woodward, *The Age of Reform*, pp. 142–8.
†J. L. and Barbara Hammond, *The Age of the Chartists*, p. 283.

another Lancashire Vicar, Canon Wray, took the same part at Manchester; the Vicar of Leigh prepared a petition at his own expense.'* The Hammonds end their account of the struggle for the Bill by saying: 'The Factory agitation, starting as a crusade for the protection of children, had ended as a successful campaign for the right of the working class to a larger life.'†

Since those early struggles still greater improvements in the conditions of work have been gained by the efforts of the workmen themselves. The Trade Unions, once condemned as illegal combinations, increasingly made their influence felt. The workman was no longer a solitary individual dependent upon his weekly wage against the wealth of a capitalist employer who could dismiss the man who refused to accept his terms. Workmen by united action obtained concessions which otherwise would never have been granted. The strike weapon was a powerful lever to obtain redress against injustice and to secure shorter hours and higher wages. There have been strikes which had no justification and a few have been marred by violence, but a general view over a considerable period of time shows that the strike has only been used when negotiations have failed and there has been a real grievance to redress. Frequently the strikers have shown great endurance and self-sacrifice, accepting severe physical deprivation, in refusing to return to work until some wrong had been remedied. Strikes often have been due to unselfish sympathy with fellow workmen elsewhere. The Trade Unions have now become powerful and valuable organizations; their influence is as great as that of the employer in the last century. They have used their power with a deep sense of responsibility and with commendable restraint. No Government can afford to ignore their views, and for national policy their co-operation is essential. Through Parliament, too, the wage-earners are now able to assert great influence: and it would be impossible for either party to secure victory at the polls without the support of working-class voters. Both parties have to pay careful attention to the views of their supporters among the wage-earners. Labour organized in the Trade Unions, and

Op. cit., p. 288.   †*Op. cit.*, p. 290.

largely represented in both parties, is now one of the predominant political factors in the United Kingdom.

Capitalism has also changed its nature. While there are still thousands of small privately owned firms employing a few score of men, the larger industries have been transformed. They first became companies, the original owner often remaining either as managing director or as chairman of the board of directors; next they combined or amalgamated with other companies engaged in the same or kindred industries, and thus reduced the danger of competition and effected large economies. Almost everywhere the responsibility for control, policy, and administration has passed into the hands of a new class, the highly trained, expert manager. This is as true of the nationalized industries as of those larger industries which are still privately owned. In the great industries, side by side with the managers responsible for the conduct of the business as a whole, there are the personnel managers, again a highly trained class of men and women, whose aim is to see that the human beings engaged in the industry are working together happily and smoothly. In addition, too, there are welfare workers who are concerned with the well-being of the employees and their families. From within capitalism there has thus come a remarkable movement for humanizing the machine, and for gaining from those working it willing and intelligent co-operation. The old conception of the 'hand' has given way to the policy of treating the workers with respect and consideration, for it is now understood that the work will benefit if employees are not regarded as cogs in a machine, but as fellow workers in the united effort to increase production. One of the most pleasing features of modern industry is the way in which so many of the large firms now provide for the recreation and education of their employees. Since I have been Archbishop of York I have visited a large number of the industries of the North, and I have been greatly impressed by the splendid playing-fields, recreation-rooms, libraries, and lectures provided for employees of all ages. This goes far beyond anything required by the State or the Trade Unions. Never before has big business shown such concern for the welfare of those who work for it. This development calls for the highest praise.

The State is no longer content with controlling industry from without, but has taken over some of the most important national industries. The mines, the railways, road transport, electricity and gas, and now steel, are owned and worked by the State. The owners have been given compensation, but in most cases the administrative personnel have been retained, so that their experience is still available and an abrupt change in day-to-day working has been avoided. There are, however, still great problems to solve before the nationalized industries can claim to be working with perfect smoothness and efficiency.

The change from uncontrolled private ownership to control or ownership by the State has brought with it new problems. There is the danger of over-centralization, which takes all responsibility and initiative from the men 'on the spot'; there is the loss of the personal touch – the employees are not always certain who really is the man who is over them and who decides on their work and promotion; there is the inevitable growth of a bureaucracy which will be slow in working, frightened of experiments, and mechanical rather than human in its dealings with individuals. The chief problem to be solved under changed conditions, both in the nationalized industry and in the vast far-spread combinations, is how best to reconcile centralized authority with local freedom and responsibility.

6

King Demos

HUMANISM is the religion of the *élite;* it makes its appeal to the few and not to the multitude; its tolerant spirit evokes little enthusiasm and rarely produces martyrs. Democracy, on the other hand, makes its appeal to the multitude, calls forth fanatical devotion, numbers its martyrs by tens of thousands, and often fiercely persecutes those who oppose it.

ATHENIAN DEMOCRACY

In its simplest and original meaning democracy is government by the people, and not by a dictator or an oligarchy. Athens for a short period in its history is the classical example of a city-state governed by the whole body of its citizens. Pericles in his funeral speech over his fellow-countrymen who had died in defence of their city declared: 'Our constitution is named a democracy, because it is in the hands not of the few but of the many. But our laws secure equal justice for all in their private disputes, and our public opinion welcomes and honours talent in every branch of achievement, not for any sectional reasons, but on grounds of excellence alone.'* Its citizens had equal rights; they could assemble in one place where all could hear the voices of the orators as they debated some problem of public interest; they decided on the laws that were to govern them, on the declaration of war or the making of peace, on the acquittal or condemnation of those charged with offences against the State; they could even decide that a citizen whose power and ambitions might prove a public danger should be banished from the city for a period of years. This self-government in matters both great and small was possible only because Athens had a population which was very small compared with any modern State. In the fifth century B.C. its adult male citizen population was not

*A. E. Zimmern's translation in *The Greek Commonwealth*, p. 201.

more than 35,000, and if women and children were included it might have been 120,000. The attendance at the public assemblies usually fell far short of the total number entitled to be present; the only record of a division shows 3,616 taking part in it.

Every citizen of Athens had responsibilities as well as rights. It was his privilege and duty to make great contributions towards its buildings; he must be ready to give time to its concerns and administration; he must bear arms in its defence, and be willing to lay down his life for its cause. Pericles in the same speech claimed that 'our citizens attend both to public and private duties, and do not allow absorption in their own various affairs to interfere with their knowledge of the city. We differ from other states in regarding the man who holds aloof from public life not as "quiet" but as useless.'*

There are two striking differences between ancient and modern democracy. In addition to the free citizens of Athens, there were a large number of slaves who did most of the menial work. At one time it was usual to think of them as living under hard and debasing conditions, but Professor Zimmern denies this, and says they were treated not as mere living tools but as fellow-workers with the free citizens. But they had no voice in the government of the city, and no personal freedom beyond that which their owners might grant them. Secondly, ancient democracy was static; its aim was to preserve unchanged the polity which had been inherited from the past, for it was taken for granted that the upward movement from barbarism had reached its final stage and no further progress could be anticipated, but the danger of retrogression and corruption was always present. In contrast with ancient democracy, modern democracy is progressive and confidently assumes that the future ordering of society will be a great advance on all that has been experienced in the past.

Op. cit., p. 202.

King Demos

During the great part of the Christian era democracy was unknown. Government was by sovereigns or by oligarchs. The
medieval republics of Florence and Venice were controlled by
small groups of men qualified by birth, wealth, or ability. The
so-called 'Free Cities' of Northern Europe were under the
rule of wealthy burghers. In the eighteenth century France
was governed by a king with almost absolute power, and
Germany by a number of petty kings, princes, and dukes.
Democracy in its modern form was a revolt against irresponsible government; in many European countries the people,
supported and sometimes led by members of the middle class,
demanded that government should be with the consent of the
people and based upon their will. The same principle was
clearly stated in the opening sentences of the American
Declaration of Independence, 'Governments are instituted
among men, deriving their just powers from the consent of
the governed. That whenever any form of government
becomes destructive it is the Right of the People to alter or to
abolish it and to institute new Government, laying its foundations on such principles and organizing its powers in such
form as to them shall seem most likely to effect their safety
and happiness.' This is echoed in the third and sixth Articles
of the 'Declaration of the Rights of Men and of Citizens' of
the French Revolution and agreed upon by the National
Assembly of France in 1789: 'The principle of all sovereignty
resides essentially in the nation; no body and no individual
can exercise any authority which is not expressly derived from
it.' And again: 'All citizens have a right to concur, either
personally or by their representatives, in its formation.' As it
was impossible in the modern State for each citizen to exercise
personally his rights in the large community of which he was
a member, so much larger in population than the city-states of
the Greek world, he had to act through his representatives
chosen from time to time by popular election. Later on,
Abraham Lincoln condensed in a famous sentence the political
aspect of democracy: 'government of the people, for the

people, by the people.' For over a century political democracy swept like wildfire through Europe, destroying autocratic and tyrannical rule, and substituting for it popular representation. In 1910 it was possible to write: 'In Europe itself one of the most remarkable features of the most recent period has been the steady advance of democracy . . . Even Turkey is making the democratic experiment. If it succeeds every country in Europe, not even excepting Russia, will have recognized to some extent the democratic principle.'* Forty years later this statement seems strangely optimistic; but it stands as evidence of the spread of democracy until the first half of the twentieth century.

In Great Britain there had been for many centuries an elected House of Commons, but except for brief periods and rare occasions it had been controlled by the Crown or overshadowed by the House of Lords. In the eighteenth century the government was in the hands of a few families with great possessions in land. At the beginning of the last century there had been only minor changes in parliamentary representation since the reign of Charles II. The industrial towns often had no member of parliament, while small boroughs and even villages sent members to the House of Commons, although, in any case, the rural areas were fully represented by the landowning classes in the Lords. In 1827 '276 out of 658 seats in Parliament were at the disposal of landed patrons and 203 of those seats were under Tory control, eight peers alone controlled fifty-one seats.'† Elections were often disgraced by orgies of drunkenness and rowdyism, and the free electors gave their votes to the candidate who paid them most. Charles Dickens' account in the *Pickwick Papers* of the Eatanswill election (recently translated into Russian to show the degradation of democratic elections!) was only a caricature of what actually took place. 'During the whole time of polling, the town was in a perpetual fever of excitement. Everything was conducted on the most liberal and delightful scale. Excisable articles were remarkably cheap at all the public houses; and

Cambridge History of Modern Europe, Vol. XII, p. 5.
†E. L. Woodward, *Age of Reform*, p. 24.

spring vans paraded the streets for the accommodation of voters who were seized with any temporary dizziness in the head – an epidemic which prevailed among the electors, during the contest, to a most alarming extent, and under the influence of which they might frequently be seen lying on the pavement in a state of utter insensibility.' In 1832 the first Reform Act was passed; it took away seats from nomination boroughs – some hundred and forty were extinguished in England alone – and redistributed them to places where there had been no previous representation, and opened the franchise in all boroughs to £10 householders. But this was only the first step in the movement towards government by general consent: the overwhelming majority of the members of the House of Commons still came from the landed interest, and there was no representation of the labouring classes. In 1867 another step forward was taken – the franchise was extended so that 938,000 voters were added to an electorate of over a million in England and Wales. Thomas Carlyle described this as 'shooting Niagara'. Fear of intimidation of the voter was removed by the Ballot Act of 1872, which secured for him secrecy at the polling-booth. In 1884 there was another extension of the franchise, raising the United Kingdom electorate from three million to about five million, and a new redistribution of seats. Since then the franchise has been enlarged so that for all practical purposes it is universal; women as well as men are now entitled to vote. Two Acts gave eight million the franchise: property qualifications were also abolished; lunatics, criminals, and peers of Parliament are now the only adults who have no right to vote. While the House of Commons was becoming based on a wider representation, the powers of the House of Lords were reduced; by the Act of 1911 it could only stop for two years a Bill sent to it by the Commons; at the same time it was deprived of the right to reject or amend any money Bill, certified as such by the Speaker. By the Parliament Act of 1950 it can delay the passing of an Act approved by the House of Commons for the period of one year only. The ideal of the Chartists has been realized of a House of Commons elected by universal adult franchise. In Great Britain rule by the majority is now accepted; the minority opposes and criticizes, but in the last resort, however unwillingly, it accepts the decisions of the majority when an Act has been passed by both Houses of Parliament and has received the Royal Assent.

Against political democracy two objections are urged. It is said that the great mass of the people cannot understand many of the problems on which they are asked to express their opinion; that they are swayed by appeals to self-interest; that bribery under the more respectable guise of promises for the future is as powerful an instrument in securing election as the open corruption of pre-Reform days; and that emotion and sentiment often sweep away sound judgement. Many critics of democracy would echo Dr Stockman in Ibsen's *Enemy of the People* when he declared, 'The majority is never right. Never I say. That is one of the conventional lies against which a free thoughtful man must rebel. Who are they that make up the majority of a country? Is it the wise or the foolish? I think we must agree that the foolish folk are at present in a terribly overwhelming majority all around and about us the wide world over. But, devil take it, it can surely never be right that the foolish should rule over the wise!' No one would deny that there is some truth in this criticism, but stupidity and selfishness are found in every form of government; the Christian would say that neither autocracies nor democracies are free from original sin. The multitude and the oligarchy equally with the tyrant are tempted to act in accordance with what seems likely to promote their selfish interests. Plato's philosopher king might rise above self-interest, but probably he would lack the soundness of judgement which would enable him to deal with practical problems. The ordinary man inexpert in the details both of foreign and domestic politics usually possesses a kind of rough horse-sense which helps him to form a sound judgement on the broad issues presented to him from time to time; frequently he will prove to be right when the expert was wrong. With the general spread of education the citizen now takes an intelligent interest in politics beyond those of the parish pump. The right to vote encourages him in this; it gives him a sense of responsibility in the government of his country which otherwise he would not acquire; for there is no other form of government which gives this to such a high degree. The responsibility is not on one man, nor on a small group, but upon all.

It is also objected that democracy cannot produce the right men to lead the nation, that it is at the mercy of demagogues who by their rhetoric and promises corrupt or confuse the judgement of the voter. From the days of Aristophanes there has always been this criticism of democracy. In the *Knights* the sausage-seller is told that he can easily manage the affairs of democracy:

> Why nothing's easier. Do what now you do:
> Mince, hash, and mash up everything together.
> Win over Demos with the savoury sauce
> Of little cookery phrases. You've already
> Whatever else a demagogue requires,
> A brutal voice, low birth, a market training.
> Why you've got all one wants for public life.*

Over two thousand years later Bernard Shaw in *The Apple Cart* makes Boanerges say: 'I talk democracy to these men and women. I tell them that they have the vote, and that theirs is the kingdom, and the power, and the glory. I say to them "You are supreme, exercise your power." They say, "That's right: tell us what to do," and I tell them. I say exercise your vote intelligently by voting for me! And they do. That's democracy and a splendid thing it is too, for putting the right men in the right place.' Second-rate candidates are sometimes successful in obtaining election through their gifts of oratory, their lavish promises, and their ingratiating manner. But the average elector is no fool; he is not easily taken in by fustian or humbug; he is very quick to detect the man of straw and the wind-bag. This is also true of the House of Commons; most of its members on both sides of the House are ordinary men of good common sense quite capable of discriminating between the man of real worth and judgement and the ambitious thruster with the gift of the gab; many members have had

*Translated in the Loeb Classical Library.

some practical experience in administration and in public affairs on borough or country councils, in business, or in their Trade Union. The members of the House have repeatedly shown that at a time of crisis they can suspend their controversies on minor matters and unite in a common resolve. When the nation is in danger, a democratic Parliament has silenced party differences and loyally followed the leaders required by the emergency. While the two wars lasted both Lloyd George and Winston Churchill received the unswerving support of men of all parties.

The dangers inherent in political democracy can only be avoided if behind all differences there is a common background of accepted principles. Where this is absent, democracy fails, for opposition may then be carried to such an extreme that it either results in civil war or is crushed out of existence by the majority. The British form of representative government by those elected on a popular franchise has failed when transplanted to countries in which there is no common ground on which all citizens stand. The acceptance of the same outlook on life and of the same ideals has enabled the majority to respect the views of the minority, even when outvoting them, and the minority to obey the law against the passing of which it has protested by voice and vote. Political democracy in Great Britain did not emerge suddenly from the ground, nor was it imposed arbitrarily from above; it is the result of centuries of trial and error. Through bitter strife, especially over matters of religion, the nation learnt that toleration is a necessary condition for the working of democracy. Foreigners are astonished at finding in this country that there is 'Her Majesty's Opposition' as well as 'Her Majesty's Government', and are both baffled and amused at finding that the State pays a salary to the Leader of the Opposition. When Mr Churchill was defeated at the election after the last war, a Rumanian lady wrote to an English friend, 'Now I suppose they will shoot poor Mr Churchill'! Our democracy has not been threatened for centuries with a crisis likely to lead to national disruption; and this has been due not to the constitutional machinery but to the essential principles on which all parties agree notwithstanding their differences on many matters both theoretical and practical. For democracy is far more than a political method; it is a way of life. It is a political and social philosophy as well as a system of government. It is the general agreement on a way of life which enables it to work in the United Kingdom and for the political machine to survive severe strain.

DEMOCRACY AS A WAY OF LIFE

It is easier to describe than to define democracy as a way of life. Definitions and descriptions of democracy as a way of life may be multiplied to almost any extent, but all of them imply or declare explicitly that it means equality, liberty, the rule of law and duty to the State.

(*1*) *Equality*. The demand for equality does not mean that at any given time, or at any time in the future, men will be equal either physically, morally, or intellectually. There is the greatest variety in the capacities of men and women born in the same environment; but when the social environment is different, either more or less favourable, the inequalities are even more marked. Those brought up in the same surroundings, receiving the same education, and inheriting the same wealth are often unequal in ability, knowledge, and enterprise. But natural inequality has been increased and sometimes made permanent by unjust social and economic conditions. At the time of the French Revolution the demand for equality was a violent protest against privileges and restrictions which gave the few every advantage, and left the multitude in destitution, ignorance, and wretchedness. Democracy called for the abolition of the artificial barriers which divided mankind into the 'haves' and 'have-nots', and the opening of doors to the poor which for centuries had been closed to them. It insisted that all men had equal human rights which neither autocrat nor arbitrary law should take from them. The extension of the franchise to all classes was a means to an end – the equality of all citizens in the social, political, and economic opportunities of a full life.

This demand for equality comes directly from Christian doctrine. Christ did not teach that all men are equal in position or in ability; in one of His parables He took it for granted that men have different 'talents', but they are equally responsible for the use they make of them. He taught that God is the Father of all, that all therefore are of value in His sight; all are called by Him to love and serve Him, all are offered eternal life. The material differences which separate men from each other are as nothing compared with the redeeming love God has equally for all, and with the greatness of the inheritance to which He calls all. Rich and poor are admitted to the family of God by the same baptism; they are given the same spiritual help; they kneel side by side for the same Bread and Wine of Life; the same service is used for the marriage of the daughter of a king as for the marriage of a daughter of a bricklayer in a back slum. When death comes the same service is used over the bodies of sovereign and cottager. It is said that when an Emperor of Austria was buried and his body was carried to the door of an abbey, the door remained shut when admission was demanded in the name of the Emperor; it was opened only when the request was made in the name of Brother.

The Christian should insist as strongly as the democrat, and even more strongly, for his conviction comes from his faith in the Fatherhood of God, that all men are of equal value and demand equal consideration. Equality of consideration is not to be limited to one nation or race; the Athenians treated as equal only those who were Greeks, the Jews only those of their race and religion. Christianity claims equality for men of all colours and races, though accepting as a fact that many are far behind in their culture and intelligence, belonging to child races, compared with those more advanced in civilization. Christianity therefore is opposed to the Nazi theories of a master race, and to the South African Dutch policy of *apartheid*, which would mean the segregation of the black people from the white; it condemns the contempt shown by many of the citizens of the United States for the Negroes in their midst, and by some of our own countrymen for the African and Asiatic. The Christian looks for greater equality by levelling up rather than by levelling down, and is confident that, through Christian teaching, improved education, and more favourable economic and social conditions, those now low down in the scale of civilization will gradually reach a higher level. The motive of the Christian in aiming at this will always be the love of all men as children of the One Father.

(2) *Liberty*. A second characteristic of democracy is its demand for liberty. The revolution in America was caused by the attempt of a distant government to control the affairs of colonies which resented its interference. The French Revolution was caused by the tyranny and selfishness of a despotism which allowed the poor to starve while the king and his nobles squandered the taxes they had extorted from the people. It was a fierce protest against a feudal system in which privileges survived while duties had been forgotten. Both the American and the French Revolutions demanded freedom for all as a natural right. The First Article of the American Declaration of Rights asserted: 'That all men are by nature equally free and independent and have certain inherent rights of which, when they enter into a state of security, they cannot by any means deprive or divest their posterity; namely the enjoyment of life and liberty with the means of acquiring and possessing property and pursuing and obtaining happiness and security.' In the same spirit the French Declaration of the rights of men and of citizens declared: 'Men are born, and always continue, free and equal in all respects of their rights.' In France the demand for freedom naturally took the form of the abolition of class privileges which deprived the poor of their freedom. The storming of the Bastille was a dramatic protest against a system which sent men to prison without trial. Personal security against arbitrary arrest was one of the aims of the revolutionaries, though they themselves later on frequently violated the rights they had demanded.

But after security of person and freedom to vote had been won, there was still no true freedom for the multitude. In most democratic countries the proletariat, consisting of those whose chief functions were menial work and the production of offspring (proles), had freedom to vote and security from arbitrary arrest, long before they had freedom in the wider sense; they still had no certainty of a livelihood, no freedom to choose their work, no freedom to decide on the conditions under which they worked, only the freedom to starve if they refused the employment offered to them, however unjust its terms might be. There was no true freedom for millions as long as the fear of unemployment compelled them to work for long hours and poor wages, under miserable and unhealthy conditions. They were at the mercy of an industrial system in which the isolated individual was almost as helpless as the slave threatened by his owner's whip. Economic freedom was as necessary as political freedom. As soon as this was realized, democracy demanded better conditions of work, which would give a larger freedom than the mere possession of the vote. The vote was a means to an end, but for long it failed to win for the workers their demands. It was eventually through the action of the Trade Unions, armed with the weapon of the strike, through the rise of a new political party, and through the growth of humanitarianism among the employer class which weakened their resistance to change, that the giants of unemployment and hunger which had so long held the masses in thrall were successfully attacked.

Democracy, however, asks for more than physical freedom. It demands the right to freedom of discussion, both in speech and in the Press, without fear of penalty. If the citizen is to know how to use his vote intelligently he must have the right to engage in controversy, to speak freely, to hear different views and, through debate with others, to form his own opinion. This is impossible without toleration; there can be no freedom in a nation where there is a rigid censorship and where speakers and writers express their views under the menace of prosecution if they incur the disapproval of the Government. Jan Masaryk is reported to have said, 'I look forward to the day when in a tram in Prague I can say, "I hate the Government."' Western democracy is bound up with toleration; this is one of the characteristics which distinguishes it from Russian democracy, which refuses to allow any criticism of the views held by the governing party in the State.

Respect for the other man's conscience has become part of the very life of British democracy. The Englishman attaches more importance to liberty than to equality; he takes equality for granted, but he knows that liberty can be preserved only by incessant vigilance.

By a strange paradox, modern democracy, notwithstanding its zeal for liberty, sometimes unwittingly creates a danger to it. The full social and political freedom of the individual citizen can only be secured by the State; but the State in carrying out its plans is compelled to create a vast organization of officials; so gradually there comes into existence a powerful bureaucracy, too complicated for the State to control and too impersonal for the individual citizen to influence. It issues endless regulations and numerous questionnaires, and builds up a large army of officials to detect infringements of its rules, until at last the hapless citizen has lost much of his liberty. 'What we have to fear, to speak in terms of prehistoric animals, is not the sabre-toothed tiger, but the diplodocus, the vast creature with a small brain a very long way off and very heavy feet.'* This is a danger to which all democracies are exposed, and it can be defeated only by continual vigilance on the part of the electors, for, in the last resort, Parliament can control the executive which it has called into being.

Freedom in its modern form has its origin in Christianity. The strongest argument for it is that all men are the children of God and are of value in His sight; they must therefore possess the freedom which will enable them to do His will and to use rightly the talents with which He has entrusted them. Christ taught that no man must be despised, that the man who looked down with scorn upon his brother whom God had created was in danger of hell fire. Without freedom man cannot fulfil his responsibility either to God or to man. Christianity did not in the early days of the Church embark on a campaign for the liberation of the slaves, but it taught that the master and his slave were both children of the one Father, and therefore

*G. Kitson Clark, *The English Inheritance*, p. 47.

they had duties to each other. At first the Church was content with mitigating the lot of the slaves and with encouraging their masters to free them, but in course of time it was realized that slavery in any form was inconsistent with the Christian doctrine of man, and so under the leadership of Christians like William Wilberforce, Great Britain freed the slaves throughout its Empire, and used its navy to stop this horrible traffic in human beings. There were other causes besides those of Christian conviction which might have led in time to the abolition of slavery: economically it was becoming unprofitable; but Christian action was the strongest force which resulted in its suppression by all civilized nations.

(3) *Rule of Law.* Unrestrained liberty would result in anarchy. Only in a perfect world could men be trusted neither to injure their neighbours nor to act against the well-being of the community; only an absolute ruler who combined perfect wisdom with complete unselfishness could be trusted to govern without law. Force is necessary in any form of government for the protection of its citizens against the dishonest and violent, but in a democratic State it will be used in accordance with law which has been made with the consent of the people. In Great Britain, when a law has once been passed by both Houses of Parliament and received the Royal Assent, it is binding upon all, and it is subject to the interpretation of the judges, who can protect the citizens from its misuse as well as from the arbitrary acts either of the Government or of private individuals.

The rule of law is necessary to protect individuals from the irresponsible action of a Government, whether it is that of a dictator or a bureaucracy, which has either seized, or inherited power, or has been given it by the people. In a primitive society custom hallowed by long tradition takes the place of written law; obedience to it is unquestioning, and any deliberate or accidental breach of it is followed by severe penalties. But when society has become more complicated and large numbers live in a city or nation, law is essential for the security of the community and the protection of its citizens. If the law is enforced or ignored, or even changed, at the will of the ruler, what was legal yesterday may become treason to-day; the citizen then would never be certain what laws were still in operation or what new edict might be issued to-morrow. Life would become full of unexpected pitfalls, and social and economic stability an impossibility. Life in a community whose laws depended solely on the will of the ruler and which could be made or abrogated according to his whim, would be like the game of croquet in *Alice in Wonderland*, where the balls were live hedgehogs who wandered about the lawn, the mallets were flamingoes whose long necks were difficult to manipulate, and the hoops were soldiers who doubled themselves over in arches, and when tired walked away; no wonder Alice complained, 'They all quarrel so dreadfully one cannot hear oneself speak – and they don't seem to have any rules in particular; at least if there are nobody attends to them.' Uncertainty as to the nature of a law may be more harmful than a bad law which is understood by all. Democracy demands not only just laws in accordance with the will of the people, but also their impartial administration. In a totalitarian State the judge is an instrument of State policy, he must support the State in its own wrong-doing and decide cases not on the evidence or on the merits of the arguments, but in accordance with the interests of the State.

In a democratic State as we know it in Great Britain the law is an expression of the will of the people. The judges exist to see that law is not used unjustly and to ensure that the individual citizen is given both protection from its abuse and the benefits of its operation. Laws constitutionally made and passed are binding on all; none can claim exemption unless the law explicitly allows it; all, rich and poor alike, are equally under it, and no privilege can be claimed against it. If the law is disobeyed those who break it must suffer the penalties it prescribes; it can be changed only by the parliament which passed it. Good laws protect both equality and liberty, for they defend the citizens against the arbitrary actions of the State, they secure to them justice and peace, and they demand obedience from all, for in the sight of the law all men are equal.

In an Age of Revolution

Democracy insists on equal rights for all men, but duties are the corollaries of rights, and disaster falls upon the State in which the citizens claim their rights but forget their duties. We have seen how in the Athenian State every citizen was expected to make his contribution to the community of which he was a member. In the modern democratic State there is always the danger of the citizen speaking of 'they', by which he means an impersonal government, and neglecting to say 'we', and thus recognizing the responsibility he has as an individual for the well-being of the State. This tendency is increased in a Welfare State, which is regarded as a universal provider and is expected to relieve the citizen of personal responsibility. When the individual looks upon the Government as something entirely apart from him, it quickly falls into the hands of place-seeking politicians who consider their own interests before those of the people they are supposed to represent. The good citizen must not only use his vote, but use it intelligently; he must use it not only in national but also in local elections; and when he has cast his vote he must not sit back feeling he has done all that is necessary, but he must show an active interest in the votes and speeches of those he has helped to put in office.

But the exercise of the franchise is a very small part of the duties of a citizen. A large amount of philanthropic and welfare work has always in the past been undertaken by volunteers. Most of the work once done by unpaid individuals is now passing into the hands of Government officials. 'The sense of responsibility in British society has not been confined to the political sphere. No element in it has been more salutary than the amount and variety of voluntary service which has been given in every kind of social activity. It is unparalleled in the world. Not the least part of it has come from the so-called "leisured" class which it is now the fashion to regard (so far as it survives) as an excrescence of drones and parasites. There is a real danger, in many of the plans which are now put forward, that much if not all of this unrewarded service may pass into the hands, in the name of "organization", of Government officials. If this ever comes to pass, not only will democratic life suffer a grave decline of that very "efficiency" which regimentation is intended to promote, but something vital will have gone out of the spirit of citizenship in this nation – an indispensable ingredient, as I believe, in the social cement of our particular kind of democracy.'*

Two wars have shown that a democracy is ready to make the greatest sacrifices in defence of its country and its cause. No totalitarian State could have done more than the citizens of the free democracies in subordinating their personal rights to the success of the cause for which they were fighting; they showed themselves capable of making the greatest sacrifices and enduring the most severe hardships until victory was won. But when war is over and peace has been declared the citizen is tempted to demand rights and to ignore duties. The weakness of a democracy is that its citizens tend to forget that their responsibilities to the State are as great in the time of peace as they were in war.

CHRISTIANITY AND DEMOCRACY

The revolutionary methods of democracy largely account for the opposition it met with from the Church. The Church both on the Continent and in Great Britain treated it as a dangerous and subversive movement which was attempting to overthrow the established order. In the French Revolution the goddess of reason had been enthroned in Notre Dame and Christianity had been abolished by edict. Pope and bishop denounced the movement and warned their flocks against having any part in it. The very word democracy evoked fear and anger from the ranks of the clergy, who regarded it as synonymous with atheism. On the other hand, the democrat hated and despised the Church as the close ally of the governing and landowning classes. The Church owned great possessions, and therefore instinctively opposed a movement which threatened property. Unhappily, class distinctions

*C. K. Allen, *Democracy and the Individual*.

were carried even into the public worship of the churches; in some of the baroque churches on the Continent the ornate and gilded boxes of the nobility overlooked the sanctuary, while the poor stood where they could; in country churches in England the squire sat in the dignity of a curtained and cushioned pew in the most prominent place; behind it were the more modest pews of the lesser gentry and the farmers, and at the back were the bare planks for the labourers and their families. The bishops in England in the first part of the nineteenth century belonged to the governing classes, 'eleven in 1815 were of noble birth; ten had been tutors or schoolmasters to a prince, or a duke, or a statesman.'* In the worst days of the Industrial Revolution the bishops and clergy, with a few honourable exceptions, made no protest against the long hours and inhuman conditions of the factory or mine in which men, women, and children were compelled to work to save themselves from starvation. In pamphlets and leaflets the Church was bitterly attacked for its failure to champion the cause of the poor: 'Attacks are directed against its religious teaching, but the chief cause of the Church's unpopularity was the reputation of inhumanity; the feeling that the Church gave its sanction to all the injustices and abuses that degraded the poor and outraged their self-respect.'† The failure of the Church to defend the weak and oppressed, and the revolutionary element in democracy created a gulf between the Church and the masses which in many parts of Christendom still remains unbridged.

To-day both the leaders of the Churches and most of their clergy have made it plain that the Church supports many of the demands made by democracy. The Lambeth Conference of 1948 was emphatic in stating the nature of human rights: 'all men, irrespective of race or colour, are equally the objects of God's love and are called to love and serve Him. All men are made in His image; for all Christ died; and to all there is made the offer of eternal life. Every individual is therefore bound by duties towards God and towards other men, and has certain

*J. L. and Barbara Hammond, *The Age of the Chartists*, p. 220.
†*Op. cit.*, p. 218.

rights without the enjoyment of which he cannot perform those duties. These rights should be declared by the Church, recognized by the State, and safeguarded by international law.' The Conference in the next resolution declared the nature of these rights; among them are: 'security of life and person; the right to work, to bring up a family, and to possess personal property; the right to freedom of speech, of discussion and association, and to accurate information; and to full freedom of religious life and practice, and that these rights belong to all men irrespective of race or colour.'

In England the tension between the Church and democracy has never been so acute as it was on the Continent. Many early Trade Union and labour members were Nonconformists, and had their first lessons in practical democracy in the affairs of their chapels, and as lay preachers gained their experience in public speaking. In the Church of England there have always been found clergy and laymen who have shown deep concern over social injustice. It was a great Churchman, Lord Shaftesbury, who carried on a campaign until at last Parliament abolished some of the worst of the abuses in the factory or mine; while a succession of clergy from the days of Frederick Denison Maurice and Charles Kingsley to Charles Gore and William Temple have supported democracy in its demands for social reform.

The Church is not, however, greatly concerned over democracy as a political movement. There is nothing specifically Christian in the demand for representative government or the broadest possible franchise. It is sheer nonsense, disproved frequently by history, that *vox populi* is *vox dei*. Majorities are frequently wrong, though probably not so frequently as minorities, and are nothing like so dangerous as dictatorships in which a ruler in a fit of bad temper or indigestion may do or say something which plunges the world into war. The Christian is attracted to democracy as a method of government which gives the individual citizen an opportunity of responsibility which would not be found under an oligarchy or despotism: but provided that the State is encouraging the good life among its citizens, the Church need neither accept nor reject on Christian grounds any particular form of government.

It is, however, very different when democracy is presented as a way of life rather than a political system. When it demands not merely the vote, but that social wrongs should be abolished and a new order established in which there is equality and freedom; that the sufferings of the poor and destitute should be relieved; that no child, because of the poverty of its parents, should go through life handicapped; that there should be a fairer distribution of wealth – then the Church should regard the movement with sympathy and understanding, for its Master spent the greater part of His earthly life as a working man at the carpenter's bench at Nazareth, and had His home among humble country folk; He knew what was meant by hunger and poverty, often He had only a stone for His pillow, and the sky was the roof which sheltered Him. He showed His love towards the poor, condemning the rich man who had neglected the beggar sitting by his gate, and those who failed to help the hungry, the naked, and the prisoners. He taught that God was the Father of all and cared for all. He had no possessions of His own, with the exception of the clothes He wore, and in nakedness died between two naked thieves. The disciples to whom He had given the commission to carry on His work were poor men, most of whom earned their livelihood by fishing in the Lake of Galilee. The Church in its early days consisted mainly, though not entirely, of the poor and the unlearned. When the rich and educated were admitted to it as members, they entered it on terms of spiritual equality with their slaves and freed men. St Paul boasted of this: 'There is neither Jew nor Gentile, there is neither bond nor free, there is neither male nor female, for ye are all one in Christ Jesus,' and on another occasion he wrote: 'Ye see your calling, brethren, how that not many wise men after the flesh, not many mighty, not many noble, are called. But God hath chosen the foolish things of the world to confound the wise; and God hath chosen the weak things of the world to confound the things which are mighty; and base things of the world, and things which are despised, hath God chosen.' The great hymn sung throughout Christendom breathes the very spirit of democracy: 'He hath put down the mighty from their seat and hath exalted the humble and meek; He hath filled the hungry with good things and the rich He hath sent empty away.' It is a tragedy that so often the Church has looked upon democracy with suspicion, and that democracy has assumed that the Church is opposed to its aims and aspirations. We must not, however, think that Christianity is so bound up with democracy that every believer should be compelled by his faith to be a democrat; we should be content with affirming that 'democracy is linked to Christianity, and that the democratic impulse has arisen in human history as a temporal manifestation of the inspiration of the Gospel.'*

Christianity should help democracy to avoid three dangers to which it is especially exposed: secularism in the exact sense of the word; over-confidence; and the suppression of individuality. Democracy often becomes secularized through its exclusive concentration on the problems of this life and indifference as to what happens to the individual after death; the problems, claims, and interests of this life will absorb all man's energies and hopes. The democrat believes in the millennium, but that it will be established in this world, somewhere round the corner, and he has an almost apocalyptic sense of a new and perfect world which he can create. He dismisses off-hand all belief in a future life as 'pie in the sky'. Like the humanist, his hope of progress is limited to this life. When his plans fail here no hope remains. The Christian Church teaches there is no inconsistency between belief in a future life and the determination to make this world better. The denial of all belief in a hereafter lessens the sense of responsibility which comes from a man knowing that he is destined for eternity, and that what he is and does here have consequences which are eternal. Democracy suffers from the limitations which follow from short-term views when it rejects the faith in the life everlasting.

Another defect of democracy is over-confidence. Some of its protagonists are so strongly convinced that their special brand

*J. Maritain, *Christianity and Democracy*, p. 26.

of democracy is the only truth, that they despise and hate all who cannot pronounce correctly their shibboleths. This over-confidence makes democracy peculiarly fissiparous; when victory has been gained, fierce disputes arise as to how best it should be used. Democracy, like revolution, is always devouring its own children; it closes its eyes to the weakness of human nature, and it has an idealistic picture of man's capacities and virtues, assuming that if he has any defects they can be overcome by a changed and more favourable environment. Democracy needs to learn the meaning of humility; only so will it avoid the blunders which come from over-confidence. 'Some of the greatest perils to democracy arise from the fanaticism of moral idealists who are not conscious of the corruption of self-interest in their professed ideals. It requires religious humility. Every absolute devotion to relative political ends (and all political ends are relative) is a threat to communal peace. But religious humility is no simple moral or political achievement. It springs only from the depth of a religion which confronts the individual with a more ultimate majesty and purity than all human majesties and values, and persuades him to confess, "Why callest thou me good? There is none good but One that is God".'*

In yet another way the Christian Church should give help to democracy. It champions the rights of the ordinary man, the so-called 'little man', as against the privileges of the few; it aims at removing the artificial barriers of wealth and class which prevent him from developing and using fully the special gifts he possesses. The individual is not to be submerged in the anonymous mass, but he is to be himself, upright, self-respecting, and free. Yet, notwithstanding this, there is always the danger that the very successes of democracy may iron out individual characteristics, so that eventually there is a grey mass of men and women who all speak, dress, and vote in exactly the same way. If in such circumstances a raider from Mars captured one man and carried him away as a specimen, the Martians would at once know what all the other inhabitants of the earth were like. Democracy by its

*R. Niebuhr, *The Children of Light and the Children of Darkness*, p. 104.

command of universal education, of the Press and the wireless, may smooth out individual qualities until all men are moulded into the same ways of thinking and speaking, until the number each is given becomes the chief mark of difference. Mr Charles Morgan says that with the drift of population from the country to the town individuals became submerged in numbers, and numbers began to be thought of as having reality in themselves. 'Numerical thinking dehumanized, and perhaps one should add despiritualized, men's relationship with their fellow-men ... A grey soullessness appeared in societies under numerical pressure. It caused men, at all levels, to think of others and even of themselves too easily as anonymous members of vast statistical groups, and much less easily than in the past as knowable, distinguishable beings who had, each one, been a boy or a girl, who was happy or lonely or afraid, whose hand one might touch, and whose look one might recognize; men and women who were, in brief, not "employers" or "employed", not dim categories, but creatures, each *one* a child of God.'* Christianity should help democracy against this danger of numerical pressure by insisting, in season and out of season, that every man, woman, and child is of infinite value in the sight of God, that their differences as well as their similarities must be respected; that each must have freedom to develop his personality as God intended, and not as the convenience of the State requires.

If, however, the Church is to influence democracy it must not attempt to do so from a lofty pedestal of self-righteousness; it is only to a Church which is deeply penitent for past failures that democracy will listen; a Church which is repentant and humble, which shows its Master's love for individuals, especially His care for the poor and suffering, and which has His courage in denouncing social wickedness, will be more likely to commend Christ, than a Church which depends upon its worldly authority and prestige.

*Liberties of the Mind, p. 33.

7

The God-State

In the early days of the Church, Christians were called upon to offer worship to the Emperor as divine; they had to refuse to do so, even though refusal was punished with death. In the twentieth century Emperor-worship has been revived in a new form, and Christian Churches are called upon either to submit to the all-powerful State or to suffer persecution for their refusal. Once again in many countries the Church and the State are in open conflict.

This need not have been so, for the Church has always recognized that the State has God-given authority and that within limits it has the right to demand obedience from its subjects. Our Lord taught His followers that they were to render unto Caesar the things which are Caesar's and unto God the things which are God's. St Paul told his converts that they must honour and pray for the Emperor and submit themselves to those in authority. It is true that in the Book of the Revelation the State is shown as an enemy, but this is so because it is persecuting the Christians. But usually it is accepted that the State obtains its authority from God and exists to preserve peace and to protect its citizens from injury to their persons and their property. The world Church in St Paul's teaching 'did not merely recognize the State as permitted by God, but prized it as an institution which at least cared for justice, order, and external morality. In this respect already Paul drew upon the Stoic doctrine of the moral law which is written in the heart, and ascribed also to the heathen a knowledge of goodness which is outwardly expressed in their State and in their legal system. The Empire wields the sword according to the Will of God and by the order of God.'* The authority of the Emperor, though divine in its origin, was not unlimited, and when his commands were contrary to the divine law, then

*Ernest Troeltsch, *The Social Teaching of the Christian Churches*, Vol. 1. p. 80.

they must be disobeyed, whatever the cost. With the spread of Christianity the Church became a powerful organization instead of a small sect which the Empire could disregard with safety. The Church found itself from time to time confronted with demands which its members could not conscientiously obey. It became therefore necessary to justify resistance to an authority which the Church accepted as coming from God. This became the more urgent after the conversion of the Empire, when the ruler was no longer a pagan, but a Christian, especially as a number of laws contrary to Christian teaching were abrogated. Gradually the theory was evolved that in all secular matters both the clergy and the laity must obey the State, but in all spiritual matters obedience must be rendered to the Church. This was clear in principle, but ambiguous in application, with the result that there were frequent conflicts between the Church and State throughout the Middle Ages. It was never, however, denied either by the Church or by the State, that each was supreme, with authority from God, in its own proper sphere. In practice this meant that the Pope was the final authority in all spiritual and ecclesiastical matters, the Emperor or King in those which were concerned with man's life on earth. It was the duty of the State to protect the Church and to help it in its work, and it was the duty of the Church to pray for and to bless the State.

From time to time both Church and State refused to accept the limitation of this authority and each endeavoured to rule the other. The true theory was, however, restated by Dante in the Middle Ages in his *De Monarchia*, in which he argued that both Emperor and Pope received their authority directly from God, instead of the Emperor receiving it at the hands of the Pope. The Emperor must have unlimited temporal authority, and this must be universal in its extent, but this authority is to be used for the benefit of those he ruled: 'The citizens are not there for the sake of the consuls, nor the nation for the sake of the king, but conversely, the consuls for the sake of the citizens, the king for the sake of the nation. For just as the body politic is not established for the benefit of the laws, but the laws for the benefit of the body politic, so too they who live under the law are not ordained for the benefit of the legislator, but rather he for theirs ... Hence it is clear that, albeit the consul or king be masters of the rest as regards the way, yet as regards the end they are their servants: and the monarch most of all, for he must assuredly be regarded as the servant of all.'*

In *De Monarchia* we can see the Christian doctrine of the State as from God and existing for the good of the society over which it has the government. The State is independent of the Church, but it is related to it, as both have their authority from God and both exist for the welfare of mankind. The Christian doctrine of the State is thus built on a dual foundation: its authority is from God, and its true end not the glory and power of the ruler, but the protection and benefit of the ruled. The State, being under the law of God, has no right to demand obedience to laws which are not in conformity with His law. Christianity does not demand any one special form of government; it may be rule by one man, or by the few, or by the many chosen by popular election: the Christian State can be found under very different constitutions: but always the State must recognize that it is under the sovereignty of God and that the purpose for which it exists is to defend from external foes the society which it governs, and to promote within it justice, good order, and peace between all classes and individuals.

THE HOBBESIAN STATE

With the formation of national States new problems rose as to the relationship between the ruler and his subjects. Had the ruler complete power over his subjects? What was the source of his authority? Had his subjects any rights against him? The most striking and comprehensive of answers to these questions was given by Thomas Hobbes in his *Leviathan*, which was published during the Commonwealth: it is an uncompromising apology for absolutism; as such it was denounced and a copy of the book was publicly burnt at Oxford. Hobbes was

*P. 159. Temple Classics Edition.

born in the year of the Armada, and this made him say, 'Fear and I were twins.' This element of fear in his character gave him a sombre view of man in a state of nature. All men were born equal with equal rights; no one would therefore give place to his neighbour, and men lived in a condition of perpetual strife. They had no security, 'No Arts: no Letters: no Society: and which is worst of all continual fear and danger of violent death: And the Life of man, solitary, poor, nasty, brutish, and short.' Men recognized the misery and danger of their lives; and to obtain security they agreed to surrender their independence to a sovereign who would protect them from violence and injustice. Only through such a complete surrender could they hope to gain the security which was essential to their well-being. All had to agree to this surrender, for it would be insufficient if only some entrusted themselves to his protection, while others remained in the state of nature. The surrender had to be complete and irrevocable. In future law was to be the expression of the will of the sovereign, the supreme and only legislator. Beyond the implied condition of giving protection, he is under no contract with his subjects, for they have agreed with one another to make over to him their natural rights. Far better that he should misuse his position than that they should attempt to overthrow him. The worst misgovernment cannot be worse than a civil war or a nation in anarchy. The subject, therefore, in his own interests must submit to bad laws or to a tyrannical ruler, for anything is better than a return to the state of nature in which there is no peace or security and the hand of every man is turned against his neighbour; all kinds of hardships and inconveniences should be accepted for the sake of security and a quiet life. The sovereign can do no wrong; his actions may be immoral and tyrannical, but they cannot be illegal. What the sovereign decrees is legal. Right and wrong are what the sovereign allows or forbids. Morality is therefore separated from law. The sovereign not only makes the laws, but he also interprets and enforces them. He has the right to suppress all opinions contrary to those which he holds. The clergy hold their authority from the sovereign and must teach only what he approves: 'seeing then in every Christian commonwealth, the civil sovereign is the supreme pastor, to whose charge the whole flock of his subjects is committed, and consequently that it is by his authority that all other pastors are made, and have power to teach, and perform all other pastoral offices: it followeth also, that it is from the sovereign that all other pastors derive their right of teaching, preaching, and other functions pertaining to that office, and that they are but his ministers: in the same manner as the magistrates of towns, judges in courts of justice, and commanders of armies, are all but ministers of him that is the magistrate of the whole commonwealth.'* In Hobbes we have the father of modern absolutism. Historically the theory is nonsense; at no time in history was there this deliberate transfer of power to one man; nor does modern research confirm Hobbes' picture of society in anarchy before the transfer was made.

Two reservations, however, mitigate the autocracy of Leviathan. If the sovereign is unable to protect the subjects, then they are free from his allegiance, for the sovereign has failed in the supreme purpose for which he was given the rights and independence of his subjects. If he has clearly failed to give them the security for which they surrendered so much, he can be deposed by force. Secondly, even in the case of an absolute monarch as seen by Hobbes, there were still left large fields in which he never interfered. In actual practice the individual had plenty of scope for freedom and initiative; only rarely did he find the sovereign State interfering with the larger part of his business or daily life. But the weakest aspect of the Hobbesian State is 'that it allows the State no positive function. As the offspring of fear, its sole duty, apart from defence against foreign enemies, is the maintenance of order. Leviathan is simply a policeman of superhuman size with a truncheon in his hand.'†

Leviathan, p. 245. (Morley's Universal Library.)
†G. P. Gooch, *Studies in Diplomacy and Statecraft*, p. 359.

The God-State

Since *Leviathan* was written there has been in the United Kingdom and other democratic countries a steady movement away from the political basis of the absolutist State. Instead there has come into being the State which depends upon the continued assent of the society over which it rules. Hobbes might fairly claim that the sovereign had been chosen by the consent of the people – it was of their own free will that they had transferred to him the rights they possessed – but this had been done once and for all, there was no possibility of their successors escaping from an irrevocable act which had bound the future as well as the present. But the democratic State of to-day requires the continuous assent of the citizens; a general election gives their mandate to a party, but only for a limited time – in this country of five years – and at the next election the voters may withdraw their consent, and a new government is formed by the party which was in opposition.

The House of Commons is now the Sovereign of which Hobbes wrote, but very different in nature from what he had contemplated, for though it has almost absolute power for five years, its power is derived from the people, who at the end of a definite period can change their representatives for others. Leviathan does not consist, as Hobbes intended, of an individual invested with supreme power, but of a representative body dependent for its continued existence on the good-will of the people.

While politically there has been general repudiation of the absolutism of Hobbes' State, socially and economically the powers and responsibilities of the State have been enlarged beyond anything Hobbes could have foreseen. His State was the superhuman policeman armed to protect the nation from invasion, and from disorder within its borders. This was the general view of the State held until the end of the last century. It existed to protect and not to provide. The one exception was its attitude towards the poor, though even here its action was mainly repressive; harsh legislation was directed against vagabondage and pauperism, but the parishes were made responsible for saving the very poor from actual starvation. Legislation was mainly concerned with property. Laws against any violation of property were very severe. Throughout the eighteenth century 'Parliament went on adding statute after statute to the "bloody code" of English law, enlarging perpetually the long list of offences punishable by death: finally they numbered two hundred. Not only were horse- and sheep-stealing and coining capital crimes, but stealing in a shop to the value of five shillings, and stealing anything privily from the person, were it only a handkerchief.'* Early in the nineteenth century the scope of Parliamentary intervention was enlarged – laws were passed for the better administration of the care of the poor, and though these were far from satisfactory, and the old harshness was still shown against the able-bodied out-of-work, greater sympathy was evident towards the sick and children. In the middle of the century, in the face of strong opposition, laws were passed limiting the hours of labour of women and children working in the factories. Outbreaks of cholera caused anxiety over public health, and a commission in 1842 reported on the unsatisfactory water supply of most of the large towns; but it was not until 1871 that the Local Government Board was established to deal with problems connected with public health. In 1870 an Education Act laid the foundation of a national system of education, to supplement the educational work which had been largely the responsibility of the Church of England. The Act was an early and most important departure from the view that the State should be negative rather than positive in its interventions.

In the twentieth century the State decisively abandoned the older doctrine that its functions were mainly negative and protective. A mass of social legislation soon appeared on the Statute Book; schemes of insurance for workmen from accident, ill health, and unemployment, some of these borrowed from the German example, were embodied in legislation. Gradually out of piecemeal legislation for which all parties were responsible there emerged a definite system of social

*G. M. Trevelyan, *English Social History*, p. 348 (American edition).

amelioration which is now comprehensively described as the Welfare State.

It is only recently that the term Welfare State has come into use. It is a convenient term which makes it possible to measure the immense difference between the State of the eighteenth and nineteenth centuries and the State of to-day. The modern State provides for the physical and mental welfare of all its citizens, accepting responsibility for them from childhood to old age. The great development of the social function of the State during the last few years has been due to several causes. A social conscience has been developed which condemns the contrast between extreme wealth and poverty. In all classes there is now genuine anxiety to remove as far as possible conditions which hinder the development of the individual citizen and prevent him from making the best use of life. The war revealed to large numbers the conditions under which many of their fellow-citizens lived, and made them feel they had a duty towards those who were suffering and dying in the common cause. The evacuation of children from the great cities to the country brought a shock of horror to the many who had never realized the meaning of life in the slums. During the Spanish Civil War several thousand Spanish children were given refuge in a hastily provided camp near Southampton. There was a cry of disgust when it was discovered that they had lice in their hair and fleas in their clothes. It was said that this could only happen in foreign communist countries. Those loudest in their protests that children in this condition should be brought to England were blissfully ignorant that in their own towns there were tens of thousands of children living in vermin-infested surroundings. An official inquiry showed that 'about 50 per cent of girls under fourteen years of age living in industrial areas had lousy heads: that boys returned a lower rate, declining from 45 per cent at age two to 20 per cent at age fourteen, and that pre-school children of both sexes had the highest rate of infestation – up to 52 per cent.'* Though many of the most important social reforms have been carried through with the support and

*R. M. Titmuss, *Problems of Social Policy*, p. 127.

goodwill of both the political parties, a great impetus towards the Welfare State was given by the emergence of the Labour Party, containing among its members many who have had direct experience of poverty, unemployment, and bad housing.

The Welfare State as developed in the United Kingdom has three characteristics: it aims at providing physical security from the cradle to the grave; it includes all classes; and the beneficiary as well as the State contributes to its cost. In the past those who had no private means were haunted by a sense of insecurity. 'It has been estimated that before the war there were about 4,000,000 families in Britain living from hand-to-mouth or from pay-day to pay-day. Of this number one half were continually in and out of debt.'* Illness, unemployment, or old age might eat up their savings and throw them upon the charity of voluntary societies or upon the poor law. The generosity and self-sacrifice of the poor to one another in distress have always been great; by stern self-denial the able-bodied have gladly accepted privation for the sake of ailing children or to make a home for parents no longer able to work. But even those who at normal times earned good wages knew that their position was uncertain if there should come a prolonged period of unemployment. In the years between the wars the millions unemployed in the depressed areas intensified this persistent sense of insecurity. The Beveridge Report, a great State document, showed how this fear might be removed by State action, and its proposals were in the main adopted and eventually passed into law. The Welfare State provides for the nutrition and education of the children of the nation: free milk and free meals are provided; family allowances of 5s. a week are paid for each child other than the eldest; in July 1949 some 4,700,000 allowances were paid in respect of 2,970,000 families. Regular medical and dental inspections take place in the schools. Free medical service is provided for all, and the hospitals which once were straitened by lack of means now receive liberal help from the State. The unemployed are certain of a weekly payment which they

*Op. cit., p. 116.

receive as a matter of right, and which enables them to escape the worst physical results of a long period without work, or the humiliation of depending on the charity of others. The State has given Local Authorities large subsidies for the building of houses for the working classes; and though the number yet built is far from sufficient to meet the demand, successive Governments, and both parties, have pledged themselves to carry out a programme of building until the slums and overcrowding are abolished. The aged now have pensions which save them from destitution, and attempts are being made to provide homes for the old people who need care and help. There are still gaps in this great policy of welfare, but it is nothing less than amazing that within ten years such a revolutionary and comprehensive policy of welfare should have been so successfully carried through, and with the consent of all the great parties of the State.

Secondly, this policy includes all classes. Before the second World War State assistance was confined to the lower grade of wage-earners. But class distinctions have become blurred, the well-to-do and the poor suffered side by side the anxieties and losses of the war. Wages have gone up, so that many who once were poor are now receiving week by week more than those who are dependent upon service pensions and the interest on their investments and savings. Heavy taxation and increased costs have reduced the incomes of many who used to be described as of independent means. No longer did the concern of the State for the health and well-being of the population 'rest on the belief that, in respect of many social needs, it was proper to intervene only to assist the poor and those who were unable to pay for services of one kind or another. Instead it now increasingly regarded as a proper function or even obligation of Government to ward off distress or strain among not only the poor but almost all classes of society. And because the area of responsibility had so perceptibly widened, it was no longer thought sufficient to provide through various branches of social assistance a standard of assistance hitherto considered appropriate for those in receipt of poor relief – a standard inflexible in administration and attuned to a philosophy which regarded individual distress as a mark of social incapacity.'*

The third characteristic of the Welfare State in this country is that those who benefit by it contribute towards the cost. This strangely is often forgotten, and one of the most frequent criticisms heard in the United States is that in the Welfare State anything can be obtained for nothing. On a visit to the States in the autumn of 1949 I was repeatedly asked if it was not true that the waster and indolent could on demand obtain help as a right from the State towards which he had not contributed a penny. The actual conditions of national insurance should disprove this charge. In 1951 employed men paid 4s. 11d. and the employer 4s. 2d. as their weekly contribution to the scheme, though by the end of 1951 the contribution rates for men and women were increased by 4d., the employer paying half of this. In addition, help is given under the National Assistance Act to any person who needs assistance to supplement a pension or an insurance benefit. This is, through the nature of the case, not a contributory scheme. But the National Insurance scheme is essentially contributory, and those who draw benefits from it are not receiving doles or charity, but are claiming what is their right and what they have paid for.

The modern democratic State in the United Kingdom is a planned State. If full employment is to be secure it is necessary that a central authority should control the industries of the country so that those which earn most by export to foreign countries are encouraged, and those which provide home luxuries are limited in their productivity until more pressing needs have been met. When materials and labour are limited the Government must see they are used to the best advantage. Industries which employ most usefully large numbers of men and women have special claims for State help. In agriculture it is necessary to see that the crops and livestock are produced and increased which will be of most value to the nation. Food when limited in quantity has to be so rationed that all have an equal share in it. It is tacitly assumed that if control is to be

Op. cit., p. 506.

effective most decisions have to be made at Whitehall instead of being left to the individual industrialist or farmer; a huge mass of questionnaires and regulations therefore are sent out from Government offices and a great army of inspectors is given the duty of seeing the regulations are observed. Many restrictions have been imposed upon the use of what once was regarded as private property, and licences, once viewed as permits to do something, have become instruments of veto and control. The multiplication of regulations and restrictions tends to check initiative, and often puts a serious brake on speed. Months have to be spent in endless correspondence and exasperating delays, while an application is handed on from one department to another, until it reaches an official who is prepared to take the responsibility of making a positive decision. Passing the buck has become a high art in the subordinate ranks of national planners. It is, however, impossible for a Welfare State to exist without planners, planning, restrictions, and licences. The failures of individual planners and the obvious defects in the machinery which only recently has been created, do not justify the wholesale condemnation of a planned society.

CHRISTIANITY AND THE WELFARE STATE

The Christian Church should welcome the Welfare State. It is the embodiment of the principle 'Bear ye one another's burdens, and so fulfil the law of Christ.' In bringing relief to the poor, giving food to the hungry, finding work for the unemployed, caring for the children and the aged, and providing healing for the sick it is carrying on the work of Christ. The Church for centuries has done much to help the poor and suffering; voluntary societies and individuals gave what help they could to those who were in need. But the problems of poverty were too great to be solved by the Church or by voluntary organizations. Before the State recognized its responsibilities, in town and country alike there was to be found much poverty, serious malnutrition among the children, avoidable illness and pain through the failure to obtain adequate medical or surgical treatment, and physical deprivation and mental suffering through long unemployment. The Welfare State has brought new hope to millions, and given them help which in the past was never possible. The un-Christian contrast between great wealth and extreme poverty has almost vanished, and millions have been given the opportunity of a more comfortable and secure life than was ever possible for their parents.

But there are dangers in the Welfare State against which the Christian must be on his guard. It may easily become a State concerned only with physical and mental well-being, while the spiritual needs of its citizens are neglected. Material prosperity and physical well-being do not necessarily bring happiness. There are signs that the physical health of the Welfare State is sounder than its spiritual: better education, higher wages, and greater security have not prevented an increase in crime, the break-up of home life, and a growing sense of disappointment and uneasiness. It is becoming plain that man does not live by bread alone, and that care for the welfare of the soul is as important as care for the welfare of the body.

There is also danger that the Welfare State may weaken the sense of personal responsibility. Much that was once done by the parents is now taken over by the State. From infancy to the day on which the boy or girl leaves school the parents are relieved of much of the responsibility which used to rest upon them for the physical welfare and the education of their children. Over-zealous welfare officers and teachers may resent questions, objections, and suggestions from parents as amateur interference; this is not yet the case with most of the State officials, but there is undoubtedly a tendency among some of them to disregard the opinions and wishes of the parents. As State control and planning increase it is almost inevitable that the millions of men and women concerned come to be looked upon as numbers or cases to be fitted neatly into the pigeon-holes of a vast organization. These dangers are very real, but they are the more likely to be avoided if they are frankly recognized. The risks and defects of the Welfare State are, however, of minor significance contrasted with the malnutrition, the unemployment, and the poverty of the days when the State accepted no responsibility for the positive welfare of its citizens. With all its limitations, the Welfare State is more Christian both in spirit and in actual practice than a State which confined itself to the protection of its citizens from violence, and its poor from actual starvation, but did nothing to feed the hungry, to clothe the naked, or to restore those who had fallen by the way.

TWO FORMS OF DEMOCRACY

While in one direction democracy has developed into the Welfare State built on the foundations of universal franchise and the recognition that the good of the people is the true end of the State, there has been a development in another and opposite direction which has resulted in the totalitarian State. There is considerable confusion because the supporters both of the Welfare and the totalitarian States claim that they are the logical outcome of democracy and exist for the welfare of the people. Both States are highly centralized, and in different degrees stress the vital importance of planning. But there are two fundamental differences – the Welfare State depends on popular election from beneath, and the totalitarian State on authority established by force and exercised from above. The Welfare State relies upon consent, but the totalitarian State upon coercion. Great confusion is often caused by failure to understand the different senses in which the term democracy is used.

By democracy Great Britain, the United States, and the nations acting with them mean 'government of the people, by the people, for the people'. Russia and her satellites omit the middle term of this definition – democracy, they hold, is government of the people for the people, but not by the people. The Russian Communist contends that the people are not yet capable of governing themselves in their own interests; so this must be done at the present stage of development by a dictatorship. Popular representation in the countries which describe themselves as democratic he regards as a sham, a

mere façade to conceal the bankers and capitalists who are the
real governors of the country. Until, therefore, the capitalist
system is destroyed root and branch there can be no genuine
democracy, for the children receive an education vitiated by
the tenets of capitalism, the Government is manipulated by
the wealthy, and the mind of the adult voter is corrupted by a
Press owned by the few. The Communist looks to a dictatorship of the people to sweep away capitalism and all its works,
and thus prepare the way for the classless State in which all are
equal. This may take a long time, but it will eventually be
successful. Strange as it may seem to those who have been
brought up in a different tradition, the Russian Communist
genuinely believes that it is possible to have a dictatorship
which is also democratic. The Party consisting of the *élite*
among the faithful stands between the mass of the people and
the Government. The Party chooses the leaders who are to
govern the State. The supreme leader who has either been
selected by the Party, or who, by intrigue, murder, or outstanding ability, has gained this position, becomes the
embodiment of the will of the people; through him they will
both act and speak. From time to time his authority is confirmed by the people through an election in which all adult
citizens are compelled to vote, but they will have no choice,
for only one candidate, who has been carefully selected by the
Party for his orthodoxy, will be allowed to stand. The dictatorship, whether of an individual or of a group, will purge the
nation of all vestige of feudalism and capitalism; it will crush
any elements of disaffection by liquidating all who show independence, and it will seek popularity by conferring on the
people as many material benefits as conditions allow. So far
there are no signs of the dictatorship in Russia or elsewhere
giving place to more representative government; power once
enjoyed is hard to resign; and the dictator who abdicated
would go in perpetual fear of death by the assassin who had
some wrong to avenge, or of arrest and condemnation by
those who had succeeded him. There is no encouragement for
a dictator to abdicate! The Communist, however, claims that
the dictatorship of the proletariat is a temporary expedient,

and when it has accomplished its work, either the State itself will wither away as no longer necessary in an equalitarian society, or some other means will be found through which the people can express their will. The Western and Eastern conceptions of democracy are therefore very different, and when the Russian speaks of democracy he does not mean what is implied by the Englishman and North American when they use the same term.

There is also a sharp cleavage between revolutionary and constitutional democracy; one form of democracy believes that its aims can only be secured by violence, the other trusts to popular representation in Parliament. In the early years of modern democracy it was assumed that revolution was the only method; this was due to the fact that the American and French Revolutions were carried through by force of arms, and with some justification it was felt that the rulers of Europe would never voluntarily surrender their privileges. During the first half of the nineteenth century the greater part of Europe was fermenting with revolutionary and terrorist movements, and in the forties they reached a climax in a series of insurrections which with comparatively little bloodshed overthrew autocracy, abolished feudalism, and substituted representative government. In the second half of the century, in the countries where the franchise was wide and representative government genuine, it was found that the desired reforms could be obtained by constitutional means. But where autocracy existed, notably in Russia and in States where there was no popular election, democracy continued to rely on violence.

THE TOTALITARIAN STATE

The totalitarian State is in many ways sharply opposed to the Welfare State. Its origin is to be found in the nationalism which was one of the causes leading to the break-up of Medieval Christendom. It is sometimes said that the nation State was the result of the Reformation; but before the Reformation the spirit of nationalism was becoming strong in

England, Scotland, France, Spain, the Netherlands, and elsewhere; the stronger the sense of national independence, the greater was the resentment against the shadowy claims of the Holy Roman Empire, or the more tangible demands of a Papacy which itself had become a State. The totalitarian State was foreshadowed by the absolutism of Louis XIV with his saying '*L'état c'est moi*', but autocracy in Europe was checked by the French Revolution. The totalitarian State as we see it on the Continent is of modern growth. First there was the totalitarianism of Communist Russia when Lenin took over the autocracy of the Tsars and established a régime which demanded the complete and unquestioning submission of all who live within the Soviet Union. In reaction from this there followed the Fascist Revolution with Mussolini in Italy: here the powers of the dictator were exercised through industrial corporations which theoretically had autonomy, but which in practice were controlled by the Fascist Party and its dictator; Hitler rather later in Germany borrowed much from Fascism, but intensified its tyranny and brutality, and proclaimed the doctrine of racial superiority.

The differences in the various totalitarian States can be partly accounted for by the difference in character both of their dictators and of the countries themselves. It would be interesting to examine in some detail the dissimilarities between the great dictators. Stalin, before he made a decision, took advice from many, though the final decision was always his; Hitler, on the other hand, trusted to his intuition and disregarded the opinions of his generals and other advisers. Stalin shunned publicity, very rarely showed himself, and was known chiefly through his pictures, which represented him as the resolute leader or the benevolent father; but to Hitler dramatic publicity was the very breath of life. Mussolini was a rival to Hitler in seeking the limelight; he had no love for his fellow dictator's oratory: 'that Bavarian preaching fellow' was his description of him to an English visitor; but he had more culture than Hitler, and must have mocked at the German Führer's views on art. Both Hitler and Mussolini excited the passionate adoration and homage of their followers. Once

The God-State

I saw Mussolini admitting the younger Fascisti in the amphitheatre on the Pincian in Rome; a vast crowd patiently waited long before the hour of the ceremony; as the clock struck eleven Mussolini appeared; at a run, followed by his panting Cabinet, he inspected the serried ranks of the Italian youth, who with the thousands of spectators went into a wild delirium of enthusiasm; when he reached the platform he held up his hand; there was at once dead silence, then with one voice the youth took the oath of loyalty to the movement, promising to hate all who were opposed to it. When this was finished, the Dictator kissed two of the representatives of the youth just admitted; this was followed by another hysterical outburst of enthusiasm. Hitler, to an even greater degree, excited the adoration of his followers; any sign of lukewarmness might result in arrest and punishment. Only the Pope has the power to excite the same kind of devotion from those who accept him as their head. In the totalitarian State, the will of the people is expressed and embodied in the person of the dictator, whether he is Stalin, Hitler, or Mussolini. George Orwell in *Nineteen Eighty-Four* describes the dictator in the State of the future: 'At the apex of the pyramid comes Big Brother. Big Brother is infallible and all powerful. Every success, every achievement, every happiness, all virtue, are held to issue directly from his leadership and his inspiration. Nobody has ever seen Big Brother. He is a face on the hoardings, a voice on the telescreen . . . Big Brother is the guise in which the Party chooses to exhibit itself to the world. His function is to act as a focussing point for love, fear, and reverence, emotions which are more easily felt towards an individual than towards an organization.'*

Differences in their countries also account for varieties of totalitarianism. Russia has been accustomed to despotic rule; and its vast population can only be administered by a highly centralized bureaucracy. The State was looked on as an agent of repression, so revolution against the State became an essential article in the creed of the Russian Communist until he attained power, when he appropriated and continued to use

*P. 209.

its weapons of tyranny. In Germany the people have always been ready to obey authority, and prefer to be regimented, so they soon submitted to the suppression of independent thought and action by their Nazi rulers. In Italy the people are easy-going, and harshness natural in Russia and Germany was repugnant to them. Fascism in Italy was therefore less rigid and hard than Communism in Russia or Nazism in Germany. With the exception of Yugoslavia, which under Tito has shown a sturdy nationalist independence, the other Communist States imitate, with local variations, the totalitarianism of Russia. Spain under Franco has an absolutist régime which is both stupid and harsh, but can hardly be described as totalitarian.

Four characteristics are found in all the truly totalitarian States.

(1) Each State claims complete autonomy. It makes for itself its own laws of conduct both in relation to other States and to its own subjects. It refuses to regard as binding either an absolute moral law or international law, if this should prove an obstacle to its ambitions and interests. In Mussolini's words, 'The State in fact as the universal ethical will, is the creator of right.' The State recognizes no higher authority than itself. It is a god-State, with the power to make right wrong, and wrong right. Good and evil are determined by the interests of individual States, and therefore are different in States with conflicting aims. The rules of conduct for a non-moral State are set forth in Machiavelli's *The Prince,* in which the moral laws are always subordinated to State necessity: 'A prince therefore who is wise and prudent cannot or ought not to keep his parole, when the keeping of it is to his prejudice and the causes for which he promised removed. Were men all good this doctrine was not to be taught, but because they are wicked and not likely to be punctual with you, you are not obliged to any such strictness with them; nor was there ever any prince that wanted lawful pretence to justify his breach of promise. I might instance many modern examples, and show how many confederations of peace and promises have been broken by the infidelity of princes, and how he that best personated the

fox had the better success. Nevertheless, it is of great conse-
quence to disguise your inclination, and to play the hypocrite
well; and men are so simple in their temper and so submissive
to their present necessities, that he that is neat and cleanly in
his collusions shall never want people to practise them upon.'
It would be easy to give 'many modern examples' showing
how at their convenience dictators have broken the most
solemn promises and torn up recently made treaties in the
attempt to gain some advantage for themselves or their
nation. Most of the totalitarian States aim at economic autarky
as well as at political autonomy. They plan to become entirely
self-supporting, and thus independent of all imports from
foreign countries. Only a few of the larger States are able to do
this without accepting a lower standard of living. It is a policy
which makes impossible commerce with other States, and it is
naturally ruinous to States which depend on trade overseas.
Political autonomy and economic autarky when combined
enclose individual States in prison walls of their own making,
and make impossible freedom of intercourse between the
nations of the world.

(2) The State is not only supreme, it is totalitarian. It claims
the totality of life in all its aspects and in every department of
activity. The State is the supreme reality and against it the
individual has no rights. Mussolini in 'The Doctrine of
Fascism' in the *Enciclopedia Italiana* writes: 'For the Fascist,
everything is in the State, and nothing human or spiritual
exists, much less has value, outside the State . . . Outside the
State there can be neither individuals nor groups (political
parties, associations, syndicates, classes).' The Welfare State
exists for the individual, but for the totalitarian State the individual is an instrument for its use, without any rights of his
own. The totalitarian State is all-pervasive, there is no corner
of life in which refuge can be found from its demands. No
political opposition to it is permitted; the formation of
political parties is forbidden. The Press, the wireless, the
cinema have no independence; they are used as loudspeakers
for the views of the Government. Education is used skilfully
and remorselessly to mould the children from their earliest

years into unthinking, obedient, devoted slaves of the State. The colleges and universities are staffed by those who will inculcate the doctrines approved by the State and none other. Students who might show symptoms of natural independence are refused the opportunity of higher education. Scientific and philosophic theories and discoveries are judged, not by their truth, but by their agreement with the views of the bureaucracy which controls the State. No independent cultural associations are permitted. Games, recreation, pageantry are used for the advancement of the prestige and power of the State. All industries are either owned or controlled by the State, and the workman goes where he is sent to work under conditions which are decided for him. The totalitarian State claims the whole of man and enters, as far as it can, into the very recesses of his being. It annihilates the individual as a free being, degrading him into a serf to be used as it thinks best.

(3) All the totalitarian States rest upon and glorify force. In the Communist State the dictatorship of the proletariat is defended as an interim stage between the bourgeois and completely Communist society. But for over thirty years in Russia the dictatorship has ruled with a rod of iron, and there are no signs that it is in any way weakening. Though the Communist speaks of peace and promotes peace demonstrations and organizations on a gigantic scale, Russia has not demobilized, and has ready for use huge armies and airfleets. Both Mussolini and Hitler openly mocked at peace and glorified war. Mussolini in his article on 'Fascism' states: 'Above all, Fascism, in so far as it considers and observes the future and the development of humanity quite apart from the political considerations of the moment, believes neither in the possibility nor in the utility of perpetual peace. It thus repudiates the doctrine of Pacifism – born of a renunciation of the struggle and an act of cowardice in the face of sacrifice. War alone brings up to their highest tension all human energies and puts the stamp of nobility upon the peoples who have the courage to meet it. All other trials are substitutes, which never really put a man in front of himself in the alternative of life and death.'

The God-State

The totalitarian State rules its subjects by force. No free assemblies exist, so criticism and opposition have to go underground. The rulers are fearful of any attempt to overthrow their power. For their own safety and for the unity of the nation any sign of disaffection must be dealt with at once. The totalitarian State therefore must be a police State, with a huge army of spies and informers ready to report neighbours or personal enemies for deviation from the narrow path of orthodoxy. Mere suspicion may condemn a man to months of imprisonment before he is even told the nature of the charge brought against him. There are huge prisons and still larger labour camps for political offenders as well as for criminals. Occasionally torture is used to gain information or to compel the accused to confess to crimes of deed, or even of thought, which he has never committed.

(4) In the same way, within a nation justice is exercised according to the demands of the State. The judges have no independence, their decisions must be those which agree with the interests of the State: 'the aim of a court of justice in an organic State (such as Russia) is necessarily entirely different from that appropriate to a democracy. In the latter, opposition to the State, if it takes certain clearly specified forms, is a crime. In the former it is always a sin: and the accused as well as the accusers recognize it as a sin. The question for the court to settle, then, is not "can this be proved in accordance with rather strict rules of evidence?" but simply "do we believe this?"; not "can we demonstrate that X has broken the rules?" but simply "Is X a traitor?" that is "Has he acted against the interests of the State?" If the court is satisfied that he has, it is immaterial whether the law has or has not actually foreseen the possibility of the special kind of act which he has perpetrated.'* Sin is not an offence against God, but against the State; and the greatest of all sins is opposition to or criticism of the governing party in the State. The State is supreme above right and wrong, the codes of conduct which in the past have been accepted by civilized men and women are ruthlessly swept aside as bourgeois, deviationist, or as 'dangerous

*T. D. Weldon, *States and Morals*, p. 177.

thinking'. The conception of an absolute law, the law of God, above the changing laws of nations, is treated as a relic of an age of superstition.

The process of intimidation and arrest never ceases. As the promises of the totalitarian States fail, so the murmur of criticism grows, and the methods of repression become more severe. To quote again from George Orwell: 'If you want a picture of the future, imagine a boot stamping on a human face – for ever. The face will always be there to be stamped upon. The heretic, the enemy of society will always be there, so that he can be humiliated and defeated once again. The espionage, the betrayal, the arrests, the tortures, the dis-appearances, the executions will never cease. It will be a world of terror as much as a world of triumph.' For the health of the State, culprits must always be found against whom hatred can be directed and on whom vengeance can be wrought.

The totalitarian State must always be a despotism. If it allows a representative assembly to exist, it is representative only of the Party, the names of the candidates must be approved before the election; the poll is conducted under con-ditions in which secrecy is impossible, and the absentee voter will incur grave suspicion. When the Assembly meets its chief purpose is to approve of the decrees of the dictator, and if he deigns to appear to give him prolonged ovations. In the earlier years of the totalitarian régimes, the real power rested with the Party, whether Communist, Nazi, or Fascist. But this has gradually been appropriated by a small Junta. Above the Party and the Politburo there is the Dictator, who must be perpetually flattered and propitiated by those immediately around him, and adored as a god by the distant multitude. The Communists would, however, deny that their order is a return to the older despotisms; these, they claim, were imposed by tyrants for their own selfish purposes without any responsibility for their subjects. Communist, Fascist, and Nazi alike would declare that their Government more truly represented the people than assemblies returned by popular election, that its Führer or dictator represented the will of the people and the spirit of the whole society, and that it existed for the welfare of the people; and in support of this they would point to social reforms which have been carried through. But no apologist for the totalitarian State would ever claim it brought liberty. Its propaganda, its pageantry, its public entertainments, its schemes of social welfare, are a miserable compensation for the loss of freedom.

CHRISTIANITY AND THE TOTALITARIAN STATE

The totalitarian State, with its demand for the whole of man in its service, should meet everywhere with the opposition of the Christian Church, which calls for allegiance to One who is above all dictators, and which obeys a law more imperative and absolute than any decrees of State. Frequently for a time a concordat or agreement conceals the fundamental opposition between the Church and the totalitarian State; occasionally the State may patronize the Church, or the Church may attempt to use the State for its own purposes. But sooner or later the inherent opposition comes to light. The Church demands complete obedience to God, the State complete obedience to the dictator. The State places the dictator on the throne which belongs to God alone, and calls upon all to fall down and worship. Lenin, Stalin, Hitler, and Mussolini claimed and received from millions the loyalty which should be given to God. Their utterances were treated as the Voice of God, their writings as sacred scriptures, their pictures took the place of icons, their slightest opinion was regarded as a revelation of divine truth; and in the case of Lenin his embalmed body is visited by adoring pilgrims. In a more terrible and more effective form the emperor worship of the Romans has been revived in the twentieth century. Now as then the Christian refuses to join in this worship, for he must obey the commandment, 'Thou shalt worship the Lord thy God, and Him only shalt thou serve.'

8

Communism: its Nature

OF all the foes which to-day oppose the Christian Church Communism is by far the most dangerous. From a theory held by a few extremists of the left it has become a revolutionary and dynamic force which is destroying traditional beliefs and overturning long-established institutions. By argument, fraud, and force it has made gigantic conquests both in the West and the East, and it is now threatening to burst the dykes which protect Western civilization. It has missionaries and evangelists as enthusiastic and self-sacrificing as those who spread the gospel in the early days of Christianity. The predominant form of Communism is bitterly opposed to Christian faith and practice. It is the gravest peril which the Christian Church has had to meet since the time when the victorious armies of a militant Mahommedanism threatened to over-run Europe.

The ideal of the Communist is a universal classless society in which all are equal and in which all share according to their needs through the common ownership of the means of production and distribution. The Communist recognizes that his ideal is still far from realization; Socialism he looks upon as a half-way house towards it, though he detests the British form of Socialism as a dangerous alternative to true Communism. Not even in Russia is complete Communism to be found. Its rulers have carefully avoided claiming that the Soviet Union is yet a Communist State – its official title is 'the Union of Soviet Socialist Republics' – and the Soviet Constitution of 1936 defined the Soviet Union as 'a Socialist State of workers and peasants'. But however many halting places there may be on the way, the thorough-going Communist will never rest until throughout the world there is a classless community in which all property is owned by it for the good of all.

Communism: its Nature

At different times idealists have drawn imaginary pictures of Communist societies, and occasionally small groups have lived together with all things in common. The best-known example of this is described in the Acts of the Apostles, where we read of the first Christian converts in Jerusalem that 'all that believed were together and had all things common; and sold their possessions and goods and parted them to all men, as every man had need.'* And again later we are told, 'And the multitude of them that believed were of one heart and of one soul; neither said any of them that ought of the things which he possessed was his own; but they had all things common ... Neither was there any among them that lacked; for as many as were possessors of lands or houses sold them, and brought the prices of the things that were sold, and laid them down at the apostles' feet; and distribution was made unto every man according as he had need.'† This was clearly the act of a number of men and women under the influence of a wave of religious enthusiasm. It affords no precedent for Communism as we know it to-day. The Communism of the early disciples was voluntary; no compulsion was placed on any of the newly converted to surrender their possessions. Ananias and Sapphira were not punished because they had sold their land and kept for their own use some of the purchase money, but because in giving only part of the price to the common fund they pretended they were giving all. A Christian had full right to retain his property, and if he sold it the money received was his own to use as he thought right. The experiment of owning all things in common seems to have been abandoned very soon, and the Church of Jerusalem was so impoverished by it that St Paul had to collect money from the Gentile Christians to send to the relief of believers in Jerusalem. Later on the monastic Orders repeated the attempt. In the course of time they had great possessions, though individual members possessed no property of their own. The Orders made a valuable contribution to civilization, but the

*Acts II, 44, 45. †Acts IV. 32, 34, 35.

administration of large estates was often beyond their capacity, and on the eve of the Reformation many of them were almost bankrupt. But even if economically the monasteries had been successful, it would be absurd to treat their common life, or the earlier experiment at Jerusalem, as precedents to be followed on a national, still less on a world-wide, scale, in the totally different conditions of the twentieth century. Christian Communism was always on a voluntary and self-supporting basis, but Communism to-day is compulsory, imposed by a State on its citizens, and on a scale which calls for a vast organization if it is to work efficiently.

There is nothing incompatible between voluntary Communism and Christianity; economically and politically Communism may be unworkable and inexpedient, but this does not make it un-Christian. It is possible for a man to be both a Communist and a Christian, and there are some Christians who believe that there is more in common between Christianity and Communism than between Christianity and Capitalism. Even in the States where Marxian Communism has been adopted, there are many citizens who claim to be both loyal Christians and loyal Communists. In Russia itself millions of practising members of the Orthodox Church are obedient subjects of the Soviet State. They accept it as a sound economic order, though they reject its Marxian ideology. In Poland, Czechoslovakia, and Hungary there are Communists who regularly attend the Liturgy or the Mass. It is said that in China among the university students there are some who reconcile their Christianity with their Communism. In condemning systems of Communism as hostile to Christian faith, care must be taken to avoid making it impossible for the Christian Communist to remain within the Church. His economics and politics may be hopelessly wrong, but as long as he believes it is possible to be loyal both to Christ and Communism, and witnesses to the Christian faith by his life, the Church should not confront him with the stern choice of 'Christ or Communism?' But what may be said of individuals cannot always be said of the system or movement to which they have given their allegiance; for it is necessary to distinguish between the individual Communist and Communism. While it is right for the Church to find room for those who describe themselves simply as Communists, it is impossible for it to accept as loyal members those who are convinced Marxian Communists. To-day the term 'Communist' is commonly used to describe those who are followers of Marx and Lenin, and who belong to a movement which is openly and aggressively hostile to Christianity.

MARXIAN COMMUNISM

If Communism in its modern form is to be understood it is essential to know the foundations on which it is built. For Communism is much more than a political system or an economic theory; it consists of a closely knit set of principles and opinions which are taught and held as firmly as the dogmas of the Christian Church. The Communist looks upon the Manifesto of 1848 by Karl Marx and Engels, on Marx's *Capital*, and in a lesser degree on the works of Lenin and Stalin, as his Scriptures, which contain a creed from which he may not depart.

The first article of the Marxian faith is that the material world is the fundamental reality. Christianity, according to William Temple, is 'the most materialistic religion in the world'; but it teaches that material things are created, used, and interpenetrated by spirit. The Marxist Communist holds that ideals proceed from matter, and that apart from it there is no reality. This does not mean that the Communist has no ideals, still less that he neglects art, drama, music, and the other aspects of life which are often described as spiritual; but he holds they are the outcome of matter and depend on it for their existence. If all ideals, art, and religion itself come from matter, it follows there can be no God, no revelation, no future life. Religion is the great delusion, the creation of fear, a device to stupefy the poor and the oppressed, and the opium to prevent them from revolting against the wrongs they suffer.

Secondly, history can only be understood as the conflict between economic forces. Here we come to one of the most difficult aspects of the Marxian creed, its dialectic. Dialectic is the argument and clash between contending claims and movements. The dialectic consists of a thesis – the statement of an argument; an antithesis – the contradiction and criticism of the original thesis; and from debate and conflict there results the synthesis, a new statement born of the clash between the thesis and the antithesis, a conclusion different from both, but preserving what is true in them; this now in its turn becomes the thesis, and will presently be exposed to the same process of criticism and transformation. But Marx did not confine this dialectical process to mental argument; he applied it to the whole of history. Throughout history there is persistent movement; there is nothing static; established society is attacked and criticized, until it is destroyed and a new order takes its place. But though over a long period there may be a number of minor changes, they cannot continue indefinitely, for there comes a moment when there is a jump forward, and something appears which is qualitatively, and not quantitatively, different.

The third article of faith is that this movement of history is due to continuous struggle over the possession of the means of production and exchange. The key to history, according to Marx, is to be found in the changes which have taken place in the ownership and control of the means of production and of exchange. In the past historians had interpreted history as the record of political, social, and national conflicts, but Marx saw in them only the struggle between opposing economic forces. It is now generally accepted that he made a valuable contribution to the understanding of history by the emphasis he gave to economic factors. These were almost entirely ignored by the older historians. Marx over-stated his case when he attempted to account for *all* historical changes by economic causes, and claimed that human intelligence, law, religion, and every form of culture are only the superstructure built on and conditioned by a vast economic sub-structure. But when large reservations have been made for the non-economic factors which have been present in historic changes, it remains true that Marx's thesis 'that the economic factor is fundamental for all social institutions and particularly for their historic development' is of great importance. 'It has exercised a profound influence, and all modern writers are indebted to him even if they do not know it. Any return to pre-Marxist social theory is inconceivable.'* This dialectical economic approach to history is illustrated by the present economic position. Feudalism was opposed until it gave way to capitalism, but capitalism now in its turn is attacked by the proletariat, who will continue their assaults until it is abolished and its place taken by Socialism, under which the workers will own the means of production and distribution. Marx assumes that the development from slavery to feudalism, from feudalism to capitalism, and capitalism to Socialism is inevitable; but it will not be a gradual progressive development; the final change will be the result of revolution. The belief in the inevitability of Communism has been an inspiration to millions. It is always encouraging in the midst of a severe struggle for one of the contestants to know that he is certain to win, and any danger that this might lead to slackening of effort is counteracted by an equally strong conviction that the date of victory depends upon the zeal and work of those who are striving for the new order. Though the new order is bound to come, its advent will be sooner or later according to the devotion of those struggling for it. Marx prophesies this in the closing paragraph of his chapter on 'The Historical Tendencies of Capitalist Accumulation'. 'Along with the constantly diminishing number of the magnates of capital, who usurp and monopolize all advantages of this process of transformation, grows the mass of misery, oppression, slavery, degradation, exploitation; but with this too grows the revolt of the working class, a class always increasing in numbers, disciplined, united, organized by the very mechanism of the process of capitalist production itself. The monopoly of capital becomes a fetter upon the mode of production, which has sprung up and flourished along with it and under it. Centralization of the means of production and socialization of labour at last reach a point where they become incompatible with their capitalist integument. This

*R. N. Carew Hunt, *The Theory and Practice of Communism*, p. 42.

integument is burst asunder. The knell of capitalist private property sounds. The expropriators are expropriated.'*

The fourth article of faith is that there must be continuous and relentless class warfare between the capitalist and the proletariat; capitalism must be abolished if the worker is to have justice; as the owners of the means of production will not voluntarily surrender their possessions, they must be taken from them by force. Capitalism is the great enemy. Marx advances two arguments in support of this. First, by his highly questionable theory of surplus value, he claims that all value is created by labour, some of it is returned to labour in the shape of wages, but the rest is appropriated by the capitalist for his own use. This theory would not be accepted by most present-day economists who teach that value is created by organization, by management, by the use of savings, of land and of raw materials, as well as by labour, and these all have a right to some share of the profits. Marx's other argument is stronger: he shows the injustice and misery which so often resulted from the unscrupulous use of the power given by the private ownership of the means of production. He quotes a mass of evidence from official inquiries on the evils of the capitalist system as seen in the mines and factories in the first half of the nineteenth century. Though in most countries the worst evils of the capitalist system have been abolished, the Communist agitator continues to stir up hate and anger against the private capitalist, and urges that no just society will be possible until private property is abolished, and the means of production and exchange are owned by the people and used for their benefit.

From this there follows a fifth article of faith. Everything must be subordinated to the determination to destroy capitalism and to create the Communist State. Nothing must stand in the way of this. Traditional morality must be rejected as a system of ethics for the protection of the capitalist and the bourgeois. Truth, honesty, pity are to be rejected if they obstruct the advance of the revolutionary forces. As there is no God, there can be no absolute morality. The good is that

Capital, p. 788 (Swan Sonnenschein & Co.).

which promotes the Communist cause; evil is that which hinders its progress.

A sixth article of faith is that before Socialism passes into complete Communism there will be an intermediate stage. The newly enfranchised proletariat will not be capable at once of carrying through the great changes which are necessary. For a time their interests must be safeguarded by a dictatorship, the dictatorship of the proletariat. Unlike the dictatorships of the capitalist and the bourgeois, it will act in the interests of the people. It will protect the new order both from traitors and counter-revolutionaries within the nation, and from external enemies who threaten to destroy the new State by armed intervention. It will be strong and merciless in defending the safety of the people. It will not be elected by the people, though they will be given various opportunities of expressing approval and support. The dictatorship will only pass away when all danger of counter-revolution has been finally removed. So far in the Communist States there have appeared no signs of the approaching end of their dictatorships; on the contrary, they seem more firmly established than ever and more relentless in crushing any threat of opposition or criticism directed against those in power.

To the Marxian articles of faith Lenin added yet another – namely, that imperialism is an evil which must be destroyed with capitalism. Imperialism he regarded as the logical outcome and the final phase of capitalism. When the capitalists had reached the limit of their activities in Europe and America, and great combines and trusts had covered the ground available for production and distribution, they looked elsewhere for fields on which large profits could be reaped. These they found in backward countries in Africa and Asia, in which they could not only sell their products, but could obtain raw material and labour at low prices. It thus became necessary for the expansion of capitalism that it should secure markets where there had been no economic progress. The worst evils of the Industrial Revolution were revived in countries where there were no Trade Unions to protect the worker from exploitation, and where the employer could impose upon him his own terms. The scramble for colonies commenced. This brought the capitalist Powers into rivalry which eventually must lead to war. The orthodox Marxist attributes the two world wars to imperialist rivalries and aggression. The Communists therefore make anti-imperialism part of their programme and attempt to make the proletariat of the backward countries class conscious, fomenting discontent, and inciting them to revolt as the victims of exploitation.

Marxism is an optimistic creed. The gospel it preaches is that there is a good time coming. The Communist believes in this as fervently as the early Christians believed in the immediate return of their Lord. But while the coming of the Lord would be an act of God independent of anything that man can do, the good time of Communism can be hastened by human action. Before it comes there will be days of tribulation, of war, of suffering, and of bloodshed; but these will bring nearer the final triumph. When that day comes there will no longer be conflicting classes, no longer warring nations, no longer oppression and tyranny, no longer compulsion by the State; but after capitalism has been destroyed 'democracy itself will begin to wither away due to the simple fact that, freed from capitalistic slavery, from the untold horrors, savageries, and infamies of capitalistic exploitation, people will gradually become accustomed to the observance of the elementary rules of social life that have been known for centuries, and repeated for thousands of years in all school books: they will become accustomed to using them without force, without compulsion, without subordination, without the special apparatus for compulsion which is called the State'.*
This is indeed Utopia! A Utopia only reached by ignoring the dialectical struggle on which Marx elsewhere has insisted so strongly, for there is no reason to think it would come to an end with the establishment of the Communist State; a Utopia only possible if human nature were so completely changed that envy, hatred, greed, and fear vanished with

*Quoted from Lenin in J. C. Bennett's *Christianity and Communism*, p. 16.

private property. On the contrary, the history of Communist States shows that among the party leaders, fear and hatred lead to the frequent liquidation of possible rivals and personal foes.

RUSSIAN COMMUNISM

The Russian Revolution changed Communism from a theory into a dynamic and powerful system. The long-predicted revolution took place, and the world now can see a Socialist-Communist State in existence. Marx was proved wrong in one important respect: he had expected that the revolution would take place in the more advanced industrial nations when the contrast between the wealth of capitalism and the poverty of the proletariat became intolerable. Instead, the lot of the workers became more favourable with the increased prosperity of the captains of industry. The revolution, in fact, took place in the least developed of European countries, for Russia was far behind both Western Europe and North America. Its rulers were incompetent and corrupt, its aristocracy was luxurious and selfish, its industries were inefficient and incapable of competing with those in neighbouring States, its peasantry, huge in numbers, were patient, hard-working, and uneducated, separated by a gulf from their landlords. The Russian Revolution is one of the most dramatic and stupendous events in history. Within a few years the ancient régime had been wiped out, the aristocratic and middle classes exterminated, the urban industries developed beyond recognition, the methods of agriculture transformed the land, and the means of production and distribution appropriated by the State. Russia, once regarded as a gigantic colossus with feet of clay, has become a powerful and well-armed giant, threatening the peace and freedom of the whole world. For the first time in history a working-class State has been created. I visited Moscow in the autumn of 1943 and nothing impressed me more than the fact that it was a working-class city; everywhere there were crowds of working-class men and women, in the large and prosperous-looking streets and squares as well as in those which were mean and badly built. Instinctively I looked for people of a different class in the centre of the city, but everywhere it was the same, working-class folk in the roads on their way to and from work, in the trams, in the few carriages, in the shops, in the queues waiting outside the cinemas. I saw no one in rags, none of the outward signs of poverty often seen in South Italy, but everywhere the drab and worn clothing of working folk who were suffering from the hardships of war. Occasionally the monotony in dress was broken by the uniform of soldiers on leave, or by the smart dress of some actress at the opera or theatre. It was the same in the crowded churches and in the crowds standing outside: they all consisted of working-class people. In the Opera House it was a young and intelligent audience on the night I was there, neatly dressed and well behaved, all of them belonging to the working class. It was extraordinarily impressive to find everywhere these multitudes. I had been told that the people in the streets would look over their shoulders to see if they were followed by a spy, and that I should never see a smile nor hear a laugh; this certainly was not my experience; the crowds of working men were the same, only less well fed and clothed, as I had often seen on their way to and from the dockyard at Portsmouth, no gaiety and no sullenness. They were kindly, friendly people, interested in seeing in their midst an Englishman wearing openly a purple cassock, and very ready to help him if they thought he had lost his way or needed information. Multitudes and multitudes of weekly wage-earners everywhere impressed me in Moscow even more than the Kremlin itself.

It is often thought necessary to speak as if the Russian Revolution had been undiluted evil and had brought only misery to a country which in the past had been happy and contented. I shall have plenty to say later about the evils of Communism in Russia and elsewhere, but it is absurd to deny that it has brought some advantages to backward countries. It is difficult to say to what extent there have been advances in material prosperity since the Revolution, for the war caused such widespread suffering and loss. It is not always remembered that the Germans came within forty miles or so of

Moscow. Everywhere behind the line of the enemy advance there was devastation. I was taken to see the ruins of a famous monastery which the Germans had deliberately destroyed. On the site of the town near which it had been built there could be seen standing amidst the weeds, rows of stoves, the only remains of what once had been a flourishing town of over twenty thousand people. On my way to Moscow I had been flown low over Stalingrad; there was not a house which had been left with a roof; it was a city of blackened ruin, worse than anything I have since seen in Berlin. All this destruction must be taken into account before it is said that the poverty of Russia is due to the Revolution. From all I heard, and from the testimony of Englishmen who knew Russia before the Revolution, there would by now have been a considerable advance in the standard of living if the war had not intervened with such disastrous results.

There has certainly been great progress in education. Before the Revolution four out of every five were unable to read or write, now it is only one out of every five who cannot do so. Great care is taken over the welfare of the children; they are a privileged class. I went at very short notice to a charming nursery school in connexion with one of the factories: the mothers on going to work left their children there for the day; it was a clean, spacious building, with plenty of light and air, and attractive toys for the children. I was warned that this might have been arranged for my special benefit! I put it to the test by asking if the children could sing me an action song, such as the young children are taught at home, and which I knew could not be done without many rehearsals. The children were at once called together and sang and acted beautifully, clapping their hands, pulling the ropes of imaginary bells and so on. The universities in peace-time are crowded with students. I noticed that while many of the shop windows were empty, the book-shops were well stocked with Russian and foreign books, and nearly always there were young men looking at them. The progress in Russia since the Revolution has been summed up by a competent authority: 'The nation has, nevertheless, advanced far in most fields of its existence.

Its material apparatus of production, which about 1930 was still inferior to that of any medium-sized European nation, has so greatly and so rapidly expanded that Russia is now the first industrial power in Europe and the second in the world. Within little more than one decade the number of her cities and towns doubled, and her urban population grew by thirty millions. The number of schools of all grades has very impressively multiplied. The whole nation has been sent to school. Its mind has been so awakened that it can hardly be put back to sleep again.'*

Post-Revolution Russia claims to be a Socialist and not a Communist State. It is a Socialist State, for the State owns the means of production and distribution. There is no private ownership of land or of industry. The State owns all the mines, the docks, the factories, the banks, the railways, and the air and shipping services. Private individuals sometimes possess their own cars, but no one will be found in the whole of Russia who holds a share in or draws interest from a motor-car company.

There are three marked differences between Russia to-day and the Communist State predicted by Marx and Lenin. In a perfect Communism the State will have 'withered' away; if it survives at all its functions will be greatly curtailed, for they will be unnecessary in a society in which all will be equal, in which there will be neither social classes nor money inequalities, and all private property will have been abolished. Russia is at present far from this position. It is under the dictatorship of the proletariat. This really is the Political Bureau of the Communist Party, commonly called the Politburo. This body, consisting of fourteen members chosen by the Party, is responsible for all decision and action both at home and abroad. Parallel to it is the U.S.S.R. Council of Ministers, the Cabinet, responsible to the Supreme Council or Parliament which meets about once a year. Many of the chief ministers are also on the Politburo which has the real power, while the Cabinet is only the façade, behind which the Party acts. Stalin was a member of the Politburo as well as Prime

*I. Deutscher, *Stalin: A Political Biography*, p. 568.

Minister. He was looked upon as the Dictator, the Ruler, the Father, and even the Saviour of the people.

Communism as an ideal is egalitarian: all citizens will be of the same rank, and all will receive the same payment: Lenin regarded it as a fundamental principle that State officials should receive the same pay as a qualified manual worker. It was thought that service rendered to the community would be a sufficient incentive to work. Experience soon showed that this was not the case, and in 1931 Stalin ordered equality in wages to cease, describing it as a petit-bourgeois deviation. Men were to be paid for their actual work, only under Communism would each receive according to his needs. The discrepancy in wages became more marked with the introduction of Stakhanovism: this had its origin in a miner named Stakhanov producing in one shift fourteen times the amount of coal normally produced in the same time. This feat was given the widest publicity, and all other workers were urged to imitate him. The Stakhanovites as a reward for their work received larger wages than other labourers. In the Soviet Union the difference in incomes is nothing like so great as that between a big shareholder and a labourer in Great Britain or America; but within the working class the discrepancies are greater than elsewhere. In 1935 'an ordinary non-Stakhanovite coal miner doing auxiliary work underground earned 170 roubles per month. The wage of a non-Stakhanovite coalgetter was 400–500 roubles. The monthly earnings of a Stakhanovite were more than 1,600 roubles ... In 1948 the basic pay of a coalgetter amounted to as much as 2,000 roubles per month, that of an auxiliary above ground worker was 250 roubles, one-eighth of the coalgetter's wage. Since the early thirties wage policy in the coal industry has fluctuated, now reducing the discrepancy and now widening it even more; but on the balance the trend has been towards more and not less inequality. In 1948 there were twelve categories of wages in the iron and steel industry, eight in machine-building, but only six in industries producing consumer goods. In addition to higher wages Stakhanovites enjoy important privileges: free sojourn in rest homes and sanatoria owned by the trade unions: the right to have home tutors for their children without payment, and a number of other services which have raised the Stakhanovites' standard of living far above that of the ordinary worker. Stakhanovism has made of Russia an almost classical example of a labour aristocracy.'*

Socialist Russia also allows personal property, the ownership of which would be forbidden in the complete Communist State. I had an interesting illustration of this in a visit I paid to a Collectivist Farm some sixty miles from Moscow. Through our interpreter I was able to question the chairman and some of the committee of the farm. I was told that the land, the plant, and the tools belonged to the State. The State decided what should be grown, and how much ought to be produced. When the harvest had been gathered the State agents purchased the crops at a low rate, in lieu of the rent which would otherwise have been charged. The surplus which remained was first used to meet certain charges on the farm such as the community centre, the crèche, and the aged; but after these charges had been deducted the rest was divided among the farmers; they could do with their personal share what they liked: they could save it, or they could buy with it clothes, extra food, or furniture. Over and above this each farmer had an acre of land attached to his house; here again he could use this as he liked, and the produce belonged to him entirely: he could consume it or take it to the neighbouring market town for sale.† The simple wooden house in which he lived was often built by himself, and in that case it belonged to him. I asked what happened if he should leave the farm, and the answer was he could sell the house to an incoming farmer, but as the land belonged to the State he could not sell it. In Moscow there were many registered shops to which private possessions were taken to be sold: again the owner received the purchase money, subject to the payment of a State tax. Private property on a small scale such as this is allowed in the

*I. Deutscher, *Soviet Trade Unions*, pp. 113 and 114.

†It is said that since 1950 there have been considerable changes in this system, and in the direction of a more complete Communism.

Socialist State, but there is no possibility of investment except in Government Stock. I was told that if ever there should be the danger of individuals accumulating considerable sums, the State would certainly impose a tax! If the Communist is criticized for the fact that in Russia there are inequalities in salaries and wages, and that private property is permitted, he will admit this at once, but he will add Russia does not yet claim to be Communist; it is advancing towards it, and when the goal is reached there will be no inequalities in payment and no need for private possessions.

NO JUSTICE

Russian Communism suffers from two fatal defects. There is no justice and no freedom. The Russian would deny the charge that there is no justice; but would claim that while in capitalist countries the scales are weighted against the poor in favour of the rich, in the Soviet Union all are equal before the law. There is some truth in this statement, for there is reason to believe that Soviet judges do decide justly between private litigants. But when the State is the accuser and a citizen the defendant, the citizen is condemned before he is heard. Where the State is concerned, justice must be subordinate to its welfare and safety; if it is expedient that one man, or if need be many, should suffer rather than that the State should suffer, let him suffer, and all others if they should come even under the suspicion of offences against the State. If once the citizen falls in the hands of the secret police, it is unlikely that he will be found innocent.

Both in Russia and in other Communist countries the suspected is arrested, subjected to months of imprisonment, and to day and night interrogation until his will is broken and he is ready to confess to anything when brought to trial. Or, if he is a member of the Party, though he knows he is innocent of the charge, he is often so worked on that he comes to believe that he can render a last service to the Party by confessing that the fact he has come under suspicion proves that he has sinned against the State. There is no reason to think that in all these cases physical torture is applied; the will can be broken by hunger, sleeplessness, and long suspense, until sheer weariness, combined with fear that his relatives may suffer through his obstinacy, cause the accused to admit the charges brought against him. Injustice on a larger scale is dealt out to whole classes. At one period of the French Revolution the mob made their victims show their hands; if they were soft and clean they were condemned at once to death as aristocrats. In the height of the Russian terror there was no chance of acquittal if the accused was of noble or bourgeois birth. 'While rejecting the method of individual terror of the nihilist, on grounds of expediency rather than of morals, the Bolsheviks in their struggle to seize and hold power supported and practised mass terror. The policy was clearly stated by M. Latsis, one of the chiefs of the Cheka: "We are not waging war against particular individuals. We are exterminating the bourgeoisie as a class. Don't look for evidence to prove that the accused acted by deed or word against the Soviet power. The first question you should ask him is: To what class he belongs, what is his origin, his education, his training, and his profession. This should determine the fate of the accused."'* It is impossible to discover how many million were murdered or imprisoned in the first years of the Revolution, not because of any specific crime against the State, but solely because through their parentage, education, and profession they were not members of the proletarian class. Though the mass terror is at an end, yet every month there are scores, possibly hundreds, who in Communist countries, without trial or possibility of defence, are arrested and disappear into darkness.

NO FREEDOM

In practice Communism means the loss of freedom. In all civilized countries the freedom of the individual is protected by the law; for the courts stand between him and his arbitrary arrest by the State. In a Communist country, as in all totalitarian States, the individual may be arrested at any moment,

*G. S. Counts and Nucia Lodge, *The Country of the Blind*, p. 22.

imprisoned without knowing the nature of the accusation and sentenced to long periods of imprisonment or even to death, because a charge has been brought against him by one of the State police. Nor is it only the accused who can be deprived of his freedom – his relatives may in certain circumstances also be deprived of it. A Government Decree of 1934 directed against desertion by a member of the armed forces laid down that: 'All members of his family who are of age, provided that they in any way aided the contemplated or accomplished treason, or even knew of it and failed to notify the Soviet authorities, are punished by imprisonment for five to ten years and confiscation of all their property. The remaining members of the family of the traitor who are of age and reside with him or were dependent on his support at the time of the commission of the crime are deprived of electoral rights and are subject to exile for five years to remote regions of Siberia.'

Under the guise of forced labour Russia has reintroduced slavery. Those who have been taken as prisoners of war, or compulsorily deported from their native land, or who have been convicted either for ordinary crimes or for holding opinions regarded as dangerous or subversive by the State are sentenced to long terms of forced labour. Various estimates have been made as to the number who are compelled to work for the State as a punishment. The lowest estimate is ten million, but there are some who think the figure should be twenty-five million. From time to time there leak through the Iron Curtain reports of the extreme severity of many of these camps, to which the condemned are sent to carry out work for which no free labour is available. The conditions are appalling, and the death rate very high. It is by means of this forced labour that Russia is able to accomplish many gigantic public works which would otherwise have been beyond her financial resources. She has persistently refused requests that a United Nations Commission should be allowed to investigate the conditions of those who are victims of slave labour. This slavery is a means of terrorizing those who might be disaffected, of making profitable use of enemies of the State, and of buttressing the Soviet economy; experts who have given special study to Soviet economy believe it would collapse if forced labour were abolished.

Large, however, as the numbers are of those who are working under conditions of slavery, they are small compared to the great mass of workers in the Soviet Union. In theory these have the widest possible freedom. The Statute of the Soviet Trade Unions adopted in 1949 declares in its Preamble, 'The Constitution guarantees to all citizens of the Soviet Union the right to work, the right to rest, the right to education, the right to material security in old age, in case of illness and loss of capacity for work. The woman in the U.S.S.R. enjoys equal rights with the man in all fields of economic, governmental, cultural, and social political life. Freedom of expression, freedom of the press, freedom of meetings, and also the right to associate in social organizations are guaranteed by law to the citizens of the U.S.S.R. in the interests of the workers and for the purpose of strengthening the socialist order.' This is the ideal, but practice in several respects falls far short of it. Lenin was opposed to direction of labour, in theory it had to remain 'free', but it became necessary to find workers for the new industries in the towns, and agreements were therefore made with the managements of collective farms to supply specified numbers of their redundant workers for the towns. 'This was made possible by a phenomenal influx of the rural population into the cities and towns of the Soviet Union, an influx for which hardly a single historic precedent can be found – it involved twenty-four million people between 1926 and 1939.'* The contracts between the managements of the farms and factories were voluntary at any rate in theory. They could be defended by the necessity of finding employment for a great number of peasants who lost their work when the farms were mechanized: 'On the other hand there was massive compulsion. The individual peasant singled out as redundant by the chairman of the collective farm had no choice but to leave: he was as good as expropriated.'†

The labourer, though compulsorily directed to a job, was

---

*I. Deutscher, *Soviet Trade Unions*, p. 84.
†*Op. cit.*, p. 85.

free to leave it. This freedom was exercised at first on such a large scale that industrial efficiency suffered. Steps had to be taken to discourage the excessive fluidity of labour. Encouragements were given to persuade the workers to remain in their factory for longer periods; when these failed, sterner steps had to be taken. Severe penalties were imposed in the case of notorious slackers and absentees. Those who had left their work without permission were liable to be evicted from their dwellings within ten days without alternative accommodation being found for them. 'Often this entailed deportation to a forced labour camp. The fear of the forced labour camp came now to play the rôle that the fear of unemployment had played under capitalism – it maintained labour discipline.'*

A British Trade Unionist would feel that the Trade Unions in the Soviet Union are without the freedom which he would regard as necessary for their effective working. They have no power to regulate wages or conditions of labour. These are decided by the Government. The weapon of the strike against unsatisfactory conditions is illegal. The Russian Trade Union exists to encourage production, to recruit new workers, and to see that they are properly trained and protected. Mr Deutscher says in his informative book on Soviet Trade Unions: 'No self-respecting union in the capitalist countries would act as the recruiting agent for the industrial management: but, on the other hand, few trade unions have even concerned themselves with the raw industrial recruit (as distinct from the skilled or half skilled and settled worker) as the Soviet trade unions have.'†

Intellectual as well as spiritual freedom is discouraged by Communism. Truth is what is beneficial to the State, falsehood what is harmful to it. At any moment a scientist may have to renounce some theory which he is convinced is true because the Party decides that it is inopportune or dangerous; or a writer may be condemned because his views are not in accordance with those which are favoured by the party in power. Censure by the central committee of the Party means

*Op. cit., p. 92.   †Op. cit., p. 86.

ruin, even if its members are incompetent to pronounce any intelligent opinion on science or culture. Scientists, artists, dramatists, and men of letters know that they have only relative freedom, and that unless they at all times put the interests of the State first, they may be condemned as reactionaries and enemies of the people.

An example of this was given in the dispute over heredity. Most scientists now deny that characters acquired in a lifetime can be inherited. Until recently Russian scientists appeared to agree with scientists elsewhere in this opinion. This, however, was contrary to the older theory of which Michurin had been the protagonist – namely, that characteristics could be so changed in an individual lifetime that they could be inherited by future generations. A young scientist, T. D. Lysenko, vehemently championed this view, and declared that it was false to deny the transmission of acquired traits. He attacked those who held the generally accepted view of western scientists as reactionaries and bourgeoisie. Lysenko's views were formally approved by the Party and welcomed by the farmers, who liked to think that science would rapidly enrich their crops by the transmission of improved qualities. As soon as it was known that the Central Committee of the All Union Communist Party had approved of Lysenko, the matter was regarded as closed. Critics and opponents were at once silenced or made grovelling submissions of error. Letters and telegrams by the thousand were sent rejoicing over Lysenko's triumph and denouncing his opponents. The Academy of Science immediately passed a resolution dismissing a noted Academician who had held the condemned views, closing scientific institutions suspected of unorthodox teaching, and ordering the removal of all who held these opinions from any position on teaching or editorial staffs; text-books were to be revised to bring them into harmony with the view of Michurin and Lysenko. 'This definitive, inflexible, and powerful resolution passed a death sentence on several important institutions of Soviet science and cast into outer darkness fifteen or more distinguished scientists. Also it constituted a clear mandate for the Party to conduct a heresy hunt through the ranks of biologists and workers in the related sciences. Against this onslaught the individual is helpless, being protected neither by constitutional guarantees nor by opportunities for employment under other auspices.'*

Men of science are not alone in coming under condemnation if their views do not meet with the approval of the Communist Party. In the last few years journalists, dramatists, and composers of music have been censured and exhorted either because they have not attacked Western culture with sufficient ferocity, or because they have not given unqualified admiration to the Soviet Union. The publication and presentation of plays by English and American dramatists was condemned in 1946 by the Central Committee of the Communist Party as 'placing the Soviet stage at the disposal of the propaganda of reactionary bourgeois ideology and morals. It has constituted an effort to poison the consciousness of the Soviet people with a world view hostile to Soviet society and to revive the vestiges of capitalism in consciousness and life.'† Music has also come under the censorship. Many of the best-known Russian composers were compelled to confess their deviation from the strait paths of Communist orthodoxy and to promise to amend their ways in the future. 'Zhdanov who was responsible until his death in 1948 for the doctrinal purity and aims of the Soviet State, at one time carried the heresy hunting into the world of music. Prokofiev, Shostakovich and the rest of the composers were all lined up and constrained to more or less humiliating recantations and confessions of Western deviationism. The abject grovelling of those men of genius constituted a disgusting spectacle for those who believe in freedom of thought and expression or in human dignity.'‡ Zhdanov, responsible for this correction of music, is generally reported to have no personal knowledge of any music over and above that of popular melodies and ballads!

The censorship of the Press in all Communist States is severe: no newspapers are allowed which would give news

*G. S. Counts and Nucia Lodge, *The Country of the Blind*, p. 221.
†*Op. cit.*, p. 121.
‡Maurice Peterson, *Both Sides of the Curtain*, p. 278.

not acceptable to the Government; and there is an equally severe censorship on the sale of books. Some foreign books can be obtained, but they are few compared to the many not allowed to cross the frontiers of a Communist country. In Czechoslovakia since the Revolution there has been no free Press: publishing has become the responsibility of the State, and no book can be published without the previous approval of some Government Ministry. In 1950 it was ordered that no book published before 1945 can be sold. In China 'art and literature, the theatre and the cinema, are dragooned into the Party pattern. The newspapers publish only what is acceptable to Peking, while every effort is made, for instance by the exclusion of foreign news agencies, to cut the Chinese people off from knowledge of what is happening abroad.'*

To sum it up – in a Communist State, there is no freedom of person from arbitrary arrest and condemnation, no freedom in choice of occupation, no freedom of speech, no freedom in science, literature, and the arts. The dictatorship of the proletariat exercises complete control over the lives of the citizens, and though it is claimed that this is only temporary until all danger of a counter-revolution has been removed, there are no signs of the weakening of a control more thorough and far-reaching even than that exercised in the days of irresponsible despots.

*Leonard Constantine, 'Communism and the Chinese Tradition', a broadcast printed in the *Listener*, 18th January, 1951.

9

Communism: its Methods

COMMUNISM has spread during the last fifty years with amazing rapidity. This cannot be explained solely by the use of force and of unscrupulous propaganda. There are other causes which have attributed to its phenomenal expansion.

Communism has come to millions as a gospel of hope. It offers deliverance to multitudes whose lives are hard and wretched, from whom starvation is never far off, and who see no possibility of improving their lot. It incites them to rise against their oppressors and to break the chains which bind them. To the hungry and the poverty-stricken it promises a new social order in which all will be free and equal; but before this hope is realized the exploited must rise against the exploiter, the peasant against the landlord, the dark races against their white masters, and the proletariat against the capitalist. If they do so they are assured that their victory is inevitable; only the date is uncertain, and this will depend on the degree of courage and resolution they show. This confident promise of a new and just social order has met with an enthusiastic response from millions who in the past had no hope for themselves or their fellows.

To many who have never had to suffer from poverty or social injustice, Communism has come as a substitute for Christianity. The most generous and enthusiastic of the younger men and women in every nation always feel the need for some cause to which they can give themselves with complete and self-forgetting devotion. Communism both offers them an ideal and claims their lives. Its ideal is to be realized in this world, and not in some shadowy future existence; here and now it calls for the removal of social injustice and the establishment of a new order of justice and peace; here and now in this world inequalities due to birth and money can be abolished, race divisions transcended, and a society created from which oppression and poverty will be banished and all will enjoy the natural fruits of the earth and the products of human labour and skill. To hasten the coming of this earthly kingdom Communism has its Church. Instead of a pope at its head, it has a Lenin or Stalin, the representative and father of the new community; instead of a hierarchy of ecclesiastics, it has the different grades of the Party; instead of the Bible, it has Marx's *Capital*, supplemented by the almost equally sacred books of Lenin and Stalin; instead of sin, there is private property to fight against and destroy. Communism offers a fellowship as wide as that of the Christian Church, embracing men of all nationalities and races. In a book with the title *The God that Failed*, six ex-Communists give the reasons which attracted them to Communism; one of the most powerful was membership in a world-wide fellowship, free of all race and class distinctions. Communism is a religion promising Paradise on this side of the grave, offering a world-wide brotherhood, and demanding unlimited sacrifice for the sake of the cause. It thus makes a strong appeal to youth and to idealists, who hope to find in it a substitute for the older supernatural religion, and a cause to which they can give themselves with complete surrender.

There are others, colder in temperament, who are attracted to Communism by its logical and clear-cut statement of an intellectual position from which the mysterious and supernatural have been eliminated. Its materialistic basis, its dialectical system, its uncompromising dogmatism, its carefully knit organization, and its detailed programme make a strong appeal to a certain type of intellectual. Physical scientists seem especially to be attracted by a system which is so thoroughgoing in its materialism and so relentlessly logical in its conclusions.

Opponents of Communism weaken their cause if they ignore the idealism of the motives which have led many to support it. But Communism as a world power relies also on unscrupulous propaganda, on revolution, and on the use of terror to intimidate or destroy those suspected of disaffection. These are the most powerful weapons in the armoury of revolutionary Communism, and must be understood if its nature is to be truly estimated.

PROPAGANDA

All religious and political movements use propaganda. There is nothing wrong in its use; the keen Churchman or the member of a political party will use it to spread the opinions he holds. Propaganda can be efficient or inefficient, truthful or false. Every movement, whether religious or political, is justified in making its propaganda as effective as possible; today the means of doing so are far greater than anything in the past; the Press, the wireless, the cinema, and now television enable the propagandist to speak to far larger numbers than the evangelists or agitators of previous centuries. Propaganda can either keep to facts and to legitimate deductions from them, trusting that the truth will commend itself; or it can ignore them, or distort them so that they are unrecognizable and bear no relation to anything which has taken place; or deliberate and malicious lies are broadcast to win converts and to discredit enemies. The charge directed against Communist propaganda is that it is unscrupulous and employed without any regard to truth.

The most elementary form of propaganda is through personal argument. Christianity spread through individuals knowing their faith and the reasons for it, and by their courage and skill in presenting it to their contemporaries. The Communist Party uses effectively the same method of personal witness for the propagation of its creed. Its members are thoroughly instructed until they know what Communism means and the arguments they can most effectively advance in its support. They are trained to criticize existing institutions, to reply to objections and to use the arguments most likely to persuade. There is a remarkable similarity in their reasoning, even in the very phrases they use. There is something hard and mechanical in their arguments, not unlike the records on a gramophone, which can be repeated frequently until they are worn out, though compensation for weakness in reasoning is found in the enthusiasm with which in the colleges, factories, and at the docks a number of reliable and trained Communists expound and defend their creed.

The Communist also employs to the fullest extent modern methods of propaganda. First there is the wireless: the effectiveness of the B.B.C. during the war was largely due to its accuracy; it never intentionally distorted or misrepresented and it gave bad as well as good news. The Nazi propaganda on the wireless mixed falsehood with truth, but so often the inaccuracy of its statements was known previously by those who heard them, that before the war was over it was assumed, often quite wrongly, that all statements in the German broadcasts were lies. Communist propaganda, especially that which comes from Moscow, uses the wireless with complete indifference to truth; it misrepresents, falsifies, and ridicules the events and the policies of the countries which are regarded as enemies. The news it gives is designed to spread fear and dismay in the country against which it is directed, or, by skilful manipulation, to sow the seeds of suspicion between allies. When intended for the more backward races, it stirs up discontent and revolt against their rulers, and paints an entirely imaginary picture of the prosperity and happiness of the countries which have accepted Communism.

The cinema is also used for Communist propaganda: the best of Russian films rank very high for their technique and imaginativeness, and have behind them skilled psychology, which makes them of great value in appealing to the interests or prejudices of the nation or class to which they are addressed. A good example of this was a film shown in England some years ago. The story was of a revolt in an oriental train: first there were pictures of the arrival of the different classes of passengers on the platform, the millionaire obsequiously received by the station-master; then there followed pictures showing the compartments for the three classes: the first with every luxury and comfort for sitting, eating, and sleeping; the second adequately furnished and well supplied with food; the third consisting of bare boards occupied by poorly clad members of the proletariat crowded together in discomfort, with hunks of bread instead of caviare and champagne. An outrage committed by one of the wealthy against a working-class woman leads to the rising of the third-class passengers, the murder of the bourgeoisie and the capture and driving of the train into Communist territory. Quite apart from the story, the pictures were of great interest. Films of this nature, seen again and again by many incapable of independent criticism, gradually and almost imperceptibly create a mental outlook favourable to the reception of more direct communistic teaching. In the same way Russian films skilfully present the more attractive side of life in a Communist State, the pageantry on a great occasion, the corn-fields with the combines working on them, factories with the latest machinery, or youthful athletes of both sexes engaged in gymnastic displays.

THE METHOD OF REVOLUTION

Propaganda can prepare the way for Communism, but by itself it is not sufficient. For this, revolution is necessary. World revolution is an essential doctrine of orthodox Marxian Communism. Neither Marx nor Lenin contemplated the possibility of Communism in one country alone; surrounded by capitalist States, fearing and hating it, they believed it could not long survive; soon it would be crushed by the armed force of its enemies. The leaders of the Russian Revolution were confident that their example would presently be followed by the workers of neighbouring nations, and that within a short time world-wide Communism would be a reality.

Experience, however, disappointed this expectation of world revolution. Stalin therefore substituted the policy of Socialism in one country, for he saw it was necessary to consolidate what had been gained in Russia. Interference with the domestic concerns of other States must therefore be postponed for a time, until a fully armed and industrialized Russia would be capable of promoting world revolution. On this issue there was a bitter dispute between Stalin and Trotsky – the latter accusing Stalin of abandoning the orthodox teaching on world revolution. This led to the most serious cleavage ever experienced in the Communist Party. The two men were very different in temperament: Stalin cold, calculating, far-seeing, and pertinacious; Trotsky fiery and impulsive. Already between Lenin and Trotsky there had been some occasional difficulties, due again in part to their very different characters. A keen and capable observer who spent some time in Russia shortly after the first war told me he had been greatly struck with the contrast: Lenin all intellect, remote, cold, self-confident, and unsympathetic; Trotsky, on the other hand, with personal magnetism which could stir a great audience into passionate enthusiasm and made him the centre of devoted loyalty and fierce hatred. The latent differences of Trotsky with Lenin could no longer be concealed with his successor: personal dislike and disappointed ambition found expression in violent attacks on Stalin for abandoning the cause of world revolution, and the struggle between them only ended with the exile and murder of Trotsky and the liquidation of his followers. For a time Socialism in one country became the watchword, and when Russia was attacked by Germany it became more necessary than ever that threats of world revolution should not alarm and alienate allies.

But Stalin never really abandoned the principle of world revolution. With the defeat of Germany, and with the great increase in the power of the Soviet Union, it was possible to return to the older policy, but with a vitally important change. Marx and Lenin expected the revolution to come from below, through the spontaneous rising of the proletariat of the different nations; but Stalin saw there was little likelihood of this: instead, revolution must be engineered from above. The Government of a country must be secured by the Communist Party, either by political manoeuvres, by force, or by civil war; and then the new administration would impose the necessary changes upon the whole nation. 'Broadly speaking, the old Bolshevism staked its hopes on the revolutionary momentum of the International Labour Movement. It believed that the Socialist Order would result from the original experience and struggle of the working classes abroad, that it would be the most authentic act of their social and political self-determination. The old Bolshevism, in other words, believed in *revolution from below*, such as the upheaval of 1917 had been. The revolution which Stalin now carried into eastern and central Europe was primarily *revolution from above*. It was decreed, inspired, and managed by the great power predominant in that area. Although the local Communist parties were its immediate agents and executors, the great party of the Revolution which remained in the background was the Red Army.'*

The stages in the process of making revolution from above can be clearly seen. First there is underground preparation. In every country the Communist Party has its agents, its members, and its fellow-travellers. The agents are carefully selected and given directions by Moscow as to the policy they are to carry out. The members of the Party accept an iron discipline; they must surrender personal responsibility and private opinions; they must instantly obey orders, and speak and act in accordance with the instructions they receive. They may have to change overnight the attitude they have hitherto adopted, if by so doing they can benefit the Party; within twenty-four hours the war between the imperialist States was transformed into the defence of freedom by peace-loving democracies fighting against an aggressive and tyrannical Germany. Communists must make their influence felt in Trade Unions and Labour associations. Where there is trouble they must enflame it; where there is none they must make it; they must destroy good relations between employers and employed; they must encourage the continuation of a strike, and obstruct all attempts at a just agreement through negotiation or arbitration. Where sabotage can hinder production, it is to be used. At all times and on all occasions the Party and the Cause are to be given precedence over the interests, safety, and welfare of their fellow-workers, and good of their nation. Loyalty as a citizen is to count as nothing compared with loyalty to the Cause. In country after country there are larger or smaller groups of Fifth Columnists spreading discontent

*I. Deutscher, *Stalin: A Political Biography*, p. 554.

with complete disregard to truth, honesty, and good faith. No means, however unscrupulous, are to be neglected if they are likely to hasten the day of revolution.

Fellow-travellers are not admitted into the inner counsels and plans of the agents and members of the Communist Party. But they are used as stool-pigeons. They are flattered and fêted, invited to international conferences and allowed from time to time to visit Communist countries under the careful supervision of their hosts. They are useful, for they give an air of respectability to the Party and help to disarm suspicion.

The next step is to obtain some share in the Government. This has special difficulties. The Communist looks upon Social Democracy on the Continent and the Labour Party in Great Britain as dangerous enemies and rivals, for they offer alternatives to Communism. The Communist therefore normally stands apart from the Socialist and Labour Parties, pouring scorn on their policies and their leaders. But there comes a time when he must co-operate with them if he is to have any share in the Government. The chance comes when the chief parties in the State are evenly balanced, and the Social Democratic Party can only hold power with the help of the Communist Socialist. A coalition including some Communists is therefore formed; after a short truce, dissension between the Ministers breaks out, the Communists in the Government have the great advantage of a settled and definite aim, so they gradually get possession of the key positions, especially those which carry with them control of the police and of the armed forces.

The third stage is now reached. The Communist members create a crisis. The coalition breaks up. There are popular demonstrations, which have been carefully organized, demanding the reinstitution of the Communist Ministers and the permanent exclusion of those holding more moderate views. A People's Army suddenly appears in the streets and threatens revolt unless the 'will of the people' is respected. All over the country there are strikes, cessation of work in vital industries, and mass meetings which pass resolutions demanding a popular government. Behind the scenes there is the diplomatic pressure of Russia, while in the cafés and streets there are rumours of the massing of troops on the frontier. 'For the sake of peace and security,' the Government is reconstituted, but now it is Communist in nature, pledged to carry through a Communist or advanced socialistic policy. Later on a sham election will be held; only candidates carefully chosen by the Party will be allowed to stand; the vast majorities in favour of the candidates will be used to justify the claim that the revolution has been carried through constitutionally with the approval of the people.

Frequently it is impossible for the Communists to obtain power by methods which can be camouflaged as constitutional. Civil war must then be the weapon used. Greece for years after the end of the second war was ravaged by bands of rebels, encouraged and assisted by neighbouring Communist States, which found it inexpedient or too dangerous to declare open war. It was only by the help of Great Britain and the United States that this disastrous civil war was brought to an end and Communist designs defeated. In Korea Communist armies from the north made an unprovoked attack upon the south, and if it had not been for the intervention of the United Nations a Communist régime would have been imposed upon the whole country. There is the ever-present fear that in Iran, Yugoslavia, Italy, and even in Germany, Communism may promote civil war, if it can gain power in no other way.

But whether the Communists secure power by open force or by so-called constitutional methods, the result is the same – a dictatorship of the proletariat which at once sets to work to remove all possiblity of opposition by arresting, condemning, and executing its opponents; by suppressing all independent newspapers; and by turning the judicature into an instrument for crushing opposition. Purges are conducted in the armed forces, in the Civil Services, and even in the ranks of the Communist Party. Immediately after the Revolution in Czechoslovakia in 1948 Action Committees came into existence with the object of 'purifying' all the Defence Forces and Public

Departments of unsuitable members; within two months there were over 8,000 dismissals. In 1949 large numbers of the students of the University of Prague were expelled. In 1949 the purge was directed against members and supporters of the Communist Party; by 26th May it was reported that '107,000 persons had been expelled from the Party which then had 2,000,000 members. Even in the Government there was not, apparently, the complete unity of purpose and obedience to Party directives which Communist theory and practice demands,'* and there followed a series of arrests and dismissals in Government offices: 'There has been a steady stream of arrests on charges of espionage, treason, conspiracy, rioting, terrorism, economic or "commercial sabotage", and of insulting the Soviet Union.'† Side by side with these arrests and liquidations the Communist Government proceeded with legislative and administrative action for the nationalization of the means of production and distribution, the appropriation of private property, the dividing up of the large estates, and the more gradual approach to collective farming.

THE METHOD OF TERROR

The State built on revolution is always exposed to the danger of counter-revolution. Against this possibility the dictatorship of the proletariat uses the weapon of terror. Wherever Communism is established the safeguards which the constitutional courts give to the individual citizen are abolished, and are replaced by an order of police security worked by an army of informers and spies. The police State is a grim reality in the Communist countries: it guarantees security to those in power by wholesale arrests, trials, and executions which spread fear throughout the community.

Terror may be used against a whole race or nation. In the past the Tsars used it against Poland, and the Sultans of Turkey against the racial and religious minorities under their

*The British Survey, New Series, No. 15, p. 13.
†Op. cit., p. 12.

rule. The Soviet has employed it against the small Baltic States, which already had suffered terribly in the war at the hands both of the Nazis and the Communists. There is danger that the small nations of Latvia and Lithuania may literally be crushed out of existence. Thousands of their people have already been arrested or murdered; many have been deported from their homes and possessions to distant parts of Russia. The genocide for which the Nazis were condemned has been revived by the Soviet Union in their dealings with these frontier States.

In a different and milder degree the terror is used against those living within the Soviet zone of Germany, though there it is tempered by the desire to win the people to Communism; so it is directed chiefly against individuals and groups who might give trouble to their Russian rulers. In every village there are Germans who act as spies, their own freedom often dependent on their activity in reporting on their kinsfolk and neighbours. A German who frequently visits this zone told me that while there was little ill-treatment on a large scale, there was a widespread atmosphere of dread and insecurity. Sudden arrests are frequently made at night; the arrested, without any charge being brought against them, are taken to some unknown destination, and possibly for months nothing will be heard of them. Many are taken for forced labour in the uranium mines, where they are compelled to work under conditions injurious to health, and if they are so fortunate as to be able to return to their homes after a long absence, they are often crippled for life or consumptive. The reality of the terror in the Russian Zone of Germany is proved by the large number of refugees who reach the British and American Zones: in 1949 their number was estimated to be about 5,000 a month. In Western Germany there are now between eight and ten million refugees who have escaped from the terror and insecurity of Soviet rule.

In the Communist State the terror is used ruthlessly. In the first years of the Russian Revolution there were wholesale executions and imprisonments. No member of the aristocracy or of the employer class was safe from arrest. The emergency and strain of the time may have been some excuse; but the terror was not directed only against the bourgeoisie. The more prosperous farmers – the Kulaks – incurred the hatred of the new rulers of Russia. Lenin distinguished between the richer and the poorer peasants – the former, the Kulaks, he described as 'blood-suckers' and 'vampires'. It was necessary to eliminate them before the policy of creating collective farms could be carried out. The poorer peasants were incited to act against their more thrifty neighbours, and an organized campaign was directed by the agents of the Communist Party. The Kulaks were summarily evicted from their homes; their houses, corn, and cattle were confiscated; they were refused food if they remained in or near their villages, and were deliberately left to starve. Many were carried off to labour camps, where they were treated as slaves. Tens of thousands died of hunger, of cold, and of ill treatment. Their only crime was that they had been more successful than others in their farming and had been reluctant to surrender their property to the State. The mere charge that a man was a Kulak was sufficient to bring complete ruin upon him and all his family. If a Communist had felt it necessary to defend this destruction of a whole class, he would have used the argument which Arthur Koestler attributed to Ivanov, the police investigator, in *Darkness at Noon*. 'Every year several million people are killed quite pointlessly by epidemics and other natural catastrophes. And we should shrink from sacrificing a few hundred thousand for the most promising experiment in history? ... if we shoot a few thousand objectively harmful people, the humanitarians all over the world foam at the mouth. Yes, we liquidated the parasitic part of the peasantry and let it die of starvation. It was a surgical operation which had to be done once for all; but in the good old days before the Revolution just as many died in any dry year – only senselessly and pointlessly.'

The terror may be experienced by the member of the Party as well as by those who have never belonged to it. There are frequent purges of those whose loyalty is suspect. In every Communist State there are tens of thousands of terrified citizens who know they are liable to arrest for some careless word, some chance criticism which has been overheard and may easily be repeated. There are many more who fear arrest not because of anything they have said or done, but because they may be suspected. Even their thoughts are dangerous, and cause in many what is their nearest equivalent to a guilty conscience. There is terror at the prospect of sudden arrest while in bed at night; or it may happen in broad daylight, when, with a pistol pressed against their side, they are bundled into the waiting car and hurried off to the headquarters of the police. There is terror for the safety of some relative or friend who is suddenly missing from his home or work and may never be heard of again. Those arrested dread what awaits them: detention in the filthy and crowded cells until the interrogators are ready for them, the relentless questioning, the blows, the sleepless nights, the long suspense, and at the end sentence to work in a mine, or death in an underground cellar.

The terror is increased by the fear that ill treatment, hunger, sleeplessness, and possibly actual torture may compel an innocent man to confess to crimes which he has never committed. The public confessions of the accused have caused much perplexity and have been attributed to different causes. Quite apart from physical torture, a state of mind may be reached when the wretched victim feels he can endure no more and that he must obtain some respite from days and nights of questioning and of threats. This is sufficient to account for the unexpected breakdown of the accused, without attributing it to drugs or novel methods of torture. There is, however, no doubt that torture is sometimes used to extort information or a confession. In 1949 Michael Shepkov, an employee of the American Legation in Bulgaria, was arrested and forced to sign a confession. On his release he wrote an account of the methods used to break his resistance and asked that this should be published should he again be arrested. In February 1950 he again fell into the hands of the Bulgarian Security Police, and was sent to the Sofia County Court 'to be tried, to be found guilty, and to be punished'. The United States

Information Service therefore published the statement with a foreword describing Shepkov as one who 'blended fine instincts of Christian moral ethics and honesty with a high order of intelligence'. Shepkov thus describes the methods used during his questioning: 'I was ordered to stand facing the wall upright at a distance which allowed me to touch the wall with two fingers of outstretched arms. Then to step back some twelve inches, keep up my heels touching the floor, and maintain balance only with the contact of one finger on each hand. And while standing so the interrogation continued – nor was I allowed to collect my thoughts. The posture did not appear unduly painful, nor did it particularly impress me in the beginning. And yet, combined with the mental strain, with the continuous pressure to talk, with the utter hopelessness and the longing to go through the thing and be sent down into silence and peace – it is a very effective way of breaking all resistance. I recall that the muscles on my legs and shoulders began to get cramped and to tremble, that my two fingers began to bend under the pressure, to get red and over all to ache. I remember that I was drenched with sweat and that I began to faint ... after a time I broke down.' Then, sitting down, the interrogation still continued 'hour after hour throughout the night as throughout the day without respite or end ... And if I were to stop and plead fatigue or bad memory or ask to rest – then the wall again and again, and the slaps and the blows in the nape.' Treatment like this continued over several days, combined with threats as to what would befall wife and children if obduracy were persisted in, is sufficient to break the resistance of the strongest.

Rumours about the nature of the penal camps to which so many are sent increase the fear in which the dictatorships keep the people they govern. The Soviet Union has refused to allow any inspection of these camps either by the Red Cross Society or by a committee especially appointed by United Nations. Sufficient is known, however, of their nature to justify the dread in which they are held. They are often situated in unhealthy localities, and the work which the prisoners are given is such that no free labour can be obtained for it. In the worst of them the prisoners are treated as slaves, underfed and in-sufficiently clothed, and compelled to work under the whip of their wardens. A man sent to them under suspicion of dis-affection to the State has to spend years with criminals of the lowest type. He is condemned to a living death from which there is no escape. In every Communist country these camps are set up, and political offenders are sent to them often with-out trial and sometimes with no knowledge of the alleged crime for which they have been condemned.

Death is probably the most merciful of the punishments in-flicted by a Communist State on those who have incurred its hostility. The days of public martyrdom in which the con-demned could bear open witness to the cause for which he dies are over. Usually the sentence is carried out either by hanging or by shooting in the back; the place of execution is kept secret; and if any announcement is made of it, this is delayed until some days have passed. The secrecy and sordidness of the execution increase the terror with which it is surrounded.

The police State with laws which regard the safety of the State as over-riding all other considerations, with an army of spies and informers in every tenement, industry, and village, with its methods of sudden arrest and brutal treatment of the suspected, with its penalties of torture, penal servitude under shocking conditions, and a sordid death, intimidates and terri-fies the millions over whom it exerts its authority. The very hatred with which it is regarded intensifies the relentlessness with which it suppresses all possible opposition and criticism; for successful revolt would mean the certain death of those at the head of the system.

But terror by itself is insufficient; the need for it must be reduced by plunging the people into such complete ignorance that presently they come to look upon their lot as natural, and are even persuaded to take pride in it. Terror cannot be con-tinued indefinitely, so the people must be cowed into such a condition of submissiveness that coercive measures become unnecessary. The greatest achievement and foulest crime of Communism is that by the suppression of truth and the im-planting of falsehood it renders whole peoples so incapable of distinguishing truth from falsehood that they make evil their goal, and believe that their darkness is light. Communism does this by its rigid censorship and by the deliberate and scientific teaching of falsehood.

THE COUNTRY OF THE BLIND

Through a stern censorship on all the news from outside, and through the skilful use of propaganda by the wireless, the cinema, and the Press, the rulers of a Communist State are able to keep the citizens in ignorance of the world outside their frontiers, and to give them a false impression of the past history and the present position of their own country. They have no standards by which they can judge its progress, except those which are set by its rulers. They have no means by which they can distinguish between what is true and what is false. H. G. Wells in a short story with the title *The Country of the Blind* described a race living in an inaccessible valley who had all lost their sight. When a traveller by an accident reaches their valley, and tells them of a world in which there is light and colour, and speaks to them of the beauty of the rising and setting of the sun, of the sky at night covered with stars, they believe he is mad or the victim of some mysterious disease. Their world of darkness is the only real world, for it is the only world they know, and they can imagine nothing outside it or better than it. So the Soviet rulers attempt by an iron curtain to shut out all intercourse with any other nations than their own. The iron curtain has been raised a little, and it is now more easy for approved delegations and even tourists to visit the Soviet Union. No news is allowed to come from outside, no newspapers, books, or pamphlets are admitted if they contain anything which the rulers do not wish their subjects to know. No visitors are allowed to cross the frontiers unless their views and their discretion are approved. Those who for official or business reasons have to live in Russia find themselves enclosed in glass cages, for communication with Russians is reduced to a minimum, and the Russian who becomes too familiar with the foreigner may suddenly disappear.

Lavish hospitality is shown by the Russian Government to those who are its guests, but free intercourse between them and the ordinary Russian is prevented, lest there should leak through from the outside world information which might be contrary to the statements made by the official propaganda. Most of those who live in Communist States are convinced that Great Britain and the United States are keeping their people in degradation and poverty under the rule of wealthy capitalists, while vast armaments are being built up for the destruction of the Communist world.

The people of the Communist States are given false ideas of their own history and achievements. Their victories and discoveries are grossly exaggerated. Their literature, drama, and music, which require no false praise, for their excellency is recognized throughout the world, are spoken of as if they were unique. Lately it has even been claimed that the wireless, the cinema, and the aeroplane were invented by Russian scientists! History is falsified. The treaty of Russia with Nazi Germany is ignored, while the defeat of Germany is ascribed almost entirely to the courage of the Russian army under the leadership of Stalin. A film shown in Russia on the defeat of Japan only once showed an American soldier, and then as an unimportant spectator at the signing of the surrender of Japan! Russians believe that the working classes in the democratic countries live under slave conditions, and with a standard of life far below that which the Russians themselves enjoy. They have been taught that Great Britain and the United States are obsessed with such envy and hatred of the Soviet Union that they are plotting to destroy it. Through modern methods of propaganda, unscrupulously used without any regard to truth, a whole nation may be nurtured on lies and brought up in complete and dangerous ignorance. Mr Wells described the inhabitants of the Valley of the Blind as becoming gradually blind; after the first attack of the disease 'the old became groping and purblind, the young saw but dimly, and the children that were born to them saw never at all.' There are still some in Russia who can see, they have been into Europe as members of an invading army, or on trade, or for conferences; but their number becomes fewer every year, and intercourse with foreigners becomes rarer; and before many more years have passed the millions belonging to the Soviet Union will see only what their rulers think it is expedient they should see. George Orwell in his novel *Nineteen Eighty-Four* describes to what extremes the process of historical falsification might be carried. In the Palace of Truth newspapers and pamphlets were rewritten in accordance with the changing views of the Party: 'Day by day, and almost minute by minute the past was brought up to date. In this way every prediction made by the Party could be shown by documentary evidence to have been correct: nor was any item of news, or any expression of opinion, which conflicted with the needs of the moment, ever allowed to remain on record. All history was a palimpsest, scraped clean and reinscribed exactly as often as was necessary. In no case would it have been possible, once the deed was done, to prove that any falsification had taken place ... Books, also, were recalled and rewritten again and again, and were invariably reissued without any admission that any alteration had been made.' In the same way statistics could be changed. 'For example the Minister of Plenty's forecast had estimated the output of boots for the quarter at a hundred and forty-five million pairs. The actual output was given as sixty-two millions. Winston (a clerk in the Ministry of Truth) however in re-writing the forecast marked the figure down to fifty-seven millions, so as to allow for the usual claim that the quota had been over fulfilled. In any case, sixty millions was no nearer the truth than fifty-seven millions, or than a hundred and forty-five millions. Very likely no boots had been produced at all.' No doubt this is a caricature, and yet not entirely so; this falsification of history and distortion of facts is now frequent in the Soviet Union, and if practised over a period of years the result will be a more dangerous blindness than if the people had never seen; for they will think they see, but what they see will be error and not truth.

What has happened in Russia is now being repeated in China. A missionary of nineteen years' experience in China, in a remarkable broadcast which paid great tribute to the good qualities of Communism, stated: 'The whole educational system is now simply a means of indoctrinating 475,000,000 people in Marxism–Leninism. There are new revolutionary universities, where students are given an intensive four months' course in political training, and then sent out as Government officials. I often passed their small groups as they sat in the grass on a fine afternoon discussing the morning's lecture, and heard these boys and girls of sixteen or seventeen earnestly talking about the sins of America. And when they saw me, they would say "There's an American imperialist coming along now." People's Universities are being established for workers and revolutionaries where the instruction will be of a very practical nature. The old schools and universities are being reformed to fit into the new system. But the important thing is that the whole educational system becomes a training ground in Marxist doctrine. Children now in school will never have known anything else and will take Communism for granted.'*

In Poland the same methods are now applied. A deliberate attempt is being made to substitute Marxism for national culture. No Polish man of letters can earn a livelihood unless he conforms to the Marxian pattern. Only one literary weekly is allowed to exist, all its rivals have been suppressed, and this is the organ of official instruction on matters of art and literature. Few books by Western authors are allowed to be sold or published in Poland unless they are written by Communists, while the bookshops are full of the translated works of Marx, Lenin and Stalin, sold at a low price by the million. Two weeklies very popular among children and containing moral and semi-religious stories have been taken over by the authorities and are used for Soviet propaganda and illustrated with pictures supplied from Moscow. The theatre, the cinema and music are made channels of Soviet propaganda. Western culture is derided and Russian extolled, while Polish national culture is suppressed. As the Polish peasant is only now becoming literate, he will read without criticism any literature set before him – the Soviet-inspired journals, newspapers,

*Leonard Constantine in the *Listener*, 18th January, 1951.

pamphlets and books afford him literature which is both easy to obtain and cheap, but 'it is also doctrinaire, bigoted, frequently childish and often containing scurrilous anti-Western propaganda.'*

To pass judgement on Marxian Communism it is not sufficient to know either its claims or its positive achievements; its real purpose is disclosed by the means which it uses to reach its ends. It is useless to say that these are temporary methods which are due to an age of crisis and struggle; after thirty years the methods of fraud, terror, and violence are still used, and there is no sign that they are likely to be abandoned.

It is highly improbable that Communism will collapse, though in the course of time it may undergo many modifications and lose much of its original harshness. To attempt to destroy it by war would bring universal ruin, for the use of the H-bomb would make impossible complete victory for any belligerent. Neither the democratic nor the Communist States can afford to indulge in the spirit of the Crusades; difficult as it is to do so, they must learn to live together in the hope that the danger of common ruin may prevent them from pressing to an extreme the matters on which they differ. For a time we may have to be content with an uneasy co-existence, but with patience there may come co-operation for the peace and welfare of the human race. There would indeed be greater hope of this if Marxian Communism abandoned its persecution of the Christian Church.

*The statements in this paragraph are taken from a special article in *The Times*, 12th April, 1951.

10

Communism: its Attack on Christianity

DURING the last fifty years various attacks have been made on the Christian Church. An omnipotent State demands the obedience which should be given to God alone. The resistance to its claims under the Nazis, both in Germany itself and during the German occupations of Holland and Norway, showed that the Church has many members who are prepared to suffer death rather than render to Caesar the worship due to God. The racial theories of Nazism, contemptuous of all non-Aryans, and the cruel persecution of the Jews, were a challenge to the Christian teaching that all men, irrespective of race or colour, are of value in the sight of God, the Father of all. As long as Nazism was dominant it attempted to weaken and to undermine the different Churches, sometimes resorting to physical persecution to silence their leaders and to intimidate the rank and file. The defeat of Germany removed a great danger to the Church, for if Hitler had been victorious he would not have rested until he had obtained its submission to his will.

The most dangerous and persistent attack upon Christianity comes now from the opposite quarter, from the Communism which Hitler attempted to overthrow – namely, the Marxian Communism which is dominant in Russia and its satellite States, and now threatens the peace of the world. This form of Communism, both in theory and in practice, is opposed to the Christian Church.

THE FUNDAMENTAL DIFFERENCES BETWEEN CHRISTIANITY AND COMMUNISM

There are four fundamental differences between Christianity and Marxian Communism; they are so deep that it is difficult to understand how Communism could ever be regarded as a 'Christian heresy'. On essential matters both of doctrine and

227

practice there is unbridgeable opposition between Christianity and Communism as expounded by Marx and his orthodox disciples.

(1) Marxian Communism is a materialistic creed. It asserts that matter is everything, spirit a delusion, or at the best an almost accidental by-product of matter. There is no room for God, no possibility of a revelation from without, no life beyond the grave. Religion is looked upon as the result of wishful thinking: sometimes it is a deception encouraged by rulers with the purpose of keeping the proletariat submissive, or by a priesthood greedy to gain power and wealth out of the superstition of the people. Religion is hated as an enemy which has helped to keep mankind enslaved. In the Manifesto of 1848 Marx and Engels speak with scorn of religion. 'As the parson has ever gone hand in hand with the landlord, so has clerical socialism with feudal socialism ... Christian socialism is but the holy water with which the priest consecrates the heart-burnings of the aristocrat.' Lenin is even more definite: 'The impotence of the exploited classes in struggle with the exploiters inevitably gives birth to faith in a better life beyond the grave, just as the impotence of primitive people in struggle with nature gives birth to gods, devils, miracles, etc. To him who all his life works and suffers need, religion teaches humility and patience in earthly life, comforting him with the hope of heavenly reward. And to those who live by the toil of others, religion teaches philanthropy in earthly life, offering them very cheap justification for all their exploiting existence, and selling at low price tickets to heavenly bliss. Religion is opium for the people. Religion is a sort of spiritual moonshine (bad home-made liquor) in which the slaves of capital drown their human figure, their demands for even any sort of working human life.'* The complete and uncompromising materialism of the Marxian Communist leaves no room for religion in any shape or form. Here there is no ground for compromise or reconciliation. Christianity is bound up with belief in the supernatural; Marxism denies it root and branch.

*Quoted by Barron and Waddams in *Communism and the Churches*, p. 14.

(2) There is uncompromising opposition between Christianity and Marxism over the nature of man. Christianity teaches his greatness as created by God to love and to serve Him, and with eternal life as his destiny. Marxism denies him both dignity and rights: man has come from the earth, and after a few years he will return to the earth as if he had never been. Man exists for the State, which has complete power over him; it can use him as it thinks best for its advantage; it can pamper him or send him to a slave camp; it can torture and kill him if he even appears to question its authority. The great struggle that now divides the world is over the soul of man: Christianity claims man as a son of God, made in His image; Communism claims him as an instrument to fashion and use for the welfare and power of the State. William Temple summed up this difference. 'The great and profound difference between Christian civilization and the kind of civilization which the Communists are aiming at lies in our affirmation that the primary fact of the world is God, that each individual man is the child of God, that at the root of his being he is a child of God, and that he is a child of God before he is a citizen of any national community.'

(3) Equally great is the opposition between the Christian and Marxian conception of morality. The Christian believes that there is a moral law, which comes from a righteous God who is sovereign of the universe. This law is binding on all men, at all places and in all ages. The law is not always seen clearly, and when it is seen it is often disobeyed and misapplied; but justice, truth, mercy, and love remain the same, with their absolute claim for obedience. But the Marxian denies that there is an eternal moral law. Morals are relative, and change with varying circumstances. Morality is always relative to the State – good is what promotes its strength and welfare; evil is what hinders or injures it. Morality therefore changes according to the nature and requirements of the State. Lying, treachery, deceit, cruelty may all be used in its interests. The orthodox Marxian holds that the moral theories of the past were the result of economic movements; the moral system of each age upheld the views and served the interest of the

governing class; when this was overthrown and the oppressed became the masters, their moral code was accepted and adapted to the new circumstances. There was always change through the ebb and flow of class conflict, and no immutable moral law resting on divine sanction. Lenin made this very clear in an address to a Congress of the Young Communist League: 'We repudiate all morality derived from non-human and non-class concepts. We say that it is a deception, a fraud in the interests of the landlords and capitalists. We say that our morality is entirely subordinated to the interests of the class struggle of the proletariat ... The class struggle is still continuing ... We subordinate our Communist morality to the task. We say: Morality is what serves to destroy the old exploiting society and to unite all the toilers around the proletariat, which is creating a new Communist society ... We do not believe in an eternal morality.'*

(4) Another contrast between Christian and Communist is found in their hopes for the future. Christianity looks forward to an ideal community, but it holds out no hope that it will be established in this world. It looks beyond death and beyond time for the perfect community; it will come, moreover, not by the unaided power of man, but by the goodness and power of God. The Christian is a realist, and accepts the hard fact of sin, which makes man fail repeatedly from attaining the best. The noblest schemes and most skilful blue-prints fail through the wilfulness, obstinacy, and ignorance of those for whose benefit they were intended. The Communist has his ideal of the classless State in which all are good and happy, and he is confident that it is possible to establish it in this life. Notwithstanding the scorn which Marx and Engels express in the Manifesto for Utopias, their followers are convinced that by some change in economic conditions they will be able to build here on earth the Utopia of their most optimistic dreams. They can only cling to these hopes, in spite of repeated disappointment, by ignoring the fact of sin and by a blind belief in the unaided goodness and unselfishness of the

*Quoted by R. N. Carew Hunt in *The Theory and Practice of Communism*, p. 80.

men and women whose individual value they elsewhere decry.

In view of these and other considerations, the Lambeth Conference of 1948, 'while recognizing that in many lands there are Communists who are practising Christians, nevertheless, declares that Marxian Communism is contrary to Christian faith and practice, for it denies the existence of God, Revelation and a future life; it treats the individual as a means and not as an end; it encourages class warfare; it regards the moral law not as absolute, but as relative to the needs of the State', and in the Report of the Committee on the Christian Doctrine of Man the issue is stated very bluntly: 'The most highly organized, consistent, powerful, and destructive form of secularism is beyond doubt Dialectical Materialism, and the type of communism in which it is embodied. This is perhaps the one live alternative to the Christian interpretation of man. Between the two there can be no compromise and it seems to be increasingly probable that it is between these two that the world must choose.'

If the Christian Church has recognized that Marxian Communism is its most dangerous foe, Communism, on the other hand, has treated the Christian Church as an enemy it must either destroy or subdue.

PERSECUTION IN RUSSIA

The revolution in Russia was immediately followed by an attack on the Church. The Holy Orthodox Church had immense prestige and considerable wealth, though most of the village priests were poor and ignorant. Its services were of great magnificence, conducted with the utmost care in all the details of its wonderful and complicated Liturgy. There had been no effective reform, and the hierarchy were out of all touch with modern thought. The Church produced many saints, and the devotion of multitudes of humble priests and laity was very great. But the Church was under the control of the State, and closely linked with the Tsars and governing classes. The intelligentsia both scorned and hated it as an instrument of reaction. Directly after the abdication of the Tsar in March 1917 the office of Chief Procurator was abolished and his functions taken over by a Ministry of Religion appointed by the provisional Government: this was followed by the transfer of parish schools from the Church to the Ministry of Education. The Great Council of the whole Russian Church met in August, and decided on a number of reforms and voted for the restoration of the Patriarchate, and elected Tikhon as the first of the new Patriarchs. But the proposal for reform came too late, and with the establishment of the Soviet Government under Lenin the storm broke over the Church.

The new Government at once nationalized banks, factories, building, and lands. The people seized and appropriated monastic property and land. In February 1918 a decree separated State and Church, and all property belonging to churches and religious societies in Russia was declared to be the property of the people. Meantime the new Patriarch denounced these attacks upon the Church and excommunicated those responsible for them; a sentence or two from his pastoral letter will show the vehemence of his protest: 'Come to yourselves, ye idiots, cease your bloody deeds. Your deeds are not only cruel – these acts are in reality the work of Satan, for which you are subject to everlasting fire in the life to come after death and the terrible curse of posterity in the present life on earth. By authority given us by God, we forbid you to approach the holiness of Christ, we excommunicate you if you still bear the name of Christian, and in accordance with your birth belong to the Orthodox Church.' Later in the Pastoral he calls upon the faithful to resist the attacks upon the property of the Church: 'We call all of you believers and true sons of the Church; place yourselves for the defence of our insulted and oppressed Holy Mother. The enemies of the Church seize the power over her and her property by force of deadly weapons, but you revolt against them by the power of your faith and the strength of your voices as a nation which will stop the madmen.'* A month

*Quoted by Paul Anderson in *People, Church and State in Modern Russia*, pp. 53–4.

later the Patriarch and Synod gave detailed instructions as to how priests and worshippers should resist attacks on the property of the Church. In 1921 the struggle between Church and State was intensified. The Patriarch proposed to use the movable wealth of the Church to assist the starving in the terrible famine of that year. The Government refused to allow this on the grounds that the property had already been nationalized, and that the Church's sole duty was that of worship. The Government then sent out agents to seize the property. The Patriarch again called upon the faithful to resist. The State retaliated by active persecution: Orthodox bishops, priests, and laity were arrested and tried; most of them were found guilty, large numbers were executed, and still more were sentenced to imprisonment or exiled to Siberia. Many suffered through mob violence, and many were tortured and killed without even the mockery of a trial. Roman Catholics were persecuted as well as the Orthodox. The Patriarch Tikhon in 1922 was arrested and for a time in danger of death. He was released in the following year as the result of his 'confession', in which he repented of his actions against the Government, and which he ended by saying, 'I declare hereby to the Soviet authorities that henceforth I am no more an enemy to the Soviet Government, and that I have completely and resolutely severed all connexions with the foreign and domestic monarchists and the counter-revolutionary activity of the White Guards.'*

Until 1939 the Church was subject to persecution, to atheistic propaganda, and to hostility of every kind. There were intervals when the attacks diminished, but at all times there was Government discrimination against believers, especially against the priests, who were deprived of their food rations on one excuse or the other. There were three lines of attack:

First, there was open and undisguised persecution. The clergy were often arrested and frequently without trial liquidated, imprisoned, or sent to labour camps. Churches were arbitrarily closed and their property confiscated. The work of ministers of religion was restricted to their place of

*Op. cit., p. 66.

worship. Religious associations were forbidden by the decree of April 8, 1929, to give material assistance to their members or to 'organize for children, young people, or women special prayer or other meetings, or, generally, meetings, groups, circles, or departments for biblical or literary study, sewing, working, or the teaching of religion, etc., or organize excursions, children's play-grounds, public libraries, or reading rooms or organize sanatoria or medical assistance.'*

Secondly, a schism was encouraged by the Government giving recognition to the so-called 'Living Church'. This consisted of members of the Orthodox Church who were anxious for drastic reforms. It abolished the Patriarchate and established a system of government which was largely presbyterian. It gave unconditional support to the Soviet, while the Soviet authorities helped it to appoint its nominees as bishops, deans, and rectors by removing or exiling those incumbents who refused to accept the schism. 'With many of the cathedrals and larger churches in their hands, the Living Church in 1925 claimed 12,593 parishes, 16,540 clergy, and 192 bishops.'† The new Church was radical and revolutionary in its leaders and in its policy. An American photographer and journalist who visited Vvedensky, the head of the new Church, thus describes him and his house: 'The walls of his four-room house are crammed with paintings and the table stuffed with statuary, ivory boxes, carved paper knives, and ivory fans. Crowded in amidst the statuary of this sitting-room is a grand piano that the Metropolitan plays. The portrait above the Metropolitan shows him in civilian clothes. These he wears under his bishop's regalia . . . The Metropolitan is witty, worldly, and a bit of a flirt.'‡ The contrast was great compared with the Patriarch Sergei, with his ascetic face and his plainly furnished room, with icons hanging on the walls. Though the new Church had the support of the Soviet and an imposing list of clergy and officials, the great mass of the

*Quoted by J. B. Barron and H. M. Waddams in *Communism and the Churches*, p. 18.

†Paul Anderson, *op. cit.*, p. 64.

‡Margaret Bourke-White, *Shooting the Russian War*, p. 149.

people felt it was a pretentious sham: before long many of the priests made their submission to the authorities of the Orthodox Church and the laity by the thousand returned to it. When in Moscow I asked one of the archbishops about the 'Living Church'. He replied, 'It would be more rightly called the "Dying" and not the "Living" Church'. Within a comparatively short time Vvendensky and most of his adherents made their submission. For a time, however, this schism appeared to be a dangerous threat to the Orthodox Church and caused great anxiety to its synod.

Thirdly, by education and propaganda the Communist Party attempted to destroy Christianity. The first Soviet Constitution of 1918 permitted freedom of both religious and anti-religious propaganda; but the Stalin Constitution of 1936 changed this to 'Freedom for religious cults to function and freedom for anti-religious propaganda are conceded in behalf of all citizens.' Anti-religious propaganda had been carried on by the teaching given in all schools and by the activities of private associations. The Godless Society by its literature and lectures conducted an active campaign against all forms of religion. On the great Festivals of the Church processions through the streets were organized which parodied the religious processes and ceremonies. Some of the churches were turned into godless museums, usually their exhibits were intended to bring contempt on the Christian faith and worship, and had affixed to them crude and blasphemous descriptions; but other museums were more scientific in nature, showing that Christianity had many similarities in other religions and illustrating its natural origin. The aim of this atheistic propaganda was to explain away and to ridicule religion. The Communist now takes it for granted that the older people will continue to accept the religion in which they were brought up, but relies on instilling in the younger generation a contempt and dislike of religion as a superstition which modern science had dispelled. The Soviet attitude towards religion 'is an inimical attitude, like the attitude of a gardener towards weeds in his cabbage patch, or of a soldier towards the enemy's machine-gun nest. This attitude determines the measures to be taken with regard to religion. In a broad sense one may say that these measures are like a pincer movement. One arm of the pincers is socialist construction, building and changing the order of life until exploitation shall cease, suffering can be quickly relieved by science, and the destiny of man fulfilled in the span of his earthly life – in brief where the very thought of God will not arise. The other arm is that of enlightenment, education, propaganda, neutralizing, de-energizing, or eradicating the ideas which are in any way related to the concept of God.'*

The fierceness and persistency of the attack on the Church of Russia caused it great damage. It is not possible to give any accurate figures of the number of the bishops and priests who suffered death or imprisonment. Large numbers of the laity were intimidated and fell away from the Church. Even when there was no official persecution, the discrimination against those known to be church-goers was so severe that it needed much courage to be seen attending public worship. At one time to the outsider it looked as if the Russian Church might be destroyed. But through all the darkest days in thousands of towns and villages the faithful openly or secretly continued to practise their religion. A Russian priest said to me, 'The grandmothers kept religion alive, for they always insisted on the baptism of their grandchildren.' When I was saying good-bye in 1943 to the leaders of the Russian Church, I asked them if there was anything they would like me to say from them when I returned to England, and very earnestly and emphatically their spokesman said, 'Tell them in England that our worship never ceased, it has continued without a break.' All honour to the heroic and loyal Christians of Russia who remained steadfast in their faith notwithstanding persecution and intimidation.

With the outbreak of war the position was suddenly changed. Prayers for the success of Russia were offered in all the Orthodox Churches, and as far as their means allowed, the different parishes made their voluntary contributions to the various war funds; though there were no official chaplains

*Paul Anderson, *op. cit.*, p. 108.

appointed to the army, the Patriarch told me that in the ranks and among the guerillas there were large numbers of priests. The Church of Russia made it plain that it was heart and soul with the State and the people in resisting the German invasion. The attitude of the State at once softened to the Church: the propaganda against it was brought to an end, the anti-God societies suspended their operations, and the godless museums were closed. In the autumn of 1943 Stalin received the Metropolitan Sergei, who shortly afterwards, early in September, was installed as Patriarch. Since then the State has restored to the ecclesiastical authorities the parish churches when sufficient demand has been made for them, and in various ways has given material support to the Church. It allows it to have its own printing-press and publications. In 1943 a Council for dealing with the affairs of the Church was set up by the State, and a year later another similar Council was formed to act as a liaison body between the Soviet and non-Orthodox religion. The change in policy was due to several causes: the discovery that persecution could not destroy Christianity, the recognition that opposition to the State by the Church had been replaced by loyalty to it, and the desire for national unity which could not be realized if a large section of the nation was penalized for its religious views. Probably also the State hoped that the Orthodox Church might spread Russian influence in the Balkans and elsewhere. The Church authorities have welcomed this change of attitude, and indeed have shown themselves over-ready to excuse the undoubted persecution by the State as an attack not on religion but on the Church of the Tsars, which had been used as a political instrument of reaction. The Church has tacitly accepted the condition that it should take no part in political activities and should confine its work to the fields of worship, doctrine, and ecclesiastical organization.

The Iron Curtain makes it very difficult to know accurately the position of the Church of Russia at the present time. There is no persecution; with the exception of the Church of Rome, all Churches and denominations in Russia are able to worship freely; there is no discrimination against the officers of the

Church or intimidation of its laity; the open parodies of religion and coarse attacks upon it are no longer allowed; in Moscow at any rate the churches are crowded to overflowing, though it must be remembered that there are now only some sixty churches in use, where at one time there were hundreds. When I was in Moscow in 1943 I was told there were fifty churches open; and the figure now given is only slightly above this. While the Orthodox Church has lost the great prestige it once had, it possesses self-government and the right to elect its own bishops. Within the walls of the churches there is freedom of worship and preaching. But the Church has been greatly impoverished, there are large numbers of parishes without a priest or church. A writer who knows Russia well thus describes the church in the village: 'You see that the doors are unpainted and barred, the windows broken or boarded up, the colour-wash peeling, and the gilt Orthodox cross on the dome hacked off or bent out of shape . . . It is gutted and used as a store for seed corn, or as a veterinary station, or as a stable . . . In all these villages with broken churches people pray at home before an ikon with the little lamp for ever burning at its foot. It is safe to say that all peasant women over forty are devout believers, as well as the great majority of the men.'* The Church is tolerated, and at times even assisted by the Government, but the Government and the Party are atheists; if among them there is a believer, it is in secret. The teaching in the schools and colleges is materialistic, no religion can be taught or openly practised within their walls. Lately there are some signs of revived activity on the part of the various godless societies, and it is said that young men and women are especially trained to be sent out to the villages as missionaries of atheism. The leaders of the Church have a difficult and dangerous path to tread; they do not wish to incur the hostility of the Government, and they must be faithful to their Church. If days of persecution should again come, however ready the leaders of the Russian Church may be to compromise and to yield on non-essential matters, they would face the worst forms of persecution and death

*E. Crankshaw, *The National Review,* October, 1950.

itself rather than surrender anything vital to doctrine and worship.

PERSECUTION OF THE ROMAN CATHOLIC CHURCH

Since the war in Communist-dominated countries the Roman Catholic Church has been the special object of the suspicion and hatred of the Communist leaders. Nowhere has it had to endure anything comparable with the fierceness of the attack on religion in Russia in the early days of the Revolution, but with various degrees of intensity the Communist States have attempted to intimidate and to weaken it. This is primarily due to the opposition between Marxian Communism and Christianity. But there are also special reasons for the attack which Communism makes on Roman Catholicism. It is a spiritual totalitarian society, and its members, especially its hierarchy, in every country are under the sovereignty of the Pope, who claims their spiritual allegiance. Nationalism always has been suspicious of papal interference, but this is heightened when the rulers of Communist States find among their subjects millions who render spiritual obedience to another ruler who has declared his hostility to Communism. Greed was also excited by the fact that in some of the central European countries the Roman Catholic Church was the owner of great estates, and often reputed to be a bad landlord. The same motives which helped to dissolve the monasteries in England are operative in many continental nations. There is also the vindictiveness of triumphant Communism against Roman Catholicism as the ally of their political opponents and as the supporter of reaction; sometimes, indeed, justification has been given for oppressive measures, for in Yugoslavia some Roman Catholic priests openly sided with the Italian armies and took part in harrying both the Orthodox and the Communists. Elsewhere Roman Catholic priests and monks showed active hostility to the newly established Communist Governments. But even if these subsidiary causes had not sharpened the hatred of the Communist against the Roman Catholic Church, there would still have been persecution, for the totalitarian State, whether Nazi or Communist, cannot tolerate a powerful rival which rejects its claims.

The attack on the Roman Catholic Church has taken three forms: First, attempted intimidation of its clergy and laity by threats and arrests. Secondly, the secularization of education and the confiscation of Church property. Thirdly, legislative and administrative action to bring the Church completely under the control of the State.

(1) The attack usually starts with speeches and newspaper articles accusing the bishops and clergy of anti-democratic activities. They are criticized as supporters of the capitalist Powers and of the propertied classes. Unsavoury scandals are invented or grossly exaggerated and given the widest publicity by the anti-clerical Press. As this campaign becomes increasingly fierce, threats are directed against the hierarchy, and they are warned that unless they drop their alleged anti-democratic and treasonable practises popular indignation will demand that they are brought to trial. Police agents are sent to ecclesiastical gatherings and reporters ostentatiously take down the sermons or speeches both of bishops and the better-known priests. Occasionally demonstrations are organized as expressions of popular indignation against the Church. Fear and anxiety spread among the clergy and laity; the more timid of the latter withdraw from association with the parish priests and join in the demonstrations against them. When the moment seems ripe, a number of clergy are arrested on charges of disaffection to the State, of treasonable communication with its enemies, or of illegal monetary transactions. Most of these charges are dealt with summarily, but from time to time a public trial is staged against some prominent churchmen, and after months of seclusion in a prison, often in solitary confinement, except for the repeated questioning by State prosecutors, they are so broken in spirit that they confess to their alleged crimes, and after the mockery of a trial are sentenced to long terms of imprisonment. When there is danger that an open trial might lead to popular protests, the accused are kept in confinement for months without any

charge being brought against them; or, as in the case of Archbishop Beran, they are kept indefinitely in house custody, and cut off from all communication with their clergy and laity. This policy removes from the Church its most vigorous leaders and at the same time spreads fear amongst the rank and file.

(2) Simultaneously with the attack on the bishops and priests, legislation is passed to secularize both the schools and the property of the Church. Through their control of the schools, the Communists are able to ensure that the children are indoctrinated from their earliest years with the tenets of atheistic Communism. In Bulgaria in 1948 religious instruction in the schools was forbidden, and in the Law concerning Churches passed in 1949 it was laid down that 'the education of children and young people and the establishment of youth organizations is under the special care of the State, and is outside the scope of activity of the Churches and their ministers'. In Hungary the schools were nationalized, and those who taught in them became servants of the State: religious teaching in theory remained in the hands of the clergy, but it was no longer obligatory, and parents were discouraged from allowing their children to receive it. In Czechoslovakia education was under the control of the State at the time of the Revolution, but a new law has deprived the famous Charles University of Prague and other universities of their independence; their professors are now appointed by the State, and students are not admitted to them unless they are likely to accept Communism. In Roumania all educational establishments are controlled by the State. In Communist States the teachers are carefully chosen with the purpose of giving instruction which will bias the children against Christianity even when a direct and open attack upon it is for a time avoided. One of the leaders of the Soviet Party Central Committee of the Department for Agitation and Propaganda states, 'A Soviet teacher must be guided by the principle of the Party spirit of science; he is obliged not only to be an unbeliever himself, but also to be an active propagandist of Godlessness among others, to be the bearer of ideas of militant proletarian

atheism. Skilfully and calmly, tactfully and persistently, the Soviet teacher must expose and overcome religious prejudices in the course of his activity in school and outside school, day in and day out.'* Text-books used in the schools either ignore religion or treat it with contempt. In a book issued by authority for use in the Russian zone of Germany it was stated that Jesus Christ had never existed and the Christian religion was founded on a myth.

As prejudice and opposition are stirred up against the Church it becomes more easy to deprive it of its possessions. The Church in most of the central European nations was a great landlord, so it suffered severely in the general confiscation of all large estates by the State. In Poland a law was passed in 1950 confiscating estates and farms exceeding 250 acres owned by the Church, though land used for holding religious services was exempt. This followed the precedent already set by Hungary, Czechoslovakia, Yugoslavia, and Roumania. The distribution among the peasants of the lands of the large estates was naturally popular among them, and thus strengthened the position of the Communists. Attacks were made everywhere against the monasteries; with a few exceptions their buildings and possessions were confiscated and the religious were evicted, sometimes with great brutality. In Hungary a large number of monasteries and convents were suddenly closed, and many of them were taken over by the State for educational purposes. On 9th June the secret police forced their way into religious houses and took away their inmates: 'The religious taken from their cells in the night of 9th June were given not more than half an hour to dress and to collect any personal clothing and possessions, to a maximum of about five kilogrammes in weight, and were then for the most part taken, tightly packed into sealed vans, to selected houses which are being made to serve as concentration monasteries.'† In Czechoslovakia charges of treason and

*Quoted by J. Barron and H. M. Waddams in *Communism and the Churches*, p. 32. Elsewhere in this chapter I have used freely this valuable 'documented study'.

†*Tablet*, 1st July, 1950.

of concealing arms were brought against the heads of some of the Orders, and most of the religious houses were confiscated to be used as social institutions; the so-called 'concentration monasteries' have been turned into labour camps; the religious sent to them are forced to work in the fields for eight hours a day, and have, in addition, two hours of schooling in Marxism. There are probably thousands of religious in central and south-eastern Europe who are penniless and homeless, who live on the charity of the faithful or are confined in concentration camps or prison.

(3) The above measures are part of the larger policy of rendering the Church powerless to act on its own initiative and making it dependent upon the State. Church publications, newspapers, books, and pamphlets have either been suppressed or are severely censored. The utterances of the bishops and clergy are carefully scrutinized, and in some cases they are only allowed to speak on specially authorized occasions for which permission has been obtained. The State is ready to make itself responsible for the payment of the parochial clergy when their usual sources of income have been confiscated, so if they incur its displeasure their income can be suspended or withdrawn. Repeated injunctions are issued that the clergy must confine themselves to their spiritual work and take no part in any political activities; usually the Churches are forbidden by law to own, or to work, charitable and philanthropic institutions, as these are claimed as the concern of the State. Though Church and State are separated in the Communist States, the control of the State over the Church is more thorough than it is in the case of an Established Church elsewhere. An example of this can be seen in the powers conferred on the Roumanian Government by a decree of February 1949. This 'outlined the Government's functions as follows: 1. To supervise and control all religious groups and their branches. 2. To supervise and control special religious education for training personnel for all religious groups. 3. To approve the establishment of new communities, parishes, and religious administrative units. 4. To control and supervise religious art. 5. To supervise and control all property and

funds of religious groups. 6. To execute the work, in conjunction with local representatives, of supervising relations and information between groups within the country and those abroad.'* One of the special aims of the Communists is to destroy papal authority as anti-national and anti-Communist, for they regard the Papacy as the spearhead of the ideological opposition and its bishops as the agents of a foreign and capitalist Power. A bishop's communication with the Papacy may lead to a charge of high treason against him. In Czechoslovakia the bishops have been accused by the Minister of Religious Affairs of 'committing high treason by obeying the orders of the Vatican'. But in both Poland and Hungary the bishops, or some of them, have reached an agreement with the State, and in the case of Poland the State accepts the 'principle that the Pope is authoritative and the supreme authority of the Church applies to matters of faith, morality, and Church jurisdiction; in other matters however the episcopate is guided by the interests of the Polish State'. The agreements appear to have been made without previous reference to the Vatican, possibly on account of the difficulty of direct communication with it.

The events in Czechoslovakia since the Revolution make clear the determination of Communist States to destroy the independence of the Churches within their borders. When I visited Prague in October 1947, four months before the Revolution, I had some contact with four Churches – the Czechoslovak Church, which had seceded from the Roman Catholic Church after the first war; the Evangelical Church; the Orthodox Church; and, the largest of all, the Roman Catholic Church. The Czechoslovak Church, very vague in its doctrine and with a tendency to Unitarianism, but strong in its advocacy of social and political reform, from the first welcomed and supported the Revolution; it therefore had no difficulty in agreeing to the demands of the new Government. Its General Synod sent the following message to the President of the State: 'We solemnly affirm our determination to give full moral support to our people in their efforts for the building of a socialist society in this country.' The Evangelical

*Barron and Waddams, *op. cit.*, p. 85.

Churches with some hesitation accepted both the conditions laid down by the State and the help it offered. 'The Church has decided to accept the help offered by the law, not in order to weaken the spirit of self-sacrifice in its members, but to procure for its parishes all that is needed that its spiritual work may go on.' The small Orthodox Church, under a Russian Archbishop, welcomed the new régime. The Roman Catholic Church, on the other hand, resisted the interference of the State with religion; this was stated in a memorandum from the bishops read in all its churches in August 1948: 'We are criticized for not having put forward an absolute endorsement of all that is being done like the other Churches have done. We would not endorse everything because unfortunately we had too much evidence that even in our country a hidden anti-Church and anti-religious fight had started.' The sequence of events fully justified this attitude. In 1948 a document was issued to local Communist groups with directions as how best to attack the Roman Church; they were instructed to undermine the Vatican by all means; to break down unity among the clergy; to drive a wedge between bishops and clergy, and between priests and their parishes; to 'attack the Catholic Church with all the usual weapons: celibacy, economic questions, the Church as a capitalist institution, moral delinquents, etc.'* In 1949 two State committees were appointed to deal with Church affairs, and a Minister for Church Affairs was given full control of ecclesiastical appointments and salaries; of all religious publications, religious education, and all the philanthropic work of the Church. District committees were given wide powers over religious societies and property, the supervision of religious teaching and the administration of theological colleges and seminaries. In 1950 most of the religious houses were confiscated. The fear of resistance from the Church was so great that in Czechoslovakia the clergy of all Churches were called upon to take an oath of allegiance to the State, and only those who had taken it would be permitted to carry out their religious duties – the bishops allowed their clergy to take the oath, though most of

*Quoted by Barron and Waddams, p. 48.

them did not do so themselves, with the reservation 'so far as this is not in conflict with the laws of God and of the Church and the natural rights of men.' If they had refused to take the oath they would have been deprived of their stipends and reduced to penury. Many priests and members of religious orders were brought to trial and imprisoned on one pretext or another. Special inducements and privileges were offered to those of the clergy who were prepared to accept the conditions laid down by the State, even if through so doing they incurred the penalty of excommunication. Coercion, persuasion, threats, and bribes have been used by the State to encourage the formation of a schismatic Church which would defy the Pope and obey the State. Archbishop Beran, much beloved of the people and a man of great goodness and wide sympathies, was confined for many months to his palace, and then exiled from his See. In his own words: 'I have been deprived of all personal liberty and all rights as the Archbishop, and all this without any kind of investigation, without any Court or other official decision.' Most of the bishops have also been kept to their houses, and priests who have not taken the oath of loyalty to the State are forbidden to officiate. Recently, however, some of the bishops have accepted the terms of the Government and appear to be acting in defiance of the Vatican. Possibly only by so doing can the ministrations of the Church be continued, and this course may have been adopted as an interim measure to secure the ministration of the Sacraments to the faithful in a period of persecution. The Government claims that 92 per cent of the Roman Catholic clergy have taken the oath of loyalty.

Against these attacks on the Church the Vatican has steadily and strenuously protested, though it has permitted concessions where they have been possible without the surrender of principle. In Hungary it has excommunicated those who laid sacrilegious hands upon Cardinal Mindszenty, and on 13th July, 1949, it declared that Catholics who knowingly and freely enlist in or show favour to the Communist Party, or who publish, read, or disseminate books, newspapers, periodicals, leaflets in support of Communist doctrine and practice, or write any article in them may not be admitted to the Sacraments. It also stated that 'Catholics who profess, and particularly those who defend and spread the materialistic and anti-Christian doctrine of the Communists, *ipso facto*, as apostates from the Catholic Faith incur excommunication reserved especially to the Holy See'. To this the Minister of Justice of the State of Czechoslovakia retorted: 'Let no one doubt that anybody who tries to carry out that Vatican order commits treason against the principles of his own State and people.' Excommunication has also been pronounced against all who took part in the exiling of Archbishop Beran. The issue between Roman Catholicism and Marxian Communism is joined all down the line.

The same resistance has not been offered everywhere by other Churches. The Orthodox Church has suffered from various deprivations and hardships in some of the Communist States, but as it is closely affiliated with the Church of Russia, and has not usually taken any active part in political affairs, it has not been attacked with the same bitterness as the Roman Church. An Orthodox Archbishop, now dead, told me of the obstacles which the Government of his nation was placing in the way of religious observance, arranging parades and compulsory drills at the hour when the Liturgy should be sung, or on weekdays when some special Festival should be observed; and of the loss it had suffered through the confiscation of much of its property, but he made no complaint of the kind of persecution from which the Roman Catholics were suffering in Czechoslovakia and elsewhere. When I asked him what counter-action his Church was taking, his reply was, 'To persevere, to pray, and to keep silence'.

Attacks have been made on the Protestant Churches – fifteen Bulgarian pastors were tried and condemned for espionage; and in Hungary the senior Lutheran Bishop, Ordass, was sentenced to two years' imprisonment on currency charges. In Czechoslovakia the property of the Salvation Army has been confiscated and two of its officers imprisoned. But the resistance of the reformed Churches, relatively few in number, was never very serious, and usually an agreement was quickly made with the State which guaranteed them freedom of worship and some financial support, while the Churches on their side promised to pray for and to support the State. In Eastern Germany, however, the reformed Churches have been as vigorous and outspoken as the Roman Catholics, and in April 1950 a protest signed by Dr Dibellius and other evangelicals stated, 'The Evangelical Church confesses to the truth that is in Christ Jesus. This truth is not compatible with the materialistic outlook in life. We protest therefore against the propaganda of this philosophy as the sole valid truth in schools, in colleges, in administrative bodies, and in State-owned organizations. No governing power has the right to force upon anyone a philosophy that runs counter to his faith and conscience.'* A month later Dr Dibellius again protested against the hostile attitude of the Government, and accused the Ministry of Culture of giving confidential instructions as to how anti-religious propaganda might be carried out in the schools.

It is plain, however, that the Roman Catholic Church is regarded by the Communists as their most dangerous foe. By ceaseless propaganda they attempt to discredit its doctrine and its ministers; they threaten its priests and laity; they attempt to sow division in its ranks; they have confiscated its property and closed its monasteries; on one excuse or another they have removed some of its leaders and have imprisoned large numbers of its clergy; they have secularized its schools and have taken away freedom from the religious Press; they have sought to isolate the diocesan archbishops and bishops from the Vatican; and have attacked the Pope as a supporter of capitalism and of war. Some have fallen away as the result of this incessant pressure, but the great majority of the bishops and clergy stand firm, and the loyalty of the laity is proved by the way in which the churches are thronged with worshippers. In some countries in which persecution is fiercest the congregations are larger than ever. Once again it will be shown that the Church is the anvil on which the hammer

*Ecumenical Press Service, No. 17, 28th April, 1950.

of the persecutor is broken. Christians of all Churches should support by their prayers and sympathy their fellow Christians in their hour of trial.

THE CHRISTIAN COUNTER-ATTACK

The Christian cannot regard as sufficient preparations to resist aggressive Communism by armed force. More than this is required, for Communism will never be defeated decisively by force alone. The Church must call for the removal of the poverty and destitution which have made millions turn to Communism as the only alternative to intolerable evils; and it must oppose a false ideology, the outcome of materialism and inspired by hate, with the Gospel of truth, justice, and freedom. Instead of a world-wide State established by force and maintained by violence, the Church must offer a universal visible fellowship united in love. The next two chapters, therefore, give some account of the Gospel message for our age, and of the manner in which the Church of England is presenting it.

II

The Gospel

IN the preceding chapters an attempt has been made to describe the confusion and bewilderment of our age and the
causes which have led to the widespread sense of anxiety and
insecurity. For a century and a half a series of movements have
undermined the foundations of traditional ways, and in the
last half-century changes have come so rapidly and unex-
pectedly as to be revolutionary in character. But great as the
changes have been which many have witnessed in their lives,
there is every prospect of even greater changes in the future.
It is impossible to foresee the results of the social and political
revolutions which have already taken place. Unless checked
either by internal weakness or by external resistance, Communism may sweep over the earth, blotting out civilization
as we know it and opening the way to a new and more terrible
dark age. The conflict between Western civilization and Communism may lead to the use of weapons which will destroy
great cities and make a large part of the globe uninhabitable,
driving the survivors of an atomic war to seek refuge in
the recesses of the mountains of Central Asia or Abyssinia.
Man seems to be standing on ground which is shaking
beneath his feet, while he watches helplessly a devastating
flood lashed by the wind and rain rapidly approaching
the dry land on which for a time he has found some
refuge. In this catastrophic age many are asking if

Christianity has any light to throw on the darkness, and help and guidance to give to a generation both perplexed and frightened.

CHRISTIANITY A RELIGION OF CRISIS

The Bible is the book for a time of crisis. In the Old Testament the prophets repeatedly warn their contemporaries of the judgement of God, which will fall upon them and their nation unless they repent of their evil ways. The judgement might come through some natural cataclysm, or through the invasion of a hostile nation, or through the supernatural act of God. But whatever form the judgement might take, its results would be catastrophic. 'The indignation of the Lord is upon all nations, and his fury upon all their armies: he hath utterly destroyed them, he hath delivered them to the slaughter. Their slain also shall be cast out, and their stink shall come up out of their carcases, and the mountains shall be melted with their blood. And all the host of heaven shall be dissolved, and the heavens shall be rolled together as a scroll.'* If Isaiah speaks in this way of the judgement on the nation, Jeremiah is equally stern in his prediction of the woes to come upon both Jerusalem and the nations: 'For, lo, I begin to bring evil on the city which is called by my name, and should ye be utterly unpunished? Ye shall not be unpunished: for I will call for a sword upon all the inhabitants of the earth, saith the Lord of hosts ... Thus saith the Lord of hosts, Behold, evil shall go forth from nation to nation, and a great whirlwind shall be raised up from the coasts of the earth. And the slain of the Lord shall be at that day from one end of the earth even unto the other end of the earth.'† Or to take one other example of the sense of crisis which filled the prophets, Zephaniah speaks of 'The great day of the Lord is near, it is near, and hasteth greatly, even the voice of the day of the Lord: the mighty man shall cry there bitterly. That day is a day of wrath, a day of trouble and distress, a day of wasteness and desolation, a day of

*Isaiah XXXIV. 2, 3, 4.   †Jeremiah XXV. 29, 32, 33.

darkness and gloominess, a day of clouds and thick darkness.'*

The same atmosphere of crisis is found in the New Testament; all through Our Lord's teaching there is a call for watchfulness, so that His hearers should not be taken unawares by the things about to come upon the earth: 'And there shall be signs in the sun, and in the moon, and in the stars; and upon the earth distress of nations, with perplexity; the sea and the waves roaring; men's hearts failing them for fear, and for looking after those things which are coming on the earth: for the powers of heaven shall be shaken.'† The early Christians expected a crisis; it would come in the return of their Lord, or in some great act of judgement such as the destruction of Jerusalem. It is this expectation of sudden change which runs through the New Testament that has so often made it difficult for us to understand it. Over forty years ago, when the world was far more settled than it is now, and when progress appeared to be certain in the years to come, a student of the Gospels wrote: 'Whatever we may believe as to the stability of our present civilization, the Gospels were written at times and circumstances when the civilization men saw around them was not stable, and when men's immediate duties were the duties of those who live in an unstable civilization. If we forget this when we study the Gospels, they become unreal for us and unmeaning.'‡ We no longer are able to feel that our civilization is secure; much which we once assumed as permanent has vanished, and much that we expected to remain is now threatened. In the changed circumstances of our time, when we are conscious that we are living in an age of tremendous crisis, we find in the Scriptures, both of the Old and the New Testaments, passages which might have been written for our time and guidance, for they are the utterances of men who from their own experience understood the tension and dread which follow when accustomed landmarks are removed, and who had to grope their way through the darkness in the midst

*Zephaniah I. 14, 15.   †St Luke XXI. 25, 26.
‡F. C. Burkitt in *Cambridge Biblical Essays*, p. 213.

of the raging of elemental forces over which they had no control until light was given to them from God. The Scriptures have become alive to us in a way they could not have been to those who assumed that the ages of revolution were long past, and who were confident that mankind would enjoy increasingly in the future the blessings brought by scientific discovery.

GOOD NEWS

What is most remarkable about the Biblical teaching on crisis is that the notes of joyfulness and expectation are never entirely silenced even in the darkest days of Jewish history. The prophets exhort, denounce, upbraid their contemporaries; they announce in terms of almost unrelieved blackness the judgement that awaits them unless they repent: but suddenly they strike a different note and break out into singing as they tell of the unfailing mercies of God and of the future He has prepared for His people. There is a gospel in the Old as well as in the New Testament: it has plenty of good news about deliverance, redemption, and restoration. 'The ransomed of the Lord shall return, and come to Zion with songs and everlasting joy upon their heads: they shall obtain joy and gladness, and sorrow and sighing shall flee away.'* 'Sing, O heavens; and be joyful, O earth; and break forth into singing, O mountains: for the Lord hath comforted his people, and will have mercy upon his afflicted.'† Jeremiah, as well as the writers of the prophecies collected under Isaiah's name, has good news to proclaim: 'Behold, the days come, saith the Lord, that I will raise unto David a righteous Branch, and a King shall reign and prosper, and shall execute judgement and justice in the earth. In his days Judah shall be saved, and Israel shall dwell safely.'‡ The Gospel of the Old Testament was the news that over all the whole world there is One Supreme God, instead of the many rival territorial and provincial gods of the heathen; that He is the Holy and Righteous God, not vindictive, cruel, and

*Isaiah xxxv. 10.   †Isaiah xlix. 13.   ‡Jeremiah xxiii. 5, 6.

lascivious, like the gods of the surrounding nations; and that in His good time He will deliver His people from their oppressors and will restore them to a land in which they will dwell in prosperity and peace. Later, as the age of the great prophets died away, the expectation of the kingdom and the Messiah who was to establish it became more materialistic. The Kingdom was to be a nation of which the Jews alone would be citizens, and the Messiah would come from God as a warrior who would destroy their enemies and conquer the Gentiles.

All through the New Testament there is heard the sound of rejoicing. It is heard in the song of Zacharias: 'Blessed be the Lord God of Israel; for he hath visited and redeemed his people.' It is heard in the song of the Blessed Virgin: 'My soul doth magnify the Lord, and my spirit hath rejoiced in God my Saviour.' It is heard in the song of the angels on the first Christmas night: 'Glory to God in the highest.' It is heard in the upper room on the night on which the Lord was betrayed, when He took the bread and the cup and gave thanks, and then afterwards He and His disciples sang a hymn, probably a passover psalm of thanksgiving. It is heard when the disciples after the ascension of their Lord 'returned to Jerusalem with great joy: and were continually in the temple, praising and blessing God'. It is heard again and again in the Acts. It is heard in the epistles, when St Paul calls upon his converts to go about with melody in their hearts. It is found in the last book of the Bible, when the seer hears 'the voice of a great multitude, and as the voice of many waters, and as the voice of many thunderings saying "Alleluia, for the Lord God omnipotent reigneth. Let us be glad and rejoice".' Long after the books of the Bible had been completed, the rejoicing continues: it was heard in the early Christian Fathers, who wrote, 'Sailing we sing and ploughing we praise,' and it finds expression to-day in the public worship of the Church and in the devotions of its individual members. However great public anxiety or private sorrow, the priest will always say at the altar, 'It is very meet, right, and our bounden duty, that we should at all times and in all places give thanks unto

Thee,' and the people will always join with him in saying, 'Holy, Holy, Holy, Lord God of Hosts, heaven and earth are full of thy glory: Glory be to thee, O Lord most High.' In its corporate worship the Church of the twentieth century unites its songs of praise and thanksgiving with the voice of the Church of all the centuries.

This rejoicing is due to the fact that the Christian Church has good news from God which it has to give to mankind. In Christ Himself the Church saw the good news; He was the Messiah so long expected. He had come to establish a Kingdom, but it was to be very different from that expected by popular opinion; it was not the kind of Kingdom brought about and maintained by force, but the Kingdom of grace, righteousness, truth, and love. It was not to be the Kingdom for one race alone, but for people of all tongues and races whom the Father over all has created as His children. The first missionaries carried the good news to the Jew, the Greek, and the Gentile. To the Jew they went with the news that the Christ had come, and through Him they could obtain forgiveness of their sins. To the Greek with the news that in Jesus Christ they could see the eternal God, no longer the Unknown God, but His glory made visible in the face of Jesus Christ. To the Gentile with the news that they were all members of the family of God, children of the same Father called to eternal life; and that by faith in Christ they would be set free from dread of the malignant demons whom they feared would watch for their souls after death. The Gospel was good news of God's revelation of Himself and of His action to save men from their sins. God was revealed in the love of Christ: and Christ, healing, preaching, dying, and rising from the dead, shows God not as passive, quiescent, and observant in some distant realm, but as a God who has intervened decisively to deliver man from his sins and to help him on the way to life eternal.

Christianity is thus good news. It is deprived of its dynamic power when it is regarded simply as a system of moral precepts or as the setting forth of the ideal of a good life shown in Christ Jesus. Much of the ineffectiveness in the modern preaching of Christianity comes from the fact that often the good news it brings is kept in the background. In a depressed and pessimistic age it is of vital importance that in the very forefront of the presentation of Christianity there should be its good news. It is true that the good news, the central fact of Christianity, must be the same in every age, but riches new and old are brought out in successive generations from the great treasure-house of God to meet the special needs of the time. The twentieth century shares a common heart with the men and women of the first century: birth, love, sin, pain, trouble, death, are common to all, and the good news which brought gladness to those who lived two thousand years ago is still good news to those whose fundamental needs are the same, however changed their outward circumstances. But as well as the needs and experiences common to all men in all ages, each century has its own special problems and difficulties for which help is required. It is thus necessary that different aspects of the good news should be made plain to meet the special needs of successive generations. In the industrial and scientific world of the twentieth century there are difficulties which could not have been experienced by those who lived in a rural environment in the ancient world. Christianity will fail to make an appeal to modern men and women unless it can help them in their perplexities and give them good news which will disperse the prevailing darkness.

THE SOVEREIGNTY AND FATHERHOOD OF GOD

There are four truths of the Gospel which should be stressed to-day. First, the Living God who reigns is the Father. The doctrine of the Kingship and rule of God comes from the Old Testament, but it is taken over in the New, and Christ gives a further revelation of the character of the Sovereign of the Universe. The Jews knew He was the all-powerful and the all-holy; Christ taught that He was also the Father. It is necessary to proclaim the reality of the Living God. Atheism assumes that modern thought has banished God from the Universe and has substituted for Him a mechanical system.

There are millions who do not deny the existence of God, but they think of Him as an absentee who created the world and then left it to its own devices, and who is as unimportant to the affairs of mankind as if He never existed. There are others who look upon Him as one who occasionally might be moved to interfere in some special emergency in the life of a favoured nation or individual. But they have no belief in God the living Lord as proclaimed by the prophets, or, as Arthur Balfour once wrote, as a God who takes sides.* If there is no God, the State can be its own god, or can create its own god in the person of a dictator like Stalin or Hitler, to whom its citizens give the worship and obedience which once was given to the Lord and Father of Jesus Christ. If there is no God, there is no absolute moral law; nations, individuals and even different centuries, can make their own codes of ethics as circumstances demand. If there is no God, man is left at the mercy of impersonal forces which buffet him here and there. Fate or chaos is then taken as a substitute for the true God. Too readily the evangelist often takes for granted belief in the existence of God when he is speaking to those to whom He is only a name. In the preaching of the Gospel to-day it is necessary to proclaim the nature of God as revealed both in the Old and the New Testament, for then His sovereignty as well as His Fatherhood will be made evident. The Christian doctrine of God should be good news to those perplexed by the claims of the false prophets who receive the adoration of millions and whose words are treated as law, when they learn that over and above them there is the eternal and unchanging God who will overrule the pride and wickedness of men and who through the ages is working out His purpose.

*'I mean a God whom men can love, a God to whom men can pray, who takes sides, who has purposes and preferences.' *Theism and Humanism*, p. 21.

The Gospel

The Christian Gospel also gives the explanation of the repeated failures of plans for the regeneration of the human race. The widely spread sense of frustration is partly due to the knowledge that many schemes which appeared so perfect on paper have broken down in actual practice. Time after time conventions, pacts, treaties, and leagues for the promotion of world peace have failed: great schemes for social reform have had unexpected and disastrous results; movements with noble ideals and unselfish aims have produced harvests of arrogance, corruption, and cruelty. Often the disappointments caused by these repeated failures have been explained by the theory that man is thwarted by external hostile forces which defeat his efforts. Fate, circumstances, an unfriendly environment, are all blamed; and man presently feels that he is really helpless, that he must either acquiesce in what is inevitable, or battle against it with a courage which is born of despair. Christianity gives a different answer: man's failures it explains as due not to some mysterious forces in the universe, but to his own will. The source of failure is to be found within and not without. There are obviously certain conditions over which man has no control, but most of his failures result from his yielding to an inborn tendency to serve self instead of God, and to satisfy his own ambitions rather than to help his fellow-men. Repeated disappointments are bringing many back to accept both original sin and actual sin as hard facts which explain human failure; for original sin is man's inborn tendency to choose evil instead of good, and actual sin is the deliberate choice of evil instead of good. If this is true, as the Christian faith asserts, a great step has been taken towards the cure of the disease by a correct diagnosis of its nature. Repeated failures are not due to some mysterious, unknown, external circumstances, but to man's own action in his misuse of the will which God has given him. The frequent perversion to evil of what was intended for good, and the humiliating and ever-recurring experiences of knowing the good and failing to realize it, are the results of disobedience to God. St Paul expressed this very clearly when he stated, 'To will is present with me: but how to perform that which is good I find not. For the good that I would I do not, but the evil which I would not, that I do.' To diagnose the disease is, however, only the first step towards its cure. St Paul at once goes on to say that it is life in Christ Jesus which gives freedom from sin. The good news declares that while sin turns man from what is right, nevertheless, the disease is not incurable; healing is found in Christ Jesus, who offers to those who repent and believe, both pardon for the past and the gift of a new life in the future. Man is fallen, but the fall is remediable. Christianity is very realistic: it has no false optimism about the nature of man; it refuses to accept the romantic views of the Communist and the humanist that with a change of social environment, or through education and science, man will blossom out with all the virtues. Christianity rejects entirely the Utopianism which believes that a new social order will automatically change man from his selfishness, acquisitiveness, and combativeness into a being who will ever afterwards live in peace and happiness with his fellows. Christianity knows that man by nature is selfish, proud, grasping, and quarrelsome; but nevertheless it also teaches that he has within him something godlike, for he is made in the image of God, though the image has been defaced and defiled by sin: and it gives the good news that through Christ man can be restored to what God meant him to be.

THE VALUE OF MAN

From what has already been said, it follows that the individual man is of value and has rights which belong to him as man. The great controversy which to-day is dividing the world is over the nature of man. The traditional view of man as little lower than the angels is now attacked from two directions. A scientific philosophy explains him as a machine, more complicated than those made by human hands, but all the same a machine in the sense that man is made up of a remarkable combination of matter and water, that his actions can largely be predicted, that he has no real freedom, that the psychiatrist can take his personality to pieces and then refit it so that it works in the future more smoothly. If this is so, man is really a thing, not a person, and the self-consciousness which he believes distinguishes him from the animal world is only a deep-seated inherited delusion which flatters his pride. The Marxian Communist makes the attack from another direction: he agrees with the materialist that man is made up of chemicals which work in a remarkable way, but he regards him as an instrument to be used in the service of the State, without rights of his own, and as much a slave of the community as the bee is to the law of the hive. He can be moulded by the State into the shape it requires, used as the State demands, and when he has outlived his usefulness, or if by any chance he should show some signs of independence, then it can liquidate him, throwing him on the scrap-heap with other discarded rubbish. Communism exalts the collective society, but degrades into automata the individuals who form it. The world is now witnessing on a gigantic scale a scientific attempt to destroy the dignity and freedom of individuals and to make them into helots under a privileged class – the so-called dictatorship of the proletariat, which by terror crushes individuality and responsibility. Christianity, in opposition to this degradation of man, teaches that each individual is of value in the sight of God. Man's value depends upon the love which God has for all the beings He has created. He is the Father of all, and each of His children has value in His sight. He has created them so that He may love them and they may love Him. He has called them not only to serve and love Him here, but to life which is eternal. It is because God values the individual that he possesses rights as man which none should take from him. The different conceptions of the nature of man result in the different ways in which he is treated: by the totalitarian State as a tool, by the Christian Church as a child of God. The Christian Church has frequently acted in opposition to its own teaching: it has committed fearful crimes in religious persecution; for centuries it tolerated slavery, and later acquiesced in the inhumanities of the Industrial Revolution;

but it was the teaching of the Church which softened the lot of the slave and eventually led to his freedom: history shows that the most successful protests against the cruelties and wrongs committed against humanity came from those who were convinced followers of Christ. The appeal against the oppression of the individual is to the spirit and teaching of Christ. Christianity when most true to its Master is the champion of the rights of the individual against systems which would treat him as a mere tool to be used by those politically or economically more powerful than himself.

LIFE EVERLASTING

Christianity also gives good news about life after death. Death is not the end; the strivings, the hopes, and victories of the individual are not buried for ever in the silence of the grave. Faith in the future life has become very dim in our time. It is therefore necessary that the Church should proclaim uncompromisingly, as part of the essential Gospel, belief in the life after death. At one time the stress laid by the Church on the future life was disproportionate. On the west wall of many of our churches the doom was represented showing the salvation of the chosen few and the damnation of the multitude; or on the Ladder of Salvation were painted the faithful ascending through angelic assistance, and the wicked torn away by demons and thrust into the ever-burning fires. When the churches were whitewashed and the old frescoes hidden from view, the eloquence of the preacher described in full detail the glory and happiness of the blessed, and in even greater detail the tortures of the lost. The figurative language of the Scriptures was used literally, and the interpretation given to it was often unintelligent and far beyond any warrant given by the text. In reaction from the hell-fire type of sermon many modern preachers have been unduly silent about the life to come. This has led to exclusive emphasis on the life in this world, as if it were all. Now, however, when the future of this world seems so uncertain, and that it is possible all human achievement may soon be destroyed, it is only the Christian belief in a life after death which can deliver man from a sense of futility. There must be greater boldness in teaching the reality of the life after death, though there must be great reserve in describing its nature. It is eternal life rather than an endless cessation of years which should interest the Christian. Mr Hoyle in his Reith lectures on 'The Nature of the Universe' concluded them by saying Christians 'in their anxiety to avoid the notion that death is the complete end of an existence suggest what is to me an equally horrible alternative. If I were given the choice of how long I should like to live with my present physical and mental equipment I should decide on a good deal more than seventy years. But I doubt if I should be wise to decide on more than three hundred years. Already I am very much aware of my own limitations and I think that three hundred years is as long as I should like to put up with them. Now what the Christians offer me is an eternity of frustration.'* It is surprising that a man of such learning did not acquaint himself more carefully with the Christian doctrine of the future life, for this teaches both duration and quality. Eternal life means an ever deepening entry into and appropriation of the perfect goodness, truth, and beauty which God gives to those who by faith are in union with Him. In this there is completion and not frustration.

The special good tidings which should be dwelt upon for our age is thus fourfold: the God who reigns is the Father; God redeems man; God cares for the individual so that each and all are of value; after death there is another life. But with this there must always go the preaching of the source and the authority of this good news, Christ Himself, as God and Man.

THE PREACHING OF CHRIST

It is vital that in every generation there should be the preaching of Christ, and this is far more than the description and application of His teaching, more than presenting Him as the perfect example of the good life; it means the showing forth of

*F. Hoyle, *The Nature of the Universe*, p. 117.

Christ; or, as St Paul would say, the public placarding of Jesus as Lord and Saviour. As the first step, it is usually necessary to show Christ as a man living among men. There is great ignorance about the simplest facts concerning His earthly life: many only know of Him as a good man who was killed by the Jews. The historical facts about Him must be taught: His birth in Bethlehem, His childhood at Nazareth, His baptism by John, His calling together and training of a small band of disciples, His journeys of preaching and teaching through Palestine, His announcing the Gospel to the multitudes, His works of healing, the growing hatred of the leaders of the Jews, the plotting against Him, the falling off of His popularity, His arrest, His trials, His torture and His death and His resurrection. In the midst of these events and happenings the Person of Christ should be shown standing out plainly, dominating and controlling men and circumstances. Our contemporaries should be helped to see Him as He was seen by His contemporaries: a man of authority setting aside old laws and traditions, denouncing the false values of the Scribes and Pharisees, single-handed with a whip of cords clearing the temple of its traffickers; calm and resourceful in the midst of those who attempted to trap Him with their questions into some dangerous admission or to brow-beat Him into submission during the trials between His arrest and His death. But with the authority there is seen limitless love and tenderness: the Christ who rebuked so sternly the Pharisees is the same Christ we see blessing the children, forgiving the sinner, mixing with the outcasts, healing the sick, and feeding the hungry. With this presentation of the life and person of Christ there must be shown the background of His earthly ministry, a small rural community with only one city of any size, a nation occupied by conquerors whose presence is bitterly resented by the Jews, whose hatred of the foreigner was equalled only by their internal hatreds and discords both on religion and politics. There must be shown, too, the Church intensely nationalistic and self-centred; stifling genuine piety with its rigorism; and treating petty rules of ceremonial as if they were the law of God; with its leading ecclesiastics pompous, fanatical, and bigoted. If the historical Christ is to be understood it will be necessary also to explain the passionate conviction of the Jews that one day God would intervene and by the might of the Messiah restore their national glory and independence. The historical facts about Christ must be taught before there can be any religious revival. He must be preached as a real person, and the events and people of His time must be made to live. Year by year there are written Lives of Jesus Christ, some of great distinction and beauty, but there is no popular 'Life' which is circulated by the million and sold on all the railway bookstalls, written in such a way that those who read it feel that the story of Christ is as real as the life of some political leader or philanthropist of their own time. The references made to Christ by the open-air preacher mean nothing to most of those who listen, for they know nothing about His life and times. This ignorance must be remedied if there is to be a return to Christ.

But the Christian cannot stop with the preaching of the Jesus of history. This is only the beginning. The life of the Jesus of history will interest and sometimes inspire, but it will give mankind neither the guidance nor the good news which it needs. The account of the life and person of Jesus Christ should be such that it leads to the question 'Who is this Jesus?' and the Christian answer must be given that 'the Jesus laid at His birth in a manger in Bethlehem, living for thirty years or so as a man among men, and dying as a condemned criminal on the cross, is the Lord and Saviour of the world.' He has the authority to give good news, to reveal the inmost nature of God, to show the true way of life and to summon men to follow it, because He is the very Son of God. The story of the Jesus of history may excite reverence, admiration, and sometimes pity, but it will not fill millions with the readiness to die for Him. The once-fashionable interpretation of Christ as a liberal humanitarian of the first century done to death by clerical obscurantists is no longer tenable: in violent reaction from this, Schweitzer and his school have shown Him as the vehement man of fire, who with dynamic force attempted by His death to bring the historical order to an end.

To-day a saner criticism sees Him as One who, though truly man, nevertheless made claims which no man had ever made before or has ever made since, and did works such as no other man has ever done. It is the supernatural Christ whose power and authority are proclaimed by the Church. The attempt to remove difficulties in the way of belief by explaining away everything in Christ which is not acceptable to the twentieth century will leave a Christ untrue to the only historical documents we possess on His life, and without the authority which claims obedience to His words.

THE TRUTH OF THE GOSPEL

But the doubt will arise again and again – is Christianity true? It is easy to see the beauty of the faith that the Power behind the universe revealed Himself as man; to admire the splendour of the sacrifice on the Cross, to understand how great must be the comfort and bright the hope which come from acceptance of the traditional doctrine about Jesus Christ – but is it true? Is it not too good to be true? Can the modern world believe that behind and above the myriads of stars revealed by the astronomer there is a personal God, who so loved this tiny little world that He sent His only begotten Son to live and die for the salvation of the men and women who for a brief space inhabit it? There are many who confidently and scornfully, and others with deep regret and sorrow, give the answer that this faith is now utterly incredible, though no doubt at one time it helped and satisfied credulous and ignorant people, but to-day it is not worth serious consideration. This is the root of the difficulty, for so many reject Christianity offhand without any serious consideration of its claims – they are against the spirit of the age, and that is sufficient to condemn them out of hand. Many have neither the will nor the patience to treat seriously the traditional faith. There is an interesting example of this in a letter written by Lord Keynes as a young man and published in his *Life*; referring to Henry Sidgwick's religious doubts he says: 'He ought to have got over this a little sooner, because he knew that the thing was untrue perfectly well from the beginning.'* A popular writer on scientific subjects contemptuously dismisses Christianity as one 'of the two great superstitions of the Western world.'† (Marxism is the other!) Those who dismiss Christianity so summarily refuse to recognize that there are Christian theologians as intelligent as themselves, many of them, indeed, with a wider knowledge of recent scientific discovery. But frequently those who thus lightly reject Christianity as unworthy of serious consideration have never attempted to understand it as set forth and defended by its best exponents. 'They almost always attack Christianity as they have found it represented by some poorly-educated clergyman in the next street, or some dull traditionalist who taught them at school ... By attacking Christianity in its most ignorant exponents, or even grossly caricaturing it after their own fancy, as a preparation for overthrowing it, they are able to arrive at the little chirrup of felt intellectual superiority far more easily than if they had to address themselves to a system of thought set forth by a competent and able contemporary thinker.'‡

In modern evangelism the evidential side must be given an important place. There are many books of great value in defence of the faith written by living scholars, but some of these are in language too technical to be understood by the ordinary man; and they need to be supplemented by smaller inexpensive books which contain in popular language the arguments of the scholars. There must be no writing down to the uneducated as far as substance is concerned, but there must be avoidance of technical language. Many of the terms used by the Christian teacher are unintelligible to the man who has no theological training. The language of the theologian needs to be translated into the vulgar tongue. Three groups of evidential literature are of special importance. The first should consist of books dealing simply and honestly with the difficulties caused by modern science, especially with those which come from recent discoveries on the extent of the universe;

*R. F. Harrod, *John Maynard Keynes*, p. 117.
†Barbara Wootton, *Testament for Social Science*, p. 87.
‡Edwyn Bevan, *Christianity*, p. 253.

for while the majority of educated men no longer find any difficulty in reconciling evolution with religion, the vastness of the universe seems to deprive the individual of all significance. Another difficulty comes from the tendency to interpret life in the terms of mechanism and to regard the spiritual as equivalent to unreality. Psychology as taught and practised by some psychiatrists seems to leave room neither for free will nor for the soul. The purpose of this group of books would be to show that modern thought does not disprove the existence of God, rather that it supports the belief that there is Mind behind the universe, and that the explanation of how the mind works does not explain why it works. Secondly, there must be books on the historical origins of Christianity. Christianity claims to be an historical religion; when the question is asked, 'Is it true?' the questioner usually means, 'Did Jesus Christ really live? Do we know reliably the outlines of His life and teaching? Did He rise from the dead?' These questions must be answered by giving the reasons for accepting the books of the New Testament as trustworthy and reliable documents. Recent criticism has tended to re-establish their position as such. Almost as important is the necessity of giving an historical view of the Old Testament, showing how its various books can be approximately dated, and giving some account of the circumstances with which they deal. Thirdly, there should be literature on Christian experience, describing how the redeeming power of Christ as the Way, the Truth, and the Life has been manifested through the centuries both in the history of the Church and in the religious experience of individuals. It should make plain that the mighty works of Christ continue every century and can be witnessed in the transformation of character and in the expansion of the Church. There are many admirable books already dealing with these great subjects, but it is important that their substance should be made more accessible to the general public and used as an essential part of evangelistic work; where no suitable books of this character already exist, competent scholars should be invited to provide them as soon as possible. There is a higher standard of education than in the past, and evangelism must be conducted in the terms and with the arguments which appeal to the thoughtful man who makes no claim to be an intellectual, but is no longer prepared to accept either his religion or politics on the authority of others. But the language used to help him to belief must be such that he understands it. Once again theologians are called upon to do what they have had frequently to do in the past: to translate and to express Christian truth in terms which are intelligible to thoughtful men of the twentieth century, and at the same time to retain the substance of the faith.

MODERN METHODS OF EVANGELIZATION

But however admirably the faith may be expressed in modern terms, the major problem still remains – namely, how to reach the multitude who never attend church, who never read a religious book, however clear it may be, and who take no trouble to hear the Christian message. In the past the answer to the problem would be found in the open-air service, but these now rarely arrest the passers-by; those who stand listening to the speaker are usually regular attendants at church, though now and again some may pause in their walk for a moment to listen, and then turn away unmoved and uninterested. Only occasionally, and then after the most careful preparation, is an open-air service instrumental in reaching the non-churchgoer.

To reach him, more use must be made of modern inventions. As the first Christian evangelists used the Roman roads and the Greek language, then a kind of Esperanto among the educated, to propagate the Christian Gospel, so modern evangelism should use as largely as possible the Press, the wireless, the cinema, and the drama. The Press, both in Great Britain and the United States, is friendly to religion. It reports news of the Churches, and many of the daily papers have a weekly article on a religious or ethical subject, usually written by recognized leaders of religion. Much more thought and care should be taken by Christians to use to the fullest extent the opportunities which are available for giving the gospel message in this way. The hurried reader of the national Press does not appreciate the influence of the provincial weekly Press: almost every town of any size has its own local paper, which is read from cover to cover during the week-end by those who live in the district in which it circulates. With a sympathetic editor and with the co-operation of the clergy and ministers of the neighbourhood, there is usually no difficulty in obtaining space for an article every week on some definitely religious subject, provided it is written in a clear and practical manner. In this way thousands will be reached who rarely attend any place of worship. The article will be read by them because it is in the paper which custom prescribes should be read through with a care and deliberation rarely given to the daily paper by those who obtain it on six days of the week.

The importance of broadcasting as an agency of religious teaching is now widely recognized. 'Religious broadcasting, with its immense resources and its annihilation of space, is able to take the Gospel into every home in the land.'* Christianity owes a great debt to Lord Reith, the first Director-General of the B.B.C., for the vision he had from the outset of what broadcasting might be for the nation and for his determination that religion should be given in all plans a position of primary importance. In his interesting autobiography he describes the initiation of religious broadcasting in this country: he had an interview with the Archbishop of Canterbury who 'had heard vaguely about broadcasting: what was it: where could he hear it?' Reith asked the Archbishop and Mrs Davidson to dinner. 'In course of conversation before dinner I pressed, unseen, the switch of the wireless set; in a few seconds the room was filled with music. As Dr Davidson's biographer remarks, they were "entirely amazed": inquired if it were not even necessary to leave a window open. Next day the Archbishop summoned a meeting of ecclesiastical leaders in his room in the House of Lords – the beginning of the religious advisory committee.'† I was chairman of the committee for twenty-one years. I doubt if any of its members realized at first the future importance of

Conversion of England, p. 105.
†J. C. W. Reith, *Into the Wind*, p. 93.

religious broadcasting, but from the beginning Mr Reith, as he then was, drummed into us the immense possibilities it offered. It was through his action that a Director of the religious side of broadcasting was appointed. Throughout the whole of his time as Director-General he took a keen personal interest in all that concerned religious broadcasting. Before long its importance was generally recognized, and the different Churches sent some of their ablest men to represent them on the committee. The scope of religious broadcasting has steadily widened since its early days; great care is taken over the selection of those who give the addresses and over the music and all that concerns the service to be broadcast: 'at the present time the Home audience in all parts of the country is offered fifteen religious services every week, together with talks on religious subjects and programmes of hymns.'* In addition, from time to time religious drama is presented through the medium of the radio, the most notable and successful example of this was Dorothy Sayers' play-cycle *The Man born to be King*. The broadcasting of this was opposed by the Sunday Observance Society; but it is now generally accepted that this was one of the greatest evangelistic appeals made in this century. In various ways the wireless helps millions who never go to a place of worship to keep in contact with Christian prayer and teaching. It is preparatory and supplementary to the more definite evangelistic work of the Church, and its value is very great. Closer co-operation between the Churches and the B.B.C. is still required; the Churches are sometimes inclined to look upon the broadcast service as unfair competition, while from the B.B.C. there come complaints that the Churches do not make sufficient use of the opportunities offered to them in this way and fail to follow them up.

The influence exerted by the cinema is perhaps even greater than that of the wireless. What is seen usually leaves a deeper impression than what is heard. Over forty million attend the cinema every week. 'The cinema has almost unrivalled power to enrich and delight the mind and can be a great cultural

*Report of the Broadcasting Committee 1949, Appendix H, Paragraph 65.

medium as well as a source of fun and entertainment.'* It can form, especially on the minds of children, lasting impressions either for good or for evil. Often it creates a false view of life, glamorous, sentimental, and luxurious. But it is much more difficult to use the cinema for evangelistic purposes than the wireless. One obvious difficulty is due to the fact that it is not under any central control, but the industry is owned and worked by a number of competing companies. Occasionally some film which is directly religious is shown, usually in connexion with the Roman Catholic Church, for films of this nature are almost certain to be welcomed in the large Roman Catholic population of North and South America. But there is nothing comparable in the cinema world to the regular opportunities of teaching and worship given by the B.B.C. To some extent the cinema is used both in public worship and in the Sunday School, and several religious institutions make praiseworthy efforts to produce suitable films for the causes in which they are specially interested, but these are usually exhibited to those who already are members of a Church, and make little or no appeal outside a small circle. The larger films which would be of interest to an ordinary cinema audience are very costly to make and produce. So far no attempt has been successful to use films on a large scale for evangelistic purposes. The possibility of this is before the minds of those who are responsible for evangelism, but the practical difficulties remain very great. Probably the Church of England Report on *The Conversion of England* is right in suggesting that 'the best policy may well be for the Church to be in the film world, suggesting themes and offering stories, even as it is in the B.B.C. . . . But there is no one as yet in the cinema industry to suggest the right themes, or to guide, theologically and religiously, the script writer and film director.'† The influence of the cinema is so great that every attempt must be made to see that it is not only used for the instruction of those who are already Christians, but as a means of bringing home to the non-churchgoer the nature and

Report of the Departmental Committee on Children and the Cinema, p. 8.
†P. 401.

teaching of Christianity. It is not sufficient for the Churches to protest against the exhibition of films which are harmful to morals, but some policy should be reached which would encourage the production of those intended either directly or indirectly to promote the cause of Christ.

The cinema, especially in the provinces, is a serious threat to the popularity of the drama. But a successful play has a more lasting influence than a successful film, though it is not seen by so many; and there is always the possibility that it may be adapted for the screen. Throughout the Middle Ages the drama was one of the most common and popular methods of teaching the Christian faith. The Passion Play at Oberammergau is the best-known survival of sacred drama, but at one time almost every city had its own performance of miracle plays. In York during the Festival of Britain there was a revival of the plays which in the pre-Reformation days were performed by the trade guilds in different parts of the city on stages which were moved from place to place. On this occasion they were performed before large audiences in the ruins of St Mary's Abbey. Recently many parishes have had Nativity plays at Christmas and Passion plays in Lent, and in addition there have been a number of morality plays, like *Everyman*. Many of these plays are poor in quality and would not be tolerated by a regular playgoer. Few of them are evangelistic in the sense of reaching those outside the Churches; usually the spectators consist of the friends of the performers and of those who are already churchgoers. The devotional value of this type of play is often greater than its artistic or literary qualities. Occasionally, however, religious plays are written of such outstanding merit that their appeal is general. *The Just Vengeance* by Dorothy Sayers, produced in Lichfield Cathedral; *The Rock* and *Murder in the Cathedral* both by T. S. Eliot are plays of this nature. Sometimes on the secular stage there is presented a play which would not be labelled as religious – to do so would be fatal to its success – and which yet deals from the Christian standpoint with profound religious or ethical problems in a modern setting. The most recent play of this character is Mr Eliot's *The Cocktail Party*, which had long runs both in London and in New York. Plays of this nature written by men and women of ability, produced and acted well, would provoke questioning and discussion which might prepare the soil for the Gospel message. This would be especially the case if, like *The Cocktail Party* or *The Family Reunion*, they are relevant to modern life.

The Press, the wireless, the cinema, and the drama can all be used as opportunities of evangelism, if the goodwill of those who are responsible can be obtained. But this will be useless, and worse than useless, if it is thought that religion can be advanced by anything which is second rate. At one time 'sacred concerts' were permitted on Sundays when the usual concert was taboo; the chief difference was that the 'sacred' concert usually consisted of inferior music performed by second-rate musicians. The same principle has been applied to Sunday cinemas, for which inferior secular films are sometimes reserved. Only the best should be given for religious purposes, and it is wiser not to attempt to use these modern methods for evangelism if the performances compare unfavourably with those which are frankly secular.

Too much must not, however, be expected through the use of the Press, the wireless, the cinema, and the drama for the spread of the Gospel. Their value to the evangelist is great because they enable millions to be reached who never come within the sound of the preacher's voice; they keep alive seed which possibly was sown in childhood, they retain familiarity with prayers and phrases which might otherwise have been forgotten, they remove prejudices and kindle the desire for greater knowledge, and they can prepare the way for definite Christian teaching in association with fellowship and worship; but this fuller presentation is the special duty of the Church which has been given the responsibility of evangelizing the world. Without the Church much of the seed sown by the Press, the wireless, the cinema, and the drama will fall on stony ground, and soon will wither away if exposed to the scorching sun of tribulation and persecution.

For the Church is the field in which the seed of faith will come most naturally to fruition. The truth of Christianity cannot be proved by reason alone, still less by the methods used in physical and biological research. Reason can remove difficulties in the way of faith, and it can lead the inquirer some distance on the road towards complete conviction; but there comes a gap which must be bridged either by the direct action of the Spirit of God on the soul, or by the traveller making a venture of faith to accept as true and to act upon what has not yet been completely proved by the reason; and then through experience, he finds that his venture has been justified. Within the Church he should find the environment which will nourish and strengthen the beginnings of faith.

12
The Church

THE great changes which have taken place during the last half-century have formed a challenge to the Church to meet problems which could not have been foreseen in the past. The reaction of the Church in an age of revolution has been slower than that of most secular societies. This is inevitable, for the Church is built upon a rock which no storms can destroy, and it has a gospel which is unchangeable, even though everywhere else there is change. It must hold fast to the truth which has been revealed to it, however unpopular it may be. But the golden treasure of the truth with which it has been entrusted is contained in earthen vessels which can be changed and adapted as the circumstances require. History affords repeated illustrations of the way in which the Church has proclaimed in new surroundings the eternal Gospel in terms more appropriate to them than those used by the first evangelists; and its organization, while always retaining the threefold apostolic ministry of bishops, priests, and deacons, has been frequently altered to meet new circumstances. In the last half-century all through Christendom there can be seen to a greater or less degree the reactions of the Church to an age of rapid change. In Russia the Church, deprived of its State connexion and wealth, now carries on its work in simplicity and poverty, concentrating on its worship. The Roman Catholic Church in countries where attendance at morning Communion has been made impossible, or when work in the factories makes it difficult, now allows Communion to be received in the late afternoon or evening after a very short fast; and in France priests work in factories and mines to enable them to minister from within to an industrial population. In this chapter an account will be given of some of the ways in which the Church of England is meeting conditions unlike anything it has experienced in the past.

The Church

EVANGELIZATION

For the first time since Christianity was brought to Great Britain, the great majority of its people look upon religion as something irrelevant to their lives. There is very widespread indifference to the Christian faith and a still wider ignorance about its nature. While in the past the Church had to minister to those who, at least in name, were Christians, to-day it has to bring the faith to millions who are pagan in outlook. In the past the Church had to build up in the faith those who nominally accepted it; to-day it has to give the good news to those who are ignorant of it. Christianity is a minority religion in the midst of a heathen world; the work of the Church must therefore be largely evangelistic if it is to fulfil the commission given to it by its Lord. In the past, missionary work was looked upon as preaching to the heathen in distant lands, to-day it is of equal necessity at home; the latter may be even more important, for the home Church has to supply the personnel and much of the money required in non-Christian countries; certainly it is in some ways more difficult, for home evangelization is among men and women to whom the Gospel does not come with a shock of surprise, for most of those to whom it is preached have some dim knowledge of Christian terms, occasionally from some faint recollection of religious teaching received in their childhood, sometimes from no more authoritative sources than that of singing hymns like *Abide with Me* before a Cup-tie; this conventional knowledge may act as a prophylactic against the living Gospel.

There is so much to-day in English life which still bears the marks of Christian influence that it is very hard for Church-people to appreciate the extent of the paganization of England. The sessions of Parliament are opened with prayer, the bishops have their seats in the House of Lords, Lord Mayors and Mayors have their chaplains, the cathedrals and parish churches are thronged with worshippers on great public occasions, the majority of people still bring their children to be baptized and come to the Church for a blessing on their marriage and for a religious service at the burial of their dead.

It is difficult to see how behind this façade of outward observance religious conviction has disappeared. There are many regular church-goers who, while deploring the decline in Sunday worship, comfort themselves by saying that at heart the people are really Christian and before long will feel the need of God, or by hoping that suddenly there may come a great religious revival which will once again fill the churches. Those, however, who are most capable of forming a judgement know how serious the position is, and that it calls for the most strenuous evangelistic work if England is not to lapse into complete paganism. Once it was assumed that the ninety and nine sheep were safe within the fold and the one which was missing could be sought at leisure; now for one safely in the fold there are multitudes who have not the slightest intention of entering it.

Thus the primary duty of the Church is evangelization, which has been defined as 'to present Christ Jesus in the power of the Holy Spirit, that men shall come to put their trust in God through Him, to accept Him as their Saviour, and to serve Him as their King in the fellowship of His Church'.* Recognition of the need of national evangelization came in the First World War, when the chaplains, especially those who had had no previous experience of parochial work, were astonished and horrified to find that the majority of the men to whom they were ministering had no knowledge of the Christian faith. There was little aggressive atheism among either officers or men, most of them would claim to be Christians, but they had the vaguest ideas of the nature of Christianity, and only a small minority were actively connected with any Church or denomination. It was in view of these facts that in 1915 the two archbishops decided 'to call the men and women of England to earnest and honest repentance of our sins and shortcomings as a nation and to claim that in the Living Christ, in the loyal acceptance of Him as the Lord of all life, individual and social, lies the one sure hope.' This National Mission was called the Mission of Repentance and

*Archbishops' Committee on the Evangelistic Work of the Church, 1918.

Hope. The decision to hold it was by no means universally approved; the parochial clergy felt they had not been sufficiently consulted and that already the war had thrown almost intolerable burdens on their under-staffed parishes. The Mission, however, went forward, and those who had been most doubtful did their best to give its message in their parishes. Care was taken to prepare the clergy by gathering them together at different centres for prayer and conference, a number of valuable pamphlets were issued, and five commissions were appointed by the archbishops to consider matters such as 'The Teaching Office of the Church' and 'The Church and Industry'. In most of the parishes there were special sermons and services, and some rural deaneries had large teaching conventions. It is difficult to estimate the value of this venture – the laity disliked the call to national repentance, and would have preferred to have had solely a message of hope. But on the whole the meetings and services in connexion with it were well attended; to many of the clergy it afforded a welcome change from the strenuous round of parochial work; and undoubtedly it strengthened the conviction that the Church must break away from self-complacency and realize more fully the strength of secularism. Archbishop Davidson in a foreword to the five reports summed up the results of the mission: 'The call told: not, of course, universally, but very widely. We found that people were ready to face familiar facts afresh: that a new spirit was breaking upon dry bones: that we must, and could, be up and doing. As we appraised the outcome of the Mission call five subjects in the life of the Church and nation stood out with obvious claim for our rehandling – the character and manner of our teaching: our worship: our evangelistic work: the discovering of removable hindrances to the Church's efficiency: the bearing of the Gospel message on the industrial problems of to-day.'

In the interval between the wars there were many local evangelistic efforts; it was, however, becoming plain that the old-fashioned ten-day parochial mission was no longer the converting agency it had been in the past: it taught and strengthened the faithful, but it won few who were not already Christians. When Vicar of Portsea I had a mission for the parish: we had a strong team of experienced missioners, the most careful preparations were made for it over a period of many months, the congregations throughout the ten days were very large, and the climax was reached when, at five o'clock on a cold December morning, there were over a thousand communicants at its closing service. Large numbers of resolution cards were signed, and many who had lapsed from the Church returned, but the number of those who had been altogether outside the Church and who were converted by the mission was extremely small. This has been the general experience in the years between the wars. It was presently felt that what was most needed was the strengthening of the spiritual and intellectual life of the clergy and laity. So in 1929 the two new archbishops, Lang and Temple, made an appeal to 'all members of the Church, clergy and laity alike, to make some continuous study of the Gospel of God's revelation of Himself in Christ, of the Bible and the Creeds wherein that Gospel is set forth, part of the corporate life and work of every parish throughout the land.' From this there followed what came to be called 'The Way of Renewal': most of the dioceses arranged for central synods or meetings of the clergy on the renewal of the spiritual life, retreats were multiplied and well attended, but, most important of all, small groups of the clergy arranged to meet together in one another's vicarages for prayer and study, many of these groups continuing in existence until the outbreak of the Second World War.

It was hoped that the deepening of the spiritual life of the clergy and laity would prepare the way for a new evangelistic attempt. The dislocation caused by the war was general; so many of the parochial clergy were absent on national service and their congregations were so often dispersed through war work and air raids, that the evangelistic work of the Church was largely suspended. There was danger that much existing work might collapse in the stress of wartime conditions, and all thought of new evangelistic efforts seemed impossible to men already overworked; but in June 1943 the Church Assembly asked the two Archbishops (William Temple and myself) to appoint a commission 'to survey the whole problem of modern evangelism with special reference to the spiritual needs and prevailing intellectual outlook of the non-worshipping members of the community, and to report on the organization and methods by which such needs can most effectively be met.' The Commission was appointed with Dr Chavasse, the Bishop of Rochester, as Chairman, and the Report was completed by Whitsuntide 1945. It was published under the title of *Towards the Conversion of England*, and was almost at once sold out; within a short time it became a best seller and new issues had to be printed; it created general interest and was widely discussed both in the secular and religious Press. It reached the conclusion that 'the present irrelevance of the Church in the life and thought of the community in general is apparent from two symptoms which admit of no dispute. They are (1) the widespread decline in church-going; and (2) the collapse of Christian moral standards.' The underlying causes of the present position are summarized, a chapter followed with a brief statement of the content of the Gospel, and then a full discussion of methods of evangelism, with many practical suggestions as to how the Church in modern days can best fulfil its divinely given commission of evangelism.

The Report has had a great influence in bringing before the laity as well as the clergy the call to evangelization. In its recommendations it rightly insists: 'The first, chief, and essential method of evangelism is for every parochial ministry to be an evangelistic ministry. To be effective an evangelistic ministry cannot be exercised by the parish priest alone, but needs the co-operation of the congregation.' As a result of the impetus and guidance given by the Report, in almost every diocese there has been a quickening of the spirit of evangelism – conventions, teaching missions, parochial missions, either for ten days or a shorter period, have been held. The most striking instance was the 'Mission to London', a courageous campaign led by Dr Wand for the conversion of the huge city of which he has the spiritual oversight, and of a diocese so vast and impersonal that the Church at times seems to consist only of a number of separate congregations struggling to hold together without any visible influence on the secular world which surrounds them. In connexion with the Mission great central meetings were held – the Albert Hall on one occasion at least was taken for a meeting of workers, and crowded from the topmost balcony to the body of the hall. Striking notices on the hoardings called attention to the Mission. During the time it was held carefully chosen missioners addressed large congregations. The Mission undoubtedly brought home to London the fact that it had within it a living Church; it helped the clergy and laity to escape from a narrow parochialism into the atmosphere of a great fellowship; it gave new courage and inspiration to many who were downhearted and defeatist, while some who had hitherto been indifferent or hostile to religion were attracted to active membership of the Church. There have been elsewhere on a smaller scale missions to great cities. Both in Oxford and Cambridge missions to under-graduates have been held, and very well attended. Many dioceses have decided on evangelistic appeals on a large scale, calling upon the stronger parishes to help the weaker. All kinds of methods are being used and new experiments are being tried. In some cases whole congregations are asked to assist in the missionary effort of a neighbouring parish; in other cases companies of clergy and laity descend on a parish by invitation of the incumbent and visit house to house preparatory to services in church. An imposing list could be made of the variety of methods used both by the dioceses and the parishes. In the diocese of York the Archbishop in 1947 addressed at various centres the laity on the call to loyalty to Christ. In the next year the clergy and laity were urged to visit the nominal Churchmen in every parish and to supplement by personal appeal a letter they were to deliver from the Archbishop; at the end of the year at central meetings a call for personal witness was made by laymen as well as by the clergy. In the following year schools for the clergy were held on the subjects of worship and preaching. In 1951 and 1952 every deanery and parish has been asked to make its own arrangements for some form of evangelistic effort; this will occasionally embrace the whole of great cities like Middlesbrough and Hull, but more often the parish will make its own plans with the help and advice of the diocesan evangelistic committee. In every diocese there can be heard the noise of the wind in the tree tops; the Spirit of God is awakening a sense of missionary responsibility. The cumulative effect of numerous small efforts undertaken with prayer and thought may mean that the tide will turn and the empty places in our churches gradually be filled. Already there seem to be some signs of this in the towns. There is most certainly stronger interest in religion than was the case a few years ago, and side by side with incessant criticism of the Church there is found a keen desire to know if it has some Word from God which will guide and strengthen man in these days of darkness and fear. This has been shown in a remarkable way by the large crowds which night after night have attended the missions conducted by Dr Billy Graham.

THE APPEAL TO SOUND LEARNING

There are many who hold that there will be no return to the Church by the educated until it can be shown that its Creed is not inconsistent with modern thought. The Church of England makes an appeal to sound learning in support of the doctrines of the Christian faith. Our Church believes firmly that the Holy Spirit will lead it into all truth, and that He will guide its scholars and theologians to judge rightly how far the new views under discussion agree with the Scriptures, with the teaching of the Fathers, and with reason. The Church is convinced that as all truth comes from God, there is no reason to be afraid of new discoveries: for if true they are a further revelation of the mind of God and of the manner in which He works. The Church rightly is cautious over the acceptance of new theories, for further discussion may show that they are mistaken, but it must not denounce them if at first they may seem irreconcilable with the ancient faith; often it will be found that there is no fundamental opposition to it and that they throw new light upon it. The theologian must also see how far the teaching he gives requires to be modified and should be ready to use the discoveries and terms of contemporary thought to restate the faith, so that it may be more easily understood by intelligent men and women. Sometimes there seems at first to be no possibility of reconciling the historic faith with a new philosophical theory or scientific discovery, but even here great patience must be shown, lest unintentionally, what comes from God is rejected. Ultimately the inquirer may have to choose between Christian faith and contemporary thought, and often he may have to wait in patience and suspense while the search for reconciliation continues. But however great the dangers may be, the Church of England is emphatically on the side of free inquiry, and gives no support to those who in the mistaken interests of religion would suppress freedom of thought. Bishop Gore insisted on this: 'The vocation of a scholar requires that he should think freely. It is mocking him to tell him to investigate and form judgements of truth, and at the same time to dictate to him what those judgements are to be. He must be free to go where the argument, duly weighed, leads him ... he must be prepared to receive light from every quarter, however hostile, and to follow the light. He must not "reason in fetters". The test of the truth of the tradition is that it can bear the whole light. If his thought leads him plainly and finally outside the Christian Creed, of course he must cease to hold the office of a Church teacher. Freedom for thinking has no connexion with freedom to violate one's engagements. He must no doubt take the risk of such an event. Anyway, the Church must sanction free inquiry, praying earnestly for its scholars that their faith fail not. If such freedom is refused inside the Church, it will assert itself outside: and that way lies revolution or schism.'*

It is in this spirit of free inquiry and in readiness to accept new truth that the best thinkers in the Church of England have met the intellectual changes of the last half-century. This has led to considerable reinterpretation and restatement of the

*C. Gore, *The Holy Spirit and the Church*, p. 188.

traditional faith. One illustration of this will be sufficient. The Bible in the last century was regarded by most Christians as verbally inspired and free from all error. The so-called Higher Criticism has, however, shown that some of the books of the Bible were not written by the authors whose names they bear, that often the date when they were actually written was considerably later than had been supposed, that in them there are occasionally accounts of events which are inconsistent with one another, and statements which are unhistorical and contrary to scientific knowledge. At first these views caused indignation and dismay. To-day they are generally accepted by all intelligent Christians, who now see in the Bible the record of the gradual unveiling of the character and Will of God, of His dealings with nations and individuals, of the revelation of Himself in Jesus Christ, and of His work of redemption wrought by Christ and carried on after His ascension through His Church. No attempt is now made to defend every action ascribed to God in the Old Testament, or to accept as historical every event it relates. The Christian believes the Bible to be truly inspired by God, not for instruction in science or secular history, but to give a progressive revelation of Himself and of the nature and purpose of man. Experience has abundantly proved it is a channel of saving grace. There never has been a dogmatic definition of inspiration; it has been interpreted differently at various periods of Church history, and thus the modern view of the Bible has been gradually accepted by instructed churchmen without any disloyalty to their faith, though the militant atheist still criticizes theories of inspiration which have long ago been abandoned.

In other directions Christian thinkers have made themselves familiar with new scientific and philosophical views, and have either controverted them when mistaken or when true have shown that they throw new light on the Christian faith. In the last half of the nineteenth-century apologists were mainly concerned with showing that the theory of evolution was not inconsistent with the Christian faith, and that the Higher Criticism did not disprove the inspiration of the Bible. But as the century drew to a close theologians became interested in problems of even greater importance concerning the nature of God, and the personality of man. One of the earliest of those who wrote on these subjects was Dr J. R. Illingworth, whose Bampton Lectures in 1894 on 'Personality Human and Divine' met some of the difficulties which were troubling many; later he supplemented these lectures by books on 'Divine Immanence' and 'Divine Transcendence'. The former of these made a great impression, especially upon the younger clergy, and for a time the immanence of God revealed in man and nature was the theme of many sermons. A greater and more permanent influence was exercised by Dr Inge's Bampton Lectures in 1899 on 'Christian Mysticism'; there are many who are profoundly grateful for these lectures and for his later books on mysticism. Dr Inge taught that a direct experience of God was possible for sane and level-headed Christians not easily swept away by emotional revivals. This teaching was followed by that of Evelyn Underhill, who showed the close connexion between mysticism and the organized sacramental and devotional life of the Church.

Throughout this half-century the Church has had a series of theologians who have used the terms of modern thought. Outstanding among these was William Temple, one of the greatest men of our time, whose personal faith gave courage to others and who by his Gifford Lectures and other writings showed that a man could be both a Christian and a modern philosopher; his aim was expressed in an article in *Theology*: 'We saw as folk who desired to think like Christians, a little farther into the meaning of our world than those who sought no illumination from that faith. We had to lead as many as we could to see life in that light of the knowledge of God, which we had ourselves received. We tried, so to speak, to make a map of the world as seen from the standpoint of Christian faith.'* There are many others who have undertaken this work of interpretation: among them are Dr F. R. Barry, the Bishop of Southwell, Dr Matthews, the Dean of St Paul's, Canons Hodgson, Raven, Streeter, Quick, Richardson, Father Thornton, and Miss Dorothy Sayers. Dr Kirk, the Bishop of Oxford,

*F. A. Iremonger, *William Temple*, p. 521.

and Mr C. S. Lewis have written notable books on Christian conduct.* There have been also several volumes of essays in the succession of *Lux Mundi*, in which the contributors dealt with various aspects of the Christian faith: in 1909 appeared *Biblical Essays*, with essays by a number of Cambridge scholars on problems which had arisen from the critical study of the Bible; in 1912 there came *Foundations – a Statement of Christian Belief in Terms of Modern Thought*. In the introduction it was stated that Christian theology had been formed in a different age from our own, 'an age when the sun and stars moved round the earth, when the meaning of natural law and evolution was only dimly apprehended, when the psychology of religion, the historical method, and the critical study of ancient documents were yet unborn,' so the seven essayists (past or present Oxford tutors) had undertaken a careful re-examination and, if need be, re-statement of their faith. This was followed in 1927 by *Essays Catholic and Critical*, edited by Dr E. G. Selwyn, now Dean of Winchester; it was written, like *Lux Mundi*, from the Catholic standpoint, and its purpose was to continue under modern conditions what the earlier book had done thirty years before. In 1938 there was published the Report of the Commission on Christian Doctrine. The chairman was William Temple, and in the Introduction he stated its scope: 'Our task has been, as far as we were able, to discuss the unchanging truths of the Christian revelation, and the various interpretations of these current in the Church of England, in such a way as to be intelligible to those of our contemporaries who have some acquaintance with theology.'

Sufficient has been said to show how untrue it is to criticize the Church for concentrating on improvements in its organization or on matters of liturgy and ceremonial, while ignoring the intellectual attacks on its faith. The Lambeth Conference of 1930 called upon the Church to renew and redirect its teaching office 'by a new emphasis upon the appeal to the mind as well

*I am only mentioning theologians of the Church of England, but I am not unmindful of the great contribution made to Biblical study and Church theology by many scholars of the Church of Scotland and by Free Churchmen in England.

as to the heart in the preaching of the Word as an element in Christian worship,' and both before and since that call the Church of England has steadily kept in mind the vital importance of expressing and teaching the faith in the terms which are most appropriate in relation to modern thought and are most easily understood by educated men and women.

CHANGES IN WORSHIP

Since the time of the Oxford Movement there had been an ever-increasing demand for an enrichment both in ceremonial and ritual of the public services of the Church. Many changes had been introduced, often at the price of bitter controversy and opposition. Most of these changes were originally due, either to the wish to bring the worship of the Church of England into greater agreement with the rest of Western Christendom, or to introduce into it elements of richness and beauty which often had been absent. With the first war there came another call for change. It was discovered by the chaplains to the forces that the majority of the men to whom they were ministering found the services provided for them largely unintelligible. From the chaplains there came a strong demand for Prayer Book revision, not so much for the sake of greater liturgical correctness, but to make the public worship of the Church more popular. It was thought by the more optimistic that brighter, shorter and simpler services would attract many who were unaccustomed to church-going. An official attempt was made to meet this need by the Revised Prayer Book of 1928; this preserved the framework of the Book of Common Prayer, but simplified the language, shortened the services, and provided a number of additional prayers. If this had been all, the book would certainly have received the approval of Parliament, but the authorization of the Reservation of the Consecrated Elements and the alternative form of the Holy Communion caused violent controversy and the rejection twice by the House of Commons of the resolutions necessary for the legalization of the book.

The necessity for Prayer Book reform was, however, so

great that in most of the services in the parish churches a considerable number of changes have been made. With the exception of the proposed Canon in the Order of the Holy Communion, most of the prayers and revised services of the 1928 book are generally used with the full approval of the congregation. Apart from the more controversial proposals, Prayer Book revision in the parish churches has had three characteristics – the services are shorter, very rarely would modern congregations remain in church for the length of time regarded as natural fifty years ago; prayers are used which are not in the old Prayer Book, but which are either taken from the 1928 book or from some manual of intercessions or devotions which has commended itself to the officiating minister; and in many churches it has become the practice to have a parish communion at nine-thirty or ten as the chief service of the Sunday. Nearly all these changes are in agreement with the spirit and teaching of the Prayer Book, though probably many of them are illegal if judged by a strict interpretation of the law. Sometimes, however, the changes introduced by the incumbent on his own authority seem to have no sufficient reason except a love for novelty, and can be justified neither by liturgical knowledge nor by practical utility.

Since the second war there has been some reaction from liturgical individualism, and in more churches the Prayer Book services are faithfully followed – even to the reading in full of the 'Dearly Beloved'. Churches are becoming rare in which an individualist imposes upon his congregation a mingle-mangle consisting of alien liturgies clumsily joined to portions of the Order of Holy Communion in the Book of Common Prayer. There is increasing recognition of the beauty and associations of the Prayer Book services which have been used for over four hundred years. Mr Charles Morgan writes: 'The miracle of the Prayer Book, if allowed to speak in its own order plainly, is that it speaks both timelessly and to the occasion,' and of the Litany, 'It is wonderfully comprehensive. One would venture to say there is no human need, spiritual or temporal, that is not remembered in it ... As the necessities of men change, and from youth to age or from generation to generation their joys and sufferings alter their forms and names, the words of the Litany open to include them.'* But it is still necessary for lawful authority to be obtained for prayers and services already in general use; it is not right that those who use them should be indefinitely exposed to the charge that they are breaking the law. It is reasonable to ask that our services should be enriched by the greater knowledge we now possess of the ancient liturgies of the Church; that some at least of the services should be made simpler both in terminology and structure, and that special services should be provided for those occasions when the congregation is likely to include many who are unfamiliar with the ordinary worship of the Church. It is hoped that the new canons may provide the lawful authority for provisional and experimental changes in public worship; and that authority for changes in or additions to the Prayer Book of a more permanent character may be obtained from the Crown without the necessity of debates in Parliament.

THE CLERGY

Both evangelism and sound teaching depend largely on a sufficient number of qualified men and women who will both convert and teach. For centuries it has been customary to look upon the clergy as set apart with special responsibilities both for evangelization and teaching. The decline in numbers of the clergy has therefore been a matter of the gravest concern to the Church. In 1905, irrespective of those who had retired, there were 19,053 clergymen in the two provinces of Canterbury and York, in 1914 there were 18,180, in 1930 there were 16,745, in 1941, 17,001 and in 1949, 14,380. In 1937 there were 558 ordained to the diaconate, in 1939, 589, and in 1950, 407. These figures are the more serious when it is remembered that during the last twenty years there has been an increase in population of nearly four million.

The results of the shortage of clergy are very serious. Parishes which at one time had a staff of four or five assistant curates now think they are fortunate if they have one priest in

Reflexions in a Mirror, Second Series, pp. 53, 54.

addition to the incumbent. Parishes which always had a curate in the past have been worked since the outbreak of war by the incumbent alone. Much work which was of great importance has had to be left undone: house-to-house, or at any rate general, visitation – the normal evangelistic method of the Church of England – has become impossible; the single-handed vicar finds it takes all his strength and fully occupies his time to take the regular round of services, the baptisms, marriages and funerals, as well as visiting the sick and special cases. He has no time either for visiting those who are not members of the congregation, or for the running of clubs and socials for the young. Sometimes through lack of helpers the Sunday School has had to be abandoned. Many of the older clergy are breaking down through overwork. The pressure of existing work is so great that the clergy find it difficult to use new opportunities which present themselves for Church extension. Incumbents write to their bishops telling them they are finding the strain intolerable, and churchwardens and parishioners protest that it is unreasonable that their parish should remain so long without a curate. The bishops are keenly alive to the necessity of additional help, but they have not the men to send, unless they detach a curate from some other parish where the difficulties are almost as great. They have to leave parishes without an incumbent for months through inability to fill the vacancy caused by death or resignation, and often they are in despair as to how they may provide for the spiritual needs of the population of a new housing estate which has suddenly come into existence.

The Church has long recognized the urgent necessity of additional ordained men if it is to meet all the claims made upon it. It has been trying to solve the problem in three ways – by increasing the number of ordinands; by raising their standard of efficiency; and by redistributing the clergy so that they work where they are most needed. In the past the clergy were usually drawn from the professional classes, who paid for the training of their sons at the universities. The ministry was justly criticized as a class ministry; but in the second decade of the twentieth century it became obvious that ordinands in the future would come chiefly from parents who could not afford to pay for their training. If the Church was to obtain a sufficient supply of ordinands it would be necessary for it to contribute largely towards the cost of their training. Kelham and Mirfield were rendering great service to the Church by the thorough and careful training they were giving to those who had the vocation to Holy Orders but could not have paid for the cost of preparation. Something on a wider scale was needed, so in 1916 the two archbishops made an appeal for large sums of money for the training of ordinands and gave a pledge that no one who had served in the Forces should be debarred from Ordination solely because he could not afford the training. Over a thousand service candidates were helped and trained in this manner, an old prison at Knutsford was used for pre-university training of nearly seven hundred men. Between the wars increasing financial help had to be given by the Church for the training of its ordinands: most dioceses had their own funds from which men were given grants on the condition that they promised to work for some years in the diocese which had helped them. From 1932 there was a steady increase in the number of those ordained every year, until at last the annual losses through death and retirement were exceeded. But the war of 1939 again reduced the number of ordinands to a minimum. On its outbreak the theological colleges were emptied as men joined up in one of the fighting services. The number of clergy working in the parishes sank to an unprecedentedly low figure. Since the cessation of hostilities the numbers have again been increasing, but not yet sufficiently to replace the losses due to the war and to normal shrinkage. The State and the Local Education Authorities are helping to solve the financial problem by making grants to men who are training for various professions, but the Church still has to raise large sums for many of its ordinands, without which they would be unable to meet the heavy cost of their time at college.

Never has greater care been taken over the selection and training of the clergy. The old days have long passed when an ordinand was accepted on the strength of a degree at one of the universities and a hurried interview with a bishop. The fewer the clergy the more important it is that they should be carefully chosen and trained. In 1912 the Central Advisory Council of Training for the Ministry (C.A.C.T.M.) was established to advise the bishops in the selection and training of candidates for Holy Orders. The younger candidates appear before Selection Boards, which, after three days of residence with some twenty of them, reject, approve, or advise. A longer period of training is required than in the past – normally three years at a university and two at a theological college, or, if a university course is not recommended, three years at a theological college. A general ordination examination (usually known as G.O.E.) sets a standard for all the dioceses, and it is understood that a bishop will not ordain men who fail to pass this examination, unless there are strong reasons for an exception. After his ordination the deacon and priest is placed by the bishop under the supervision of some competent clergyman who directs and advises him on his studies. For the older clergy from time to time 'schools' are arranged at which there are 'refresher' courses to help them in their own spiritual and intellectual life, and to assist them to keep in touch with recent thought.

The supply of clergy during the last fifty years has been insufficient for the needs of the Church. There are no longer either the men or the funds for the traditional parochial system, by which every parish small or great had its own incumbent. While many town parishes with populations of ten thousand to twenty thousand have only one priest, small country parishes with populations of under five hundred continue to have their own incumbent. It is difficult to exaggerate the value of the parochial system; it has been in the past of the greatest service both to the Church and the nation: in every village of England, however poor or remote, there was a man who had been sent there to guide and help the people in the way which led to eternal life; usually he became the leader in all that concerned the social life of the community, and the friend and counsellor of its people. A succession of men whose names were known only to a few have helped through many centuries to build up all that is best in the English character. The lazy, self-indulgent, and quarrelsome among the clergy are heard of and their failings broadcast and caricatured; but the quiet work and witness of the many are taken for granted and often ignored. But times have greatly changed since the parochial system came into being. England has become an industrial instead of a rural nation, a nation of great towns instead of small villages; the villages, moreover, are no longer remote and isolated, the car and the bicycle make inter-communication easy and quick; village life itself is no longer self-sufficient, as in the past; the younger folk especially, have many of their interests outside its boundaries, while the children at the age of eleven are often sent to a school elsewhere to complete their education. With the shortage of clergy it was plainly the right policy to group together parishes so that one clergyman might minister to two, three or even four, instead of each one of these little communities having its own resident priest. By plurality and schemes of union large numbers of parishes have been temporarily or permanently united, and thus it has been possible to pay more adequately the country clergy, and at the same time to check an excessive flow of the men from the town to the country parishes. The recent Pastoral Reorganization Measure has given each diocese the power to survey its parishes as a whole and to regroup and reorganize them so that both men and money are used to the best advantage.

Change in the value of money has brought great hardship to most of the clergy. Their incomes have never been large, and from time to time in the past attempts have been made to relieve their poverty. Like everyone else, they have suffered from the heavy income tax, increased rates and the rise in the cost of living; but unlike other members of the community they have not had a corresponding rise in stipends and wages. The large parsonage house, once an attraction, has now become a burden; the cost of keeping its fabric and the garden in good order and the high wages of any domestic help have added to the financial burden of the clergy. Great efforts have been made by the Church Commissioners, the dioceses, and in many cases by the parishes, to raise the incomes of the clergy. Most of the dioceses aim at a minimum for an incumbent of £600 and a house, but though in some this standard has been exceeded, in many it has not yet been reached.

THE LAITY

But even with the reorganization of the parochial system the clergy alone cannot provide all the spiritual ministrations required in the parishes. When parishes are united, and one vicarage takes the place of two or three, the churches still remain with the duty of seeing that they are used for public worship. Frequently on a Sunday the parish priest hastens by car or bicycle from one church to another, but distances, time and physical infirmity sometimes render this impossible. It is here that the help of laymen has been found invaluable. In every diocese there are to be found a devoted band of laymen who, without payment of any sort, except for their expenses in travelling, assist the clergy in their pastoral work. They take the services and give the address when there is no clergyman present, and often when he is present assist him with the service. They hold the licence of the bishop, which is only given after their qualifications for this work have been carefully tested. But for this unselfish work in many of our churches there would be no services from one end of the week to another. Sometimes in the case of a long interregnum a lay-reader is practically in charge of the parish, and a clergyman only comes to administer the Sacraments and to visit the sick. Recently permission has been given to the readers by diocesan bishops to assist on specific and exceptional occasions with the administration of the chalice, when there are large numbers of communicants.

It is unfortunate that there has been great hesitation in allowing qualified women to take services and give addresses in church. This has been partly due to the fear lest this might lead to a demand for the priesthood of women, though there is not the slightest possibility of this ever being permitted in the Church of England; and partly on account of a deep-rooted prejudice against women speaking in church, which claims some justification in St Paul's refusal to allow women to speak in the congregation of the early church, when conditions were very different from what they are in the twentieth century. But now that women take such an active part in public life, and that the whole standard of their education has been so greatly raised in recent years, it is much to be regretted that the Church has not made fuller use of the many educated and capable women it has among its members. It has its deaconesses, a small but most valuable order; it has its sisters; it has thousands of women teaching, visiting, administering relief, conducting various church and parochial organizations; but it has been reluctant to allow them to take any part in leading public worship. Lately, however, there have been signs that the hesitation is passing away, for the Convocations have given their approval in somewhat guarded terms to women both taking public prayer and preaching in church at services other than those intended only for women and children.

In 1918 Church Councils were set up, and this gave the laity a recognized place in the work of their parishes. The church-wardens, the sidesmen, and in ancient parishes the ratepayers had their legal rights, but except at the invitation of the incumbent the ordinary Church layman was given no responsibility for Church work. The Enabling Act, which gave power to the Church Assembly, also 'provided for statutory councils on which the laity were to be fully represented at every level of the church's life. Through Church Assembly, Diocesan Conferences, Ruridecanal Conferences, and Parochial Church Councils, all of which were forced by law to meet at regular intervals, every geographical area and district of spiritual competence was provided with its representative, responsible body which must be consulted, and on which lay people were fully represented by democratic election. Only the actual ordering of public worship was withheld from their competence. This was much more than an act of justice bestowing on the laity a voice of right instead of a voice by grace. The vital thing was the establishment of a principle that the lay members of the Church were equally responsible with the clergy for all the Church did.'* The success and usefulness of a Parochial Church Council depend largely on the incumbent's ability to lead and to trust it. When this is done the Council can be of great value to the parish.

With the increasing responsibility of the laity it becomes a matter of importance that they should know the faith of the Church of which they are members, and the reasons for it. Hardly anything would strengthen the Church of England more than a great body of laymen ready to bear witness to their faith by their understanding as well as by their lives. Often the case for the Church goes by default through the layman being unable to reply to the critic. The churchman in this compares unfavourably with the Roman Catholic convert or the Communist, who know the very different creeds they hold and are eager to convince others of their truth. Too much care and trouble cannot be taken over the instruction of the laity in their faith. Already there is much useful and un-technical literature on sale in our churches; in some dioceses special lectures are organized for the laity; many of the clergy make a practice of preaching teaching sermons; and teaching missions are frequent. But much more must be done if the laity are to take a full and intelligent part in the defence of the Christian faith against its adversaries and in presenting it persuasively and reasonably to the inquirer.

CHURCH AND STATE

With the rapid growth in the activities and power of the State in the last half-century there has come the demand that there should be some readjustment in the relationship between Church and State, so as to secure greater freedom for the Church. There is no longer any agitation for disestablishment and disendowment. It is widely felt by churchmen that through disestablishment there would be lost valuable opportunities of spiritual service to the nation, and the average

*Roger Lloyd, *The Church of England in the Twentieth Century.* Vol. II, p. 153. These two volumes give an admirable and well-documented account of the Church of England in the last half-century.

citizen feels that the establishment is a national recognition of religion which should not be thrown away at a time when an aggressive atheism is persecuting Christianity in many parts of Europe. But various causes have led to the demand that the Church should not be so closely bound up with the State as it has been for many centuries. In the past every citizen was a member of the Church. The House of Commons consisted of laymen of the Church. Now a large number of its members are members neither of the Church nor of any other Christian society. The Prime Minister, who nominates to the chief offices of the Church, need be neither a Churchman nor a Christian. It is inconsistent with the spiritual nature of a Church that it should be so largely under the control of those who do not belong to it. The business of the State has so greatly increased that it has neither the interest it once had in ecclesiastical affairs nor the time to deal with them. Legislation urgently required by the Church was often delayed year after year, not so much out of opposition or ill will, but through lack of time. Recently, too, the Church has gained a deeper sense of its nature as a spiritual society, and therefore feels it right that it should manage its own affairs.

The Life and Liberty Movement during the first war asked for greater self-government. It was granted by giving the Church Assembly the right to pass measures which would become law if they were approved by resolutions of both Houses of Parliament. This was a great and remarkable act of goodwill on the part of the State. Though it still retained the final decision, it gave the Church the means of expressing its mind by formulating the legislation it required, and thus saved the long, tedious, and exasperating delays of a Bill which had to pass in every detail through both Houses of Parliament.

The Church has used these facilities to forward to Parliament a number of useful measures of reform: over sixty of these have received the Royal Assent, most of them dealing with problems of administration, discipline, and finance. Only four measures have been rejected by Parliament: two dealing with the proposed revision of the Prayer Book, a third with the division of the diocese of Lichfield, and the fourth with the disposal of super-abundant City Churches. But with these exceptions the State has shown readiness to help the Church in its attempts to readjust its work to new and changed conditions. But some further loosening of the ties which unite the Church to the State is necessary. First, it is difficult to defend the appointment of the chief officers of a spiritual society by those who need not belong to it. As long as the Church is established, the final decision on the appointment of bishops must remain with the Crown on the nomination of the Prime Minister; but the cathedral chapters should be given freedom to express their views as to the kind of bishop required for their diocese and to vote freely on the name sent to them by the Crown for election. As the Chapters are not always representative of the diocese, and still less of the Church, the Church as a whole should have a recognized right to submit suggestions or criticisms to the Prime Minister, and this should be done by the Archbishop of the Province concerned. Secondly, the Church should have the right to enrich and to revise its worship without submitting its proposals to Parliament, in which there will always be a large proportion of members not belonging to the Church. As long as the Church is established the State must maintain the right to assure itself both that the proposed changes have the approval of the great majority of churchmen, and that they are not contrary to the teaching of the Scriptures and the Prayer Book. But the Church must have greater freedom than it now possesses to formulate and control its worship. Thirdly, the Church should be allowed to make canons to regulate its own life. These must, as in the past, receive the Royal licence, and those which affect previous legislation or the laity may have to obtain the approval of Parliament. The Convocations for some time have been engaged in the revision of the canons of 1603, and it is confidently hoped that there will be no serious controversy over the majority of the proposed new Canons. Fourthly, instead of the Judicial Committee of the Privy Council as the final Court of Appeal on matters of doctrine and worship, there should be substituted a Court which is definitely spiritual in its authority and composition. Until this is done the lower ecclesiastical courts will remain half paralysed, working well in a limited sphere, but unable to deal satisfactorily with questions of doctrine and worship, as their decisions must be in accordance with the judgements of a court whose jurisdiction in spiritual matters is rejected by a large number of clergy and laity.

Changes such as these would not involve the drastic measure of disestablishment, which would mean a long controversy and might seriously hinder religious work, especially as disendowment would go with it; but they would give the Church greater freedom to order and control its own spiritual concerns. The early Church survived the collapse of the ancient civilization, for it was both detached from the world and organized for catastrophe. In the greater and more terrible catastrophes which threaten our time the Church should be in the world, but not of the world, and sufficiently detached from the existing secular order to survive its possible destruction.

If the Church has greater powers of self-government it will also be more capable of resisting any attempted encroachments by a totalitarian State. This argument has been criticized on two grounds: first, that there is no likelihood of a totalitarian State in this country; but this seems a rash and optimistic prophecy when elsewhere the movement towards totalitarianism has been so great. The second argument is stronger – namely, that a totalitarian State would sweep away any constitutional barriers behind which the Church attempted to shelter; but the more strongly the Church realizes its spiritual freedom and uses it to govern itself, the more vigorous and united will be the resistance which it would offer to unreasonable and unjust demands from the State. At present the State is in the position of being able to use the control which it legally possesses over the Church to reduce it gradually or abruptly to a mere instrument of its will. Greater freedom will not give the Church security against a tyrannical State, but it will enable it to offer more effective opposition. The central argument for greater freedom, however, is neither fear nor expediency, but the spiritual origin and nature of the Church.

The Church

In these days of world crises the disunion of Christendom is seen by Christians to be a sin against God and a stumbling-block to the spread of the Gospel. The critic from outside points scornfully to the divisions and controversies of Christendom and asks contemptuously if Christians are likely to close their ranks even in the face of a common danger. The critic does not realize the difficulties in the way of reunion, and still less does he appreciate the progress which has already been made. The obstacles in the way are great, for the different Churches and denominations are each convinced that they possess some God-given distinctive truths which they dare not surrender. It is its anxiety to be loyal to its Master that makes a Church insist on doctrines and practices which cause offence to other Churches equally loyal to Christ. The country village, with its ancient parish church, large enough to hold the population of the village, and possibly with three Nonconformist chapels, all with very small, though earnest, congregations, is an example of the wrongfulness and the absurdity of our divisions. Time and energy are wasted, tempers frayed and irritability quickened, by the presence of a number of different Churches each proclaiming the one gospel of Jesus Christ.

On the other hand, it can be truly stated that never before this last half-century have such strenuous attempts been made to find a way to reunion, and to remove or at least to reduce the evils and inconvenience which result from our unhappy divisions. It is hard for those who are under fifty to realize how greatly the relationship between the different Churches has improved in recent years. When I was first ordained, over fifty years ago, there was a deep religious, political, and social gulf between Churchmen and Nonconformists, especially in the country districts. The religious differences both in doctrine and in the manner of conducting worship were stressed to the exclusion of the more important matters on which there was agreement. Political differences were due to disputes over the privileged position of a State Church and the teaching of Church doctrine in the schools. Socially the Church of England was more closely connected with the upper classes and Nonconformity with the middle classes. Many of these differences have been softened; disestablishment and religious education are no longer matters of dispute; and the social changes throughout the nation have reduced class distinction. Though serious differences remain, both Churchmen and Nonconformists see more plainly than they did in the past how much they hold in common.

There is a new spirit and a changed outlook. The collective conscience of Christians of all Churches now condemns the bitterness of past controversies; there is a genuine anxiety to avoid controversy as far as possible, and, when it is unavoidable, to conduct it with restraint and charity. A new conception of what is meant by the Church is replacing the older idea that the Catholic Church consisted of three branches: Roman, Orthodox, and Anglican, while outside there was a collection of sects which had broken away from the true Church. Now many of our theologians teach that there is one inclusive Church of which all who have been baptised are members unless they have either voluntarily left it or been expelled from it: on this view the divisions are within the Church, and between those who are already members of it. Opportunities for practical co-operation are now eagerly sought. In active work for Christ the different Churches are drawing more closely together. A striking example of this is to be found in the British Council of Churches, on which most of the Christian Churches of Great Britain are represented, and which has organized joint action on many social and moral problems which affect all Christians.

The Church of England has taken a lead in the work for Christian unity. An historic appeal was made by the Lambeth Conference of 1920 to all Christian Churches. The immediate practical results were not great, but the appeal deeply stirred the consciences and deepened the wish for reunion. Archbishop Temple probably did more than any one man had ever previously done for Christan unity. He was convinced of its necessity. He saw the movement towards it becoming stronger in the drawing together of the different Churches, and in his enthronement address at Canterbury he bore witness to it: 'As though in preparation for such a time as this, God has been building up a Christian fellowship which now extends into every nation, and binds citizens of them all together in true unity and mutual love ... Almost incidentally the great world-fellowship has arisen: it is the great new fact of our era.' The Lambeth Conference of 1948 declared 'that it is the duty of the Church to bear united witness to God's redeeming grace in Jesus Christ, to do battle against the powers of evil, and to seek the glory of God in all things. It therefore appeals to Christians in all communions, whatever the differences which may separate them in Church order and doctrine, to join in Christian action in all parts of the world irrespective of political party for the application of the principles of the Christian religion to all departments of national and international life.' The present Archbishop of Canterbury, Dr Fisher, in a sermon at Cambridge, made an appeal to the Free Churches of England to consider the possibility of taking episcopacy into their system. A committee consisting of representative Anglicans and Free Churchmen has reported on the implications which would follow if the proposal should be adopted. It is doubtful if a great body of Anglicans are prepared to enter into communion with Churches which would remain in full communion with non-episcopal Churches, or to approve of the giving of episcopacy to another Church except as an immediate prelude to corporate reunion. On the other hand, most of the Free Churches find it difficult to depart from their traditional dislike of episcopacy. But there is encouragement in the very fact that Dr Fisher's proposal has received such careful consideration; at least it has reopened discussions with the Free Churches. Though the day of corporate reunion may still be far distant, for it must be remembered that schemes of reunion which were not generally accepted by the Churches concerned would only lead to new divisions, yet there is undoubtedly a drawing together of Christians in the face of the dangers threatened by a militant atheism, and through a stronger realization of common loyalty to the One Christ. It is deeply to be regretted that the Roman Catholic Church stands aloof from movements towards Christian unity, places severe restrictions on its members who wish to take any part in them, and demands complete submission as the price of unity.

The Church of England must hold firmly to its Catholic heritage in the Creeds, the Sacraments and the Apostolic Ministry, and to the open Bible as the Word of God which contains all that is necessary for eternal salvation; but at the same time it must never cease from praying and working with passionate zeal for the reunion of Christendom. As the ancient Catholic Church of this land it has a special responsibility for the restoration of Christian unity in England. Its leaders, both clerical and lay, are making a valuable contribution both to the British and to the World Councils of Churches, but it will be visible co-operation and friendship between the different Communions in the towns and villages which will convince most effectively ordinary men and women that the fellowship preached by the Church is not a vague ideal, but a living fact. The world desperately needs fellowship; it is only the Church which can permanently satisfy this need.

CHRISTIAN OPTIMISM

An attempt has been made in this chapter to show some of the ways in which the Church of England has been reacting to an age of change. It is sometimes accused of watching helplessly world and national movements which it cannot control and on which it has no influence. I hope that in outline sufficient has been said in the preceding pages to show that the Church has been strenuously trying to meet the challenge of the time so as to adapt its work and organization to new conditions, and to give its message and witness in a world which is permeated with secularism and hag-ridden with fear.

This is not the first, though it will possibly prove the most searching, crisis through which the Church of England has had to pass. There have been times when its survival seemed uncertain. Bishop Butler's words in 1736 are well known:

'It has come I know not how, to be taken for granted, by many persons, that Christianity is not so much as a subject of inquiry, but that it is now at length discovered to be fictitious.' Thomas Fuller's preface to his history written during the Commonwealth is not so well known; in it he writes: 'An ingenious gentleman some months since in jesting, advised me to make haste with my History of the Church of England, for fear (said he) lest the Church of England be ended before the History thereof.' But three hundred years have passed since those words were written and the Church is not a dying but a living Church, which faces courageously the difficulties of the present, and is planning quietly its future work for God and the nation.

Epilogue: The Two Cities

IN the fifth century the barbarian tribes invaded Italy. In vast numbers they poured over its fair land, spreading ruin and devastation. It is said that when some envoys from Rome reached a distant city to which they had been sent with a message of encouragement they found it empty, except for the dead bodies of the citizens who had been slain. In 410 the invading hordes reached the city of Rome, captured and sacked it. When the news of this spread through the civilized world there went up a loud cry of horror and consternation,* for though Rome had lost its military and political power, it was still the sacred city. The shock of its capture was great. The end of all things seemed to be at hand. Those who secretly regretted the passing of the old gods now murmured that the fall of Rome was due to anger at the destruction of their images and the desecration of their altars. The news of this catastrophe reached St Augustine in North Africa. He saw it was a challenge to Christian faith, and replied to it by a book which has been famous for centuries throughout Christendom; he took fourteen years in writing it, and gave it the title of *The City of God* or as it might be translated *The State of God (De Civitate Dei)*. It was intended to answer hostile critics and to give courage to the fearful and perplexed.

In this great book St Augustine describes two cities – one built by love of self to the contempt of God, the other by contempt of self to the love of God. Through the centuries the interaction and fortunes of the cities can be traced. The Rome which had fallen was a city of man built to the despite of God; though it was not entirely evil, for it had maintained authority and order, and it even had some of the qualities of righteousness, for in St Augustine's view a kingdom without righteousness

*'There was one universal cry of horror and anguish when, through a thousand exaggerated voices, the civilized world heard of the Fall of Rome.' Gregorovius, *Rome in the Middle Ages*. Vol. 1. p. 163.

is a den of brigandage; but it was inflated by arrogance, enflamed by wordly ambitions, and given over to the worship of false gods. Not all its past glory, not even its virtues, could save it from the judgement of God. The other city built to the glory of God on the foundations of righteousness and truth cannot so easily be seen. It is not the Church, though the Church should possess the righteousness of the city of God and is appointed by Him to build its walls. Nor can the city be found anywhere on earth in its perfect form. St Augustine is not altogether clear in his teaching either as to how far the city can be seen on earth or on the nature of its relationship to the Church. But whatever confusion there may be over these matters, there is none over the core of St Augustine's message – namely, that the city of God is the city of righteousness and peace, and while the earthly city will disappear, the city of God will endure for ever. The destruction of the city of man will not involve in its ruin the city of God. The Christian therefore should not be dismayed at the crashing to the ground of the civilization of the world, for his true city, his homeland, is in heaven and will remain eternally inviolate and indestructible.

In some aspects our age is not unlike that in which St Augustine lived.* It has been shaken by two great wars and violent revolutions. It is now under the threat of an even more terrible war. The sense of security possessed by the Victorians has proved to be the result of a brief period of exceptional peace and prosperity in a comparatively small corner of the globe. The world storms of recent years have destroyed this confidence beyond all recall. The cities in which many had trusted as safe strongholds are now discovered to be built on sand. The city of man, gracious and attractive as it has been made with the treasures of human skill and culture, gives no sure refuge against the blasts of the storm now raging, and offers no promise of any life when man's brief existence here is finished. Great breaches have

---

*It ought to be said that Professor J. H. S. Burleigh in his book on *The City of God* writes: 'St Augustine has no consciousness of living at an end of an era, or even in a period of transition,' p. 10.

already been made in the walls of the city of Mammon, and those who once ruled it now dread the loss of their riches as well as of their authority. In the crowded city of Demos there is a growing sense of disillusionment and frustration as its citizens find that bread and circuses fail to satisfy their deepest wants. In the city of violence the citizen has become a mere slave of the State, used by it to extend its power and to destroy its rivals. In the city of the Communist no place is found either for God or for the individual; God is rejected, while man is drained of his personality until he becomes a brainless tool in the hands of a group of unscrupulous men. All of these cities came from the earth, and will return to the earth from which they came.

In the crises of our age the Church of God must proclaim the abiding reality and sovereignty of the city of God as opposed to the city of man. St Augustine did not condemn as altogether evil the city of man; he recognized it had qualities which had been useful in the service of God, so the citizen of the heavenly city, while living on earth in the city of man, should respect its laws which tend to the preservation of earthly peace, and should both make use of this temporal peace, and also obey, as far as he can with a good conscience, the moral laws of the terrestrial city as helping to the attainment of peace eternal.* We see more readily than St Augustine the contribution which the States of the world are able to make to the city of God, for they not only can protect the Church and its members in the exercise of their religion, but they can promote justice, preserve freedom and relieve poverty; and the demands they make on their citizens should develop qualities of wisdom, self-sacrifice and fellowship which exist only in perfection in the city of God. But while the Christian acknowledges with gratitude the services the city of man has rendered to the city of God, with St Augustine he also looks upon it as a rebel against God through its pride, its acquisitiveness and its violence; he sees within it the sign of dissolution, and knows that either it will gradually decay, or will be brought suddenly to an end through the misuse of

*Vide Temple Classics Edition of *The City of God*, Book xv, Chapter 17.

the knowledge which has given men such power both over themselves and over the natural world.

The Christian therefore lives in perpetual tension, for he is a citizen both of the earthly and of the heavenly cities. He must not neglect his duties to the State of which he is a member, and which has nurtured, educated, and protected him. He must not allow his certainty that it will decay or be destroyed to lead him to withdraw to the catacombs or the cloisters. St Paul rebuked the members of the Church of Thessalonica who neglected their daily work on the excuse they were waiting for the imminent return of their Lord. Rather by his diligence and uprightness the Christian should show that he is the citizen of another city. He should reproduce in the city of man the laws of righteousness, truth, freedom, and peace which he has learnt in the city of God. But at the same time he must always resist the pressure of the earthly city to make him conform to its ideals and customs as the only reality. The pressure is so great and persistent that he will succumb to it unless he is given help from the heavenly city. Through his membership of the Church he is able to receive this help, for the Church takes him frequently to the mount of vision from which, like Christian on the Delectable Mountains, he can, even though his hands shake as he holds the glasses, see 'something like the gate, and also some of the glory of the place'. Through its ministration of the Word and the Sacraments, and through its fellowship, the Church enables its members to live more worthily of their citizenship of the city incorruptible and eternal laid up in the heavens. From the mount they must return to the city in which they have their earthly homes, bringing to it the ideals and commands of the city of God.

The uncertainty of the future of existing civilization makes it the more imperative that all hope should not be bound up with an order which may soon pass away. The Church must teach the reality, the nearness, and the claims of the city of God; even in this life its walls can be seen rising from the earth, its gates wide open to receive people of all nations and races, for wherever there is righteousness the city is beginning to come into existence. But here it can never be perfect and complete; for this we must wait until the historical order has gone. The city of God already exists in its perfection on the other side of death, but here only partially, and we can have of it only momentary and fleeting glimpses, for it is hard to discern it amongst the massive buildings of the city of man. But to the eye of faith the city is already visible.

> City of God, how broad and far
>   Outspread thy walls sublime!
> The true thy chartered freemen are
>   Of every age and clime.
>
> How gleam thy watch-fires through the night
>   With never-fainting ray!
> How rise thy towers, serene and bright,
>   To meet the dawning day!

In 1934 this hymn was sung at a service in the cathedral at Cape Town in celebration of its centenary. Afterwards Field-Marshal Smuts, who had been present, said to me with great earnestness, 'In that hymn there is all my philosophy.' It was the first time he had heard it. Its idealism, its hopefulness, its stress on unity, on 'freedom, love, and truth,' its confidence in the future made a strong appeal to the philosopher states-man. For though the completeness of the city is far off, and it will never be finished in the age of history, yet it now exists, and some progress towards its freedom, truth, and love has already been made on earth.

The Church in its life and teaching must call all to citizen-ship of the city of God. If it is to do this it must be in the world, but not of the world. It must be detached from the world, not reflecting its opinions or adopting its methods. It must be other-wordly, though showing an intense love and compassion for sinning and suffering humanity. It must dis-regard unpopularity and bear at all costs its witness, setting forth uncompromisingly the Christian way of life. It must have the courage to condemn personal, social, or national con-duct, disobedient to the commandments of God. Its members should bear about with them that strange, mysterious quality of numinousness which belongs to those who by worship and prayer are frequently on the mount of vision.

But of all the qualities most necessary for the Church of this generation probably vigilance and urgency are the chief. Not long ago the Church with the rest of the civilized world assumed that millenniums would pass before the end of man's existence on earth. There seemed to be plenty of time during which man would rise to higher levels and in which the Church could evangelize the world. The old cries for vigilance and the warnings of impending catastrophe so often heard both in the Old and New Testaments seemed to be strangely out of date. Now with terrific suddenness they have again become real. Atomic and even more deadly weapons may bring within a few years terrible destruction on our civilization and possibly leave the world desolate of all life. The work the Church has to do must, therefore, be done at once. If it delays in doing it, it may soon be too late. The catastrophic nature of our age is a call for prayer and action. The Church should pray for God's forgiveness for its own sins and for the sins of the world, asking that in His mercy He may save the human race from the doom which now threatens it. But if the catastrophe comes it will be the day of the Lord for which the Church should be ready. He should find the Church vigilant and active, fulfilling with all its might the commission He has given it; not panic-stricken at the terror coming upon the earth, but confident and hopeful, for it knows that though the city of man will consume away, the city of God will abide for ever. Nehemiah describes how the walls of Jerusalem were rebuilt in the face of the enemy; all took part in the work either in the actual building or in the bearing of burdens; 'everyone with one of his hands wrought in his work, and with the other hand held his weapon.' The Church must continue day by day to build up and enlarge the city of God; but in its hands it must hold its weapons ready for any emergency which may suddenly arise.

Index

Index

Index

Index

Index

Index

Index

Index

Index